Anonymous

Magyarland

Being the Narrative of our Travels Through the Highlands and Lowlands of Hungary - Vol. II

Anonymous

Magyarland
Being the Narrative of our Travels Through the Highlands and Lowlands of Hungary - Vol. II

ISBN/EAN: 9783743417335

Manufactured in Europe, USA, Canada, Australia, Japa

Cover: Foto ©Andreas Hilbeck / pixelio.de

Manufactured and distributed by brebook publishing software (www.brebook.com)

Anonymous

Magyarland

DEFILE OF THE LOWER DANUBE.

Frontispiece, Vol. II.

"MAGYARLAND;"

BEING THE NARRATIVE OF OUR TRAVELS THROUGH THE HIGHLANDS AND LOWLANDS OF HUNGARY.

BY

A FELLOW OF THE CARPATHIAN SOCIETY,
AUTHOR OF 'THE INDIAN ALPS.'

IN TWO VOLUMES.—Vol. II.

WITH ILLUSTRATIONS.

LONDON:
SAMPSON LOW, MARSTON, SEARLE, & RIVINGTON,
CROWN BUILDINGS, 188 FLEET STREET.
1881.

CONTENTS OF VOL. II.

CHAPTER XXIX.
	PAGE
PONS TRAJANI	1

CHAPTER XXX.
THE HEIGHTS OF THE DANUBE	12

CHAPTER XXXI.
MEHADIA	29

CHAPTER XXXII.
THE FAMILY PEDIGREE	43

CHAPTER XXXIII.
GROSSWARDEIN	57

CHAPTER XXXIV.
GOOD FRIDAY IN THE GREEK CHURCH	66

CHAPTER XXXV.
THE "QUEEN OF THE ALFÖLD"	80

CHAPTER XXXVI.
HERMANNSTADT	94

CHAPTER XXXVII.

"THE GOOD OLD TIMES" 107

CHAPTER XXXVIII.

WITH THE WALLACHS 124

CHAPTER XXXIX.

THE ROTHER THURM PASS 135

CHAPTER XL.

THE GREEK HERMITAGE OF BUCSECS 146

CHAPTER XLI.

WESTWARD 160

CHAPTER XLII.

DEBRECZIN 172

CHAPTER XLIII.

THE WINE DISTRICTS OF TOKAY 185

CHAPTER XLIV.

TEMPLES OF THE NIGHT 201

CHAPTER XLV.

DICKENS *alias* "BOSCH" 215

CHAPTER XLVI.

THE GOLD MINES OF SCHEMNITZ 227

CHAPTER XLVII.

THE "CALVARY" 239

CHAPTER XLVIII.

THE MODERN BABEL 247

CHAPTER XLIX.

O'BUDA 257

CHAPTER L.

THE WITCHES' CARNIVAL 267

CHAPTER LI.

PARTINGS 276

CHAPTER LII.

AGRAM 286

CHAPTER LIII.

THE IMPALED RAÏA 301

LIST OF ILLUSTRATIONS.
VOL. II.

FULL-PAGE ILLUSTRATIONS.

DEFILE OF THE LOWER DANUBE	*Frontispiece*
ALL AMONG THE SHEAVES	*Facing page* 68

SMALL ILLUSTRATIONS.

	PAGE
GOING HOME FROM MARKET	vi
A ROUMANIAN SOLDIER	3
A PRIEST OF THE GREEK CHURCH	10
IN THE SUBURBS OF ORSOVA	11
ISLAND OF NEW ORSOVA IN THE DANUBE	17
TURKISH BOAT	28
TRAJAN'S TABLET	31
WALLACHIAN WOMEN	35
HOW WE JOURNEYED TO MEHADIA	42
GROSSWARDEIN	62
STUDY CHARACTERISTIC!	67
BEFORE A SHRINE IN A GREEK CHURCH	72
BOAT ON LAKE BALATON	79
A CITIZEN OF SZEGEDIN	80
THE MARÓS	89
LISTENING TO THE SERMON ON GOOD-FRIDAY AT GROSSWARDEIN	92
FISHING-BOATS ON THE DANUBE	93
IN THE MARKET AT HERMANNSTADT	103
LUTHERAN CHURCH AT HERMANNSTADT	106
FORTIFIED CHURCH AT HILTAU	109
A TRANSYLVANIAN VILLAGE	113
CHURCH COSTUME OF A "SAXON" MÄDCHEN	120
OLD TOWER AT HERMANNSTADT	123
YOUNG WALLACH GIRL	124
DOORWAY OF A WALLACH HOUSE	127

	PAGE
A Wallach Baby . .	134
The Transylvanian Alps .	138
Belfrey of a Wallach Church	145
Castle of Terzburg .	151
The Hermits' Cave . . .	157
Way-side Figures	159
Market-day at Koloszvár . .	162
"Common Objects"	258
The Pursuit of Art under Difficulties	263
The Blocksberg	270
The Royal Palace of Buda . .	277
Our Carriage . . .	285
Sunset on the Plains . . .	288
In a Church at Agram . .	294
Ferry-boat on the Save .	295
The impaled Raÿa . .	310
Nearing Belgrade . .	311

"MAGYARLAND."

"MAGYARLAND."

CHAPTER XXIX.

PONS TRAJANI.

"*IHR Pass, meine Herren! Ihr Pass!*" cried a ferocious Roumanian official, speaking German with an unquestionably foreign accent, as we disembark from the steamer at Sozoreny.

It is the first time we have been asked to show our passport on the arrival at a frontier since leaving England; but we are now in Roumania, and beyond the pale of Western civilisation.

There is also a strict examination of our luggage here; and whilst these ceremonies are proceeding, numerous beggars arrive upon the scene, who whine and supplicate and show their wounds and hideous deformities, thrusting them—when the size and nature of them permit—through the bars of the gates which shut us in. There is considerable competition in the profession, and it is not easy to see which carries off the palm. There are beggars of all sorts, shapes, and sizes; beggars whose shrunk and shrivelled limbs, bound with ragged and dirty bandages, are suggestive of the malady from which *he* suffered who lay "at the rich man's door;" beggars with deformed hands, arms, and legs; beggars with no arms at all; whilst in the distance we catch sight of a wretched specimen of humanity, cantering along on all fours, and whining at the top of his voice, but who, with all his speed, only arrives in the nick of time to add his supplication to that of his brethren for "kreuzers, for the love of Heaven."

Considerable delay was caused here on account of András having failed to provide himself with a passport. The necessity for his doing so had never occurred to us; but there was so much fuss and palaver made about the matter that we began to think it would either end in his being kept for a time in durance vile, or sent back whence he had come. Since the Treaty of Berlin, Roumania together with Servia has obtained its independence, and no longer owns allegiance to Turkey. The Government, however, of the former province is exceedingly afraid of Russian spies, and is also suspicious of its neighbour Austria. Its frontier regulations with regard to passports are consequently very strict.

The incident above narrated caused no small excitement amongst the bystanders. The gendarmes instantly surrounded us with their bayonets, all of whom were barbarous but handsome-looking fellows dressed in a uniform of coarse grey cloth turned up with white, and wearing black lamb's wool caps with long peaks hanging down behind; whilst the beggars, suddenly taken off their guard, and forgetting for once their respective infirmities, entirely changed their characters. They no longer whined and wept, but spoke to each other quite cheerily in their natural voices. Arms, legs, and feet which had previously been doubled up or turned the wrong way, now assumed their legitimate position; even the man on "all fours" managed to stand upright, and peer through the gates; so great and absorbing was the interest one and all manifested in the dispute that was taking place within. At length, after much expenditure of lungs on our part, and vociferation and gesticulation on that of the Roumanian officials, we  succeeded in making them comprehend the harmless and inoffensive nature of András's vocation and the precise relation in which he stood to us as our guide, and he was permitted to accompany us across the frontier; for which act of grace I feel sure we were indebted to our having an English passport.

We had already encountered a rather unpleasant episode before landing. András, thinking we might find it difficult to obtain anything to eat here, had thoughtfully laid in a little stock of cold provisions from the steward's larder; the charge for which was so exorbitant that the two came to high words on the subject. The steward was a German, and the epithet "*Swab*," and other opprobrious titles of a similar nature, were showered upon him by András, together with the favourite but by no means complimentary Magyar sentence, "*hunczfut a német*," signifying "thief," "rogue," etc.; till, failing to make any impression upon the delinquent by these epithets, he at length appealed to the passengers, declaring before them all that as a Magyar— and here the little man drew himself up to his fullest height— he neither could nor would allow foreigners, much less an *Ángolok*, to be so imposed on. Looking over the bill we certainly did think the steward had been rather overreaching, having not only charged three florins for a bottle of very ordinary wine, but a florin for a small quantity of biscuits, and other things after the same rate. The public exposure, however, of his exorbitant charges soon brought the recalcitrant steward to reason, who at once deducted half the amount. But the usually calm and even temper of a Magyar once aroused is not easy to subdue, and we began to fear that ere long András would get us into real difficulty, for a third *contretemps* occurred just as we were at length leaving the custom-house.

Our intention, on arrival at Sozoreny, was to hire some sort of conveyance, and, driving to the station of the Bucharest and Orsova line, to leave our luggage there, whilst we made a short excursion to Turnu Severin to see the remains of Trajan's noblest work, the bridge across the Danube; after which, returning to the station, we purposed picking up our luggage and proceeding to Orsova by train.

The only thing on wheels visible outside the *Douane* was an indescribably old and battered phaeton, to which a pair of small, lean horses were attached.

We were just about to enter the ancient vehicle, when the driver, in an insolent tone of voice, demanded his fare, viz., five gulden. This, of course, was also a gross imposition, and proved far too much for our guide's present state of excitability. Finding the driver unwilling to listen to remonstrance, he wrenched the whip out of his hand, and laid it vigorously across his shoulders.

Unaccustomed to take the law into our own hands in so violent a fashion, and dreading the consequences in a country like this, we expostulated with him severely on his behaviour, informing him that if he was no longer able to keep his temper under control he must forthwith leave our service. The little man replied quite calmly, assuring us that, " with all due deference to the august *Angolok*—his sweet master and mistress "—the mode of reasoning he had adopted in the present instance was not the result of any ebullition of temper whatsoever, but was the only method that ever had the slightest effect upon a Roumanian Jew; and his words proved correct, for our Israelitish Jehu, instead of resenting the assault as we expected, folded his hands, and in the most abject manner begged us to mount, offering to take us for two gulden thirty kreuzers, that being rather less than half the sum he had first demanded.

Contrary to our expectations, no one took the slightest notice of the assault. The delinquent was "only a Jew," a people cruelly persecuted in Roumania, where the popular feeling against them is scarcely less marked than that which existed in England and other countries in the Middle Ages.

Our luggage deposited in the crazy vehicle, the miserable horses, regardless of holes and ruts, took us up the steep hill at a hand-gallop, during which not only we but our belongings also were more than once threatened with a serious upset.

Having, however, survived the perils and dangers of the

way, and seen our *impedimenta* safely locked up in a little cobwebby office at the station, we drove to Turnu Severin, about a quarter of a mile further down the river, where, climbing a conical mound, upon which still stands a ruined tower of undoubted Roman origin—supposed to have been built by Trajan to defend the passage of the bridge—we threw ourselves down beneath its cool shadow, and partook of our well-earned meal with very *Trojan* appetites. Beneath us flowed the Danube, at this point more than half a mile broad; while from the "Iron Gate Pass" came the steady but peaceful roar of the cataracts, mingling with the metallic and incessant "clack, clack," of the *cicadas* fluttering in the bushes around us. But our leafy retreat proved rather a failure: for mosquitoes of a most venomous species made a violent raid upon us, and, our repast ended, we hastened to the banks of the river, where we were safer from their attacks.

It was just at this point that that noble structure of antiquity, Trajan's Bridge, was erected, the length of which is said to have been three thousand nine hundred Roman feet—a Roman foot being rather in excess of that of our English measure. Beneath the surface of the water the remains of thirteen truncated piers still exist, which once supported the arches. These piers, which are situated 170 feet apart, are visible at rare intervals when the river is unusually low, seven others being covered with a sandy deposit which in the course of ages has collected round them, and which now forms hillocks in the river's bed.

A full description of this bridge was written by Dion Cassius, who was Governor of Pannonia during the reign of Hadrian, Trajan's successor, and who wrote the history of

Rome up to the beginning of the first century. Although the greater part of this valuable history has been lost, including that portion of it which described the building of the bridge, an epitome of his writings is still extant containing a short description of this great work, in addition to which it has also been described by Merivale.

This noblest of all Trajan's achievements, however, was not permitted to be of long duration. Built in A.D. 103, it had virtually ceased to exist in 120, having been destroyed in that year by Hadrian, in order, as he affirmed, to prevent the incursions of barbarians, who might take advantage of the bridge to cross over into the Thracian Provinces. He is, however, generally believed to have been moved to destroy it by a jealous dislike to the architect Apollodorus of Damascus, who erected Trajan's Column at Rome, as well as the Forum Trajanum, and who when a young soldier in the Roman camp offended the dignity of the Emperor; for, soon after Hadrian's accession to the throne, he not only overthrew this most ambitious of all Apollodorus's works, but, on some very slight pretext, caused him to be put to death.

Little exists in the present day above the surface of the water of any interest to the ordinary observer, except the ruined walls on each side rising just above the banks, and which must originally have formed the piers from which the first arches sprang. But how even these shapeless masses of masonry link the past to the present, and bring before us, in living memory, the valour and energy of this great people!

The climate of Europe must have been much colder at that period than now; for we frequently read of Tartars and other barbarian hordes from the surrounding steppes making use of the Danube, in the second century, for the transport from one shore to the other of their infantry, cavalry, and waggons, from which it would appear that the river in winter formed a solid bridge of ice. It seldom freezes now, and even when it does so in exceptionally severe winters the ice lasts only for a very short time.

Not far from Trajan's Bridge is a hilly promontory belonging to Servia, which stretches out into the Danube, and through which it is proposed to cut a canal to enable ships to pass down the river at low water.

After leaving the banks of the classic stream, we climbed a steep hill through a herd of formidable-looking buffaloes grazing the arid pasture on its slopes, and found ourselves in the town of Turnu Severin, a newly established Roumanian colony situated on the left bank of the river, a mile and a half from the "Iron Gate Pass," containing extensive docks belonging to the Danube Steam Navigation Company. From this place may be seen, standing on the shore of the river, the Tower of Severus; whilst on the opposite side lies Skela-Gladova, with its Turkish fortifications, and its slender minarets rising above the walls. Twenty years ago Turnu Severin consisted of merely a few houses, but it is now growing quite an important place. On the promenade the beauty and fashion of the town are taking their early evening stroll, dressed in the very extreme of Parisian toilettes, and in skirts so absurdly tight that it is a marvel how they ever get into them; and, as we looked towards the buffaloes with their long horns and outstretched necks, between which and them there existed no fence whatever, we could not help wondering whether, in the event of one of those animals taking it into its head to run after them, the "crack of doom" would immediately supervene to release them from their bondage, or whether the fair ones would double up entirely, and succumb to the attack without making any attempt at flight. Oh, how I longed to see them run! It was evidently with great difficulty that they managed to put one foot before the other, and the simple act of walking appeared to be a laborious process—at least with anything like grace—as they shuffled along in twos and threes, prattling their soft Neo-Latin, and looking at us wonderingly with their long almond-shaped eyes.

We reach the station just as the train from Bucharest draws up to the platform, but its departure is considerably delayed, on account of a search amongst the passengers for a man who was supposed to have stolen three thousand ducats. The Roumanian gendarmes did their very best to look ferocious and important, as they stood at the door of the carriages to prevent egress, whilst others inside were endeavouring to take note of the passengers and find the delinquent, of whom a full description had been telegraphed. But whether he succeeded in eluding the search, or had travelled by some other train, no one seemed to know. At any rate the gendarmes had not the satisfaction of capturing him, and we were permitted to take our seats.

Our only fellow traveller was a Greek priest, an effeminate looking man, with long black hair, which he kept on endeavouring to twist up under his high stiff cap. As we did not know Roumanian we addressed him in Latin; but the only phrase he seemed capable of uttering in that language was "*Non intelligo.*" The priests of the Greek Church are supposed to study theology in Latin; but, as I have elsewhere said, they are very ill-educated men, and I doubt whether he knew much of either one or the other.

At Gladova there is another long delay: two ambassadors are in the train and they must needs have lunch. Extensive preparations have been made for them, and the restaurant is prettily decorated with flowers, whilst waiters in white gloves tear about madly, a young woman in a very pretty costume of red and white, who also waited on the illustrious travellers, being the only person who appeared not to have quite lost her head, and but for whom I suspect they would have had but a sorry chance of any refreshment whatever.

At length we reach our destination and for the third time in the course of the day have not only to show our passports but submit to an examination of luggage.

It was our intention on arriving at Orsova to have gone to the Hotel "*König von Ungarn;*" but the station is some distance from the old town, and the only carriage we found waiting at the place of exit was harnessed to such miserably lean horses, that we could not make up our minds to get into it. Their cheeks had fallen in and their heads were like those of skeletons. Nor was this all: their flanks were bleeding either from ill-usage or friction against the rope-harness, and we could not find it in our hearts to subject the poor creatures to another journey. So observing a few hundred yards from the station a small one-storied inn, bearing the imposing title, in colossal letters, of "Hôtel Tivoli," we decided to make it our headquarters, at any rate for the night.

As we leave the station and walk across to the Hôtel Tivoli—which proves on nearer acquaintance to be about the size of a mouse-trap, nothing in connection with it being large but the name—the sun is setting behind the blue mountains which form the boundary of the Danube. Snake-like vapours are ascending from the river, the air is chill and so suggestive of ague that we are glad to take shelter anywhere till twilight is past. In this climate it is dangerous to be out of doors at sunset. Later in the evening, when night may be said to have fairly set in, one may go out with impunity, for then the air is again warm. It is only when the last touch of the sun's golden finger has faded upon the highest mountain, and those blue shadows have wrapped the earth in their sombre mantle, that that peculiar chill in the air is felt which I have so frequently described, and which is so dangerous to the traveller to encounter.

CHAPTER XXX.

THE HEIGHTS OF THE DANUBE.

A FRUGAL supper, consisting of fish from the river and Moldavian cheese—the latter served with a plate of carraways—and, thoroughly tired out from our long day's excitement and fatigue, we seek "nature's sweet restorer" ere the moon had risen above the mountain tops.

As we ascend the steps leading to the creaky little balcony by which our rooms were approached, the peaks with their tree-fringed summits frowned down upon us black as Erebus, and half shut out the sky, in which here and there a star was trimming its feeble lamp.

The position of "Hôtel Tivoli" is the best thing about it after its name. Standing in the centre of a large open space covered with grass, it is consequently free from the dust with which almost everything at this time of year is smothered. It is quiet too, and here the traveller can, if he happen to be of that disposition, indulge in the "truly rural" to his heart's content.

The following morning, after dressing—a feat accomplished under considerable difficulties, our rooms being of the most limited dimensions—we descend for breakfast to the restaurant, which, detached from the house, consisted originally of a plot of garden, but now picturesquely roofed in like a châlet, whose pillars are thickly covered with the vine from which hang grapes in thick clusters.

We are reminded of our proximity to Turkey by the deliciousness of the coffee, which, however, is scarcely better than that we have usually partaken of in many northern parts of Hungary; but it is served in small white jugs of such thick delf that they contain hardly more than the cup of Tantalus, a circumstance which causes András, who waits upon us as usual, to inquire sarcastically of our host—a Moldavian Jew—whether it is his intention to charge in the bill for the coffee or the jugs?

Sitting near us at another small table is a man with a little child on his knee, holding by a long string a pet lamb—a beautiful little creature as white as snow, covered all over like a French poodle with tiny ringlets, which glisten like spun-glass. It has a scarlet ribbon round its neck, and feeds out of the man's hand.

Presently, having tied the fair white thing to the leg of the table, he leaves it for awhile, and, carrying the child with him, enters the hotel. It bleats plaintively, but is quite happy when, going along to where it is, I take my seat beside it.

The people of Hungary often make great household pets of these beautiful little animals, keeping them until they are full grown—when, alas! they sacrifice them on the altar of mutton.

The owner, who has been to fetch a glass of *schnaps*, now returns, and resuming his seat, holds it to the child's lips, who greedily imbibes the fiery liquid, its little eyes watering notwithstanding. Observing my admiration of the lamb, he offers to sell it for one gulden and a half, and, had we been on our way to England, we might have purchased it; but, in prospect of a tour through the Transylvanian wilds, an elephant could scarcely have proved a greater encumbrance.

The morning is exquisitely fine, the sky violet blue, and the air fragrant with the perfume of oleanders, which are blooming just outside the enclosure. Every now and then from afar, as the breeze bears it towards us on its wing, comes the roar of the breakers of the Greben rapids, inviting us in their direction. We are to climb the majestic heights to-day, for which purpose some strong, sure-footed quadrupeds will be necessary. We have very strong misgivings, however, as to whether these will be forthcoming, but leave our useful guide to make the needful arrangements, whilst we stroll off meanwhile to the Kroncapelle, only a quarter of an hour's walk, and a spot of great interest, being the place where, during the war of Hungarian Independence, in 1849, the sacred crown of St. Stephen was concealed. This memorable crown, superstitiously supposed to have been fabricated by angels, was for a long time kept in the "*Alba Regia*," but was removed to the castle of Buda, where it remained until the great Moslem invasion, when it was deposited for safety in that of Presburg, at which place it reposed until the Turks were expelled from Hungary, when it was again restored to Buda. The history of this crown, from the period of its bestowal on St. Stephen in 1001 up to the seventeenth century, has been one of great vicissitude. At the time of Kossuth's flight it was buried in a box a few feet beneath the surface of the soil by two Hungarian patriots named Fuelep and Szemere, in which place it lay in safety until 1853, when it was unearthed by a peasant; its hiding-place, some affirm, having been betrayed for the sum of 20,000 ducats by an officer who was in Kossuth's own staff at the time of its concealment; others declaring it to have been the result of miraculous revelation. So great is the veneration of the Hungarians for this sacred relic, that they believe their beloved country cannot prosper without it, and also that it operates powerfully upon its destinies.

In commemoration of its recovery, a small octagonal chapel has been erected, in the Byzantine style, in the centre of which, surrounded by a stone balustrade, is a well, marking the precise spot where the sacred object lay concealed. Over it rests a block of marble, on which an artificial crown is placed, the counterpart of the true one; and above, suspended from the dome, a lamp hangs, which is always burning, whilst opposite the entrance is a life-size figure of the Virgin and Child, encircled with golden rays.

The chapel was shown us by a woman in a very picturesque and Oriental costume, and whose particular mission in life, apart from keeping the keys and nursing a rampagious baby, would appear to consist in driving away lean dogs from the enclosure. We were just on the point of leaving the chapel when she requested us to write our names in a ponderous book kept for the purpose. After having complied with her request we glanced through the volume, which contains the signatures of several hundred visitors, but amongst them, strange to say, we only lighted on one that appeared English, and to it were added the words, Boston, Mass.

As English persons are not given as a rule to avoid opportunities of the kind, the inference would be that even of the comparatively few who "do the Danube," fewer still stop at Orsova, notwithstanding that this portion of the great river contains objects of real interest to the antiquary and archæologist. The entire district is, in fact, well worthy the attention, not only of the archæological student in search of historical landmarks which have survived the levelling hand of Time, but of the ordinary tourist also, who cannot but be interested in these memorials of a long-forgotten past.

An avenue of poplars leads from the chapel to the banks of the river, which are here beautifully wooded, many of the trees being festooned with the wild vine. The Danube at this spot looks precisely like a lake, being enclosed on all sides by mountains, from which no opening is visible. At their feet lies the island-fortress of New Orsova which commands the frontiers of three countries, Hungary, Wallachia, and Servia, and forms a very picturesque object with its sombre cypress trees and high mosque reflected in the water.

On the opposite side a Turkish cargo boat is struggling with the rapids, and in the foreground some men are raising their fishing net.

This island during the last hundred years has undergone various fortunes, having frequently changed from Christian to Mahomedan rule. In 1738, after a prolonged siege, it surrendered to the Osmanlis, but in 1790 was retaken by the Austrians. By the Treaty of Sistova it was again delivered up to the Turks, who finally evacuated it in favour of the Christians in 1878.

The fortress, though a heap of ruins, is still occupied by

Turks, who, after the war was over, preferring to become Austrian subjects rather than return to their own country, entreated the Emperor of Austria to permit them to remain there. In this miserable place, although in the utmost squalor, no fewer than four hundred and fifty men, women, and children manage to live. The men occupy themselves in fishing, while the women and children work at gold and silver embroidery which they sell to visitors to the island, and thus eke out a scanty subsistence.

Leaving the island and crossing over to the left side of the Danube, we throw ourselves on the ground beneath the shadow of a tree, and revel in the fair and stately beauty of the scene. How lovely is everything! Not a sign is there of human habitation anywhere, whilst from the wooded hills comes the not unmusical but perpetual din of myriads of locusts and living things, bearing witness that not man, but *they* have dominion here.

Close to our feet a chameleon comes out of a hole and looks cautiously about him. Its rough, granulated skin is of the brightest green, and it measures fully ten inches from head to tail. A large metallic-looking beetle crawling along the sand attracts its attention and whets its appetite, but at this moment the chameleon's quick ear detects the presence of foes. Turning its curious swivel eyes to the back of its head, it catches sight of us, puts up its back, and then changing colour from green to buff, bursts out all over with black spots; it does not move, but after remaining for a long time as if transfixed, stealthily returns to its hole.

On the other side of the river a long, narrow boat now comes in sight, rowed by two Turkish boatmen, whilst a third, standing at the stern, is using a pole. He wears a scarlet fez, which, creating a small speck of bright colour, is very pleasing to the eye against the background of grey mountains floating in the dreamy haze of sultry noontide. The boat hugs the shore, for there are strong eddies in mid stream even here. The river is broad and the breeze blowing from the north, but when it lulls for an instant, the song of the boatmen reaches us in peaceful and pathetic cadence.

As we sit here and watch the Danube's majestic waves roll past, and think of the great nations to whom it has in turn belonged, Greeks, Romans, Huns, Avars, Magyars, Turks, French, and Germans, we rejoice in the fact that it has come under the sway of the Magyars once more.

It was near here that Kossuth, that ardent aspirant after political freedom, and the hero of the "War of Independence," fleeing from his pursuers, crossed the Danube and sought protection in Turkish territory. Before crossing the frontier, he threw himself down for the last time on the soil of his beloved Fatherland for which he had risked so much and fought so hard, pressed on it a sobbing, passionate kiss, and planting his foot on Turkish territory, became, as he himself has so touchingly described it in the memories of his exile, "like a wrecked ship thrown up by the storm on a desert shore." A Turkish officer greeted him courteously in the name of Allah, led him to a place which he had kindly caused to be prepared for him to rest in for the night, under God's free heaven, and asked for his sword with downcast eyes, as if ashamed that a Turk should disarm a Hungarian. "I unbuckled it," he writes, "and gave it to him without uttering a word; my eyes filled with tears, and he, wishing me sound rest, left me alone with my sorrow.

"There I stood in silent meditation on the bank—but no longer the *Hungarian* bank—of the Danube, the waves of which were mingled with the tears of the Hungarian nation —and which, not far from me, grumbled and roared through the rocky pass of the 'Iron Gates.'"

"I listened," he continues, "to this roaring in rude harmony with the storm in my heart, and as I contemplated the annihilation of patriotic hopes so undeservedly extinguished, tears of indescribable grief unconsciously showered down my cheeks."

This rhapsody from the once Supreme Dictator of Hungary may sound unmanly to the ears of the undemonstrative Briton; but these brave, lion-hearted Hungarians, whom few things daunt, love their country passionately and with a love as tender as that of woman.

It is sad to think that this brave man, who, though disappointed in his attempts at achieving a recognition of Hungary as an independent state, has yet been the means of indirectly conferring lasting benefit upon his country, should—as he describes himself—still be a wanderer, "arrived at the verge of the grave with no hope for the future, and in whose past there is no consolation." No longer expatriated, he could return to the Fatherland if he would; but he refuses to do so, since, by its own act, it has allowed itself to be merged into the Austrian Empire.

It is gratifying at any rate to know that Kossuth found for many years, together with other Hungarian refugees of the revolutionary period, a safe and peaceful exile in Turkey. The very nation which for so many centuries was Hungary's most deadly foe, and which, when demanded by Russia and Austria in 1849 to deliver up all those who had sought shelter in its dominions, bravely refused to surrender them.

These thoughts, naturally suggested by this particular spot, concerning the Hungarian hero, whose history has been such a mixture of triumph and humiliation, have kept us lingering too long. It is already past noon; the sun is sending fiery arrows through the topmost branches of the trees, and if we are to make for the heights to-day, it is high time we were on our way.

Back through the long rows of poplars which like sentinels appear to be keeping guard over the little chapel. Still sitting on the steps is the young woman with her baby. She smiles sweetly as we pass, then rises to unlock the door for another visitor, who, at this moment, appears at the wicket gate of the little garden surrounding the chapel.

On nearing "Hôtel Tivoli," we observe, standing on the

green-sward beneath the windows of our room, the steeds which are to carry us "over the hills and far away." I had no hope from the first of being able to obtain such a modern luxury as a side-saddle in this old-world locality, so that I was not disappointed in that particular at all events, but I was not prepared certainly for the extraordinary arrangement which had been improvised for my especial benefit, and which András, I could see, regarded as quite a clever arrangement. Indeed it was so, and its ingenuity did him wondrous credit, but the whole thing was so droll and altogether original in its conception, that we were speechless. He had found an old wooden chair, and having broken off the legs, he placed it on the creature's back. This was to form my seat, the *back* of the chair being placed nearest the horse's head by way of pummel, to which I was no doubt expected to hold on in case of need!

Having ascertained that the animal was sufficiently padded with rugs to enable it to bear this novel and elaborate erection without injury, and having seen that the girths were safe, we started in triumph, a barbarous-looking muleteer— wearing a lamb's wool cap very like a mop, preceding us— and András, carrying a basket of the inevitable provisions —oh! that we could live on a periodical lozenge!—gravely bringing up the rear.

Passing through the ancient town we are objects of much astonishment to the natives. Women, carrying baskets and pitchers on their heads, stop to gaze at us, calling the attention of their neighbours to the strange little cavalcade, and no wonder. Others sitting at doorways run in and peep shyly at us through small dust-begrimed windows.

Orsova—pronounced Orshova, the Hungarian s being invariably pronounced as in our English word "shall"—is the last Hungarian town on the Danube, and wears quite an Eastern aspect. The costumes are also entirely un-European. The women wear a long white skirt and a bodice reaching to the throat, generally embroidered with wool in a rich Oriental pattern and well-harmonised combination of green, red, blue, and orange. A broad girdle woven in the same colours encircles the waist, from which hangs a thick fringe extending to the heels. The men, however, wear mocassins, braided jackets, and loose trousers, and look as uncivilised as their surroundings. The roads, which seem to be none other than of Nature's own making, are formed of sand and large pebbles, over which our horses stumble as they pick their way along. A wooden bridge, and a dark little cemetery as full as it can cram of iron crucifixes, bring us to the outskirts of the town, where the houses are built of unbaked brick and enclosed by strong stockades of closely-plaited withies, bristling throughout with formidable stakes sharpened to the finest point to keep away the wolves which infest this part of the country.

These stockades, which are everywhere seen in the suburbs of Orsova, and which from their thickness and strength might easily have withstood a siege in olden time, interested us immensely. They are perhaps the surviving form of those wooden palisades or hedges called *limes*, with which the Romans surrounded the frontiers of their empire, and which Spartian describes in his account of the life of Hadrian as having been composed of stakes driven into the ground and filled in so as to form a hedge or wall.

In the outskirts of the town, which extend some considerable distance, one of these stockades was being erected, the whole reminding us of the sculpture on Trajan's Column, on which is represented the construction of the *limes* that once united the Danube to the Rhine, from which it may be seen that the soldiers, or *riparienses* as they were called by the Romans, on whom devolved the construction of these stockades, proceeded in their work exactly as we saw the men of Orsova do to-day, their costume even, a short white tunic tied loosely at the waist, and the peaked lamb's wool cap, scarcely differing from that of the Roman period.

Near the mouth of the Danube the remains of a ditch and mound still exist, supposed to have been made by Trajan at the same epoch as the bridge, for the purpose of connecting the encampments of the various Legions situated along the frontier.

Arriving at the base of the mountains which bound the noble river, we see clouds hanging beneath their summits, and climbing a steep hill, pass an encampment, not, however, of Roman origin this time, but belonging to the "wandering tribe," from which a number of spindle-legged gipsies rush out and pursue us like a troop of wild animals—*Tschorelo rom* as they call themselves, words signifying "poor man" —and refusing to leave us, until, quite wearied by their importunity, we bestow upon them a handful of kreuzers.

The climb is steep and toilsome, but we are rewarded by the splendid views which, ever changing, burst upon us continually. On our way we pass through immense flocks of sheep tended by wild-looking shepherds, and presently hear from a distance the hoarse drone of the bag-pipes, the weird music of which seems quite in keeping with the savage grandeur of these rocky fastnesses; and listening to it as we zigzag up the slopes, the thought comes forcibly to the mind, how wonderfully pastoral music, the most primitive adaptation of harmonic sounds, which took its first lessons from Nature herself—the plaintive melody of running brooks meandering through green pastures, and the harsh roar of the mountain torrent dashing over rocks—both gives and takes character for its surroundings. How out of keeping with those stern and majestic solitudes of nature would be the gentle music of the flute, or the crude wild harmony of the bag-pipes with the calm and peaceful plains!

A little further climb, we reach a shepherd's hut and behold the author of the "crude, wild" sounds sitting at the doorway. An uncanny-looking man, in very truth, with his feet and legs bandaged in coarse linen and tied round with thongs of leather. The hut itself was empty, his dog and bagpipes apparently being his only companions, and probably for many months together, for these shepherds do not return to the lowlands until winter sets in, nor always even then, some leading their flocks for pasture into Bulgaria, when, as the frosts appear, it becomes scanty on these heights.

And now having reached the summit of the mountain after an ascent of two hours, we alight from our mules, thankful so far as I am concerned with any change of position, András's impromptu saddle having proved in the using the most perfectly diabolical arrangement it is possible to conceive, and having once descended from it I inwardly determine that, come what may, nothing shall induce me to mount it again.

A good luncheon and some excellent Schiller, a wine made from grapes that grow on the hills near Orsova, go some way towards restoring our peace of body and mind; after which, descending a rocky knoll, we look down upon the Danube gliding majestically between giant precipices and walls of granite, a glorious amphitheatre of weather-beaten rock and hoary crag. As we stand almost spell-bound at the grandeur of the scene, something passes over us with a "whirr," and great stirring of the air. We must have disturbed an eagle's nest, for an enormous fellow flies screeching across the gorge, his shrill cry echoing from rock to rock, whilst a few moments later another crosses it in the same direction.

Just above us rose a large serrated cone of granite, which F. determined to climb if possible, whilst I made a sketch of the wondrous scene surrounding us. The nest was doubtless there, and its formidable denizens no longer near, he had a great curiosity to have a peep at it.

Looking down a sheer precipice upon the river, we can trace the road which was constructed by the Hungarian Government, between Orsova and Alt-Moldova, as it winds round the rocky buttresses like a tiny thread; whilst opposite, on the Servian side, portions of the Roman road are also distinctly visible even from this dizzy height.

The wind—a mere zephyr in the valleys—blows roughly in our rocky eyrie, and comes howling and hissing against the jutting rocks with a noise similar to that which it makes when blowing in the shrouds of a ship at sea. We are verily in cloudland here. Like a diaphanous curtain drawn silently and gently by an unseen hand, now and then a cloud comes scudding past, encompassing us with mist, and which, veiling all surrounding objects, lends a strange and solemn mystery to the scene. There is something indescribably awful and sublime in our surroundings, and the stillness, in itself so infinite, is broken only by the scream of the eagles which, waking the echoes, seem but to make the silence more profound.

These lofty and solitary crags must be literally full of eagles, for as we sit in calm contemplation of Nature's wildest and most savage forms as exhibited in the various rock masses around us, they appear to be alive with them. At one moment we count no fewer than five, either perched upon the crags or soaring in the heavens with motionless majestic wing. The eagle is the very terror of the shepherds in these heights, and numbers of their lambs fall victims yearly to the bird of prey.

I need scarcely say the climb to the eagle's nest proved unsuccessful, for these emperors of the air choose wisely, and fix their abode in places inaccessible to the tread of man.

The shadows were lengthening when—my sketch finished—we hastened from our rocky hiding-place. Clambering over huge boulders, which in some places obstructed our exit, as if Titans had placed them there to bar these solitudes from desecration, we reached once more the peaceful green alp where we had left our horses, and found András and his companion—overcome by their fatiguing climb—lying at full length on the ground sodden in slumber, whilst the mules were grazing close by. We aroused them, eventually, and making them lead our steeds, sent them on ahead, following ourselves on foot.

Thoroughly tired, however, by the time we reach the base of the mountain, we hail the muleteers, and causing them to remove the obnoxious arrangement with which my quadruped is still equipped, and having substituted for it a folded rug, we get on magnificently. Henceforth, till we reach Orsova, we shall be passing over level ground, so that a saddle is no longer of absolute necessity to enable a somewhat practised equestrian to keep her seat, particularly on so dejected and low-spirited an animal as this.

As we enter the old town, the sun is setting and transforming its tumble-down houses into palaces of ruby gold, and bathing with rich purple shadows and vermilion lights their crazy roofs and casements. What bright pictures of semi-eastern life are seen as we proceed along our way! By the roadside is an *ágas* at which olive-complexioned women are gossiping, dressed as on a gala day, with skirts woven in various tints in which gold thread is largely intermingled. With their gay bodices, also embroidered in gold, and their crimson head-gear, what delicious bits of colour we see everywhere, mellowed by the evening light.

Having passed the crowded cemetery, the wooden bridge, and the hot and dusty town, we dismount at our little inn, and find a snowy cloth laid in readiness for our arrival beneath the vine-covered roof of the outer restaurant. But the air is chill, and, repairing to the inner room, we eat dinner all amongst the happy peasants, who sit playing a game at cards called "*Torrok*"—a quiet, well-behaved, simple folk, whose acquaintance we are glad to make.

Sitting alone, however, at a small table near us, is a Hungarian engineer, engaged at Orsova in some public works. He at first addresses us in Magyar, and finding we cannot converse in that language, tries Spanish with better success. I on my part addressed him in German, which I feel sure, from the fact of his being in the Austrian service, he must thoroughly understand; but he only shakes his head and professes ignorance of what I am saying. How intense is the repugnance with which the Hungarians regard everything German!

Whilst sympathising with the Magyars in their very natural dislike to Austrian rule, it is to be regretted they should carry their antipathy to such lengths; for, after all, it is only "kicking against the pricks" and cannot fail in the end to widen the breach already existing in the Dual Monarchy. For a long time past, the German population, finding themselves shunned by the dominant race, have resorted to the expedient of changing their names into Hungarian form.

CHAPTER XXXI.

MEHADIA.

WHAT a barbarous scene Orsova presents on market-day, and what a jabber there is of many tongues as the people in their varied costumes scream at the top of their voices and chaffer and haggle over their bargainings; Serbs, Turks, and Wallachians all adding their unintelligible gibberish to that of the Magyar; and gesticulating so violently whilst uttering their sharp, shrill cries that the uninitiated stranger expects each moment to see them come to blows.

Interesting as it is to the traveller from the civilised west to see these people in their strange costumes, sitting by their strange wares, it is still more interesting to watch them hurrying into the market from the surrounding villages.

Having been informed by our Moldavian host the previous evening, that this was the day on which the weekly market was held, we arose early to see them arrive with their merchandise, but on walking down to the Danube we found both river and mountains so shrouded in dense white vapour, that the bold outlines of the latter were alone visible, whilst nearer objects were scarcely recognisable even a few yards ahead.

The people, however, were flocking in, and, looming

suddenly out of the semi-obscurity, appeared more like gigantic spectres than common men and women as they passed us in picturesque groups, some walking, others on horse, mule, or donkey-back, one and all clad in many-coloured garments. But besides these, from distant places on the Wallachian or Turkish banks farther down the stream, came now and then a small, crazy-looking craft, its plash heard long before it came in sight itself, laden with vegetables, fruit, fish, and sometimes a living freight of men, women, and children.

Amongst the various kinds of fish found in the river are enormous sturgeon almost as large as sharks, which are cut up and sold in slices in the market.

At ten o'clock we start for " Trajan's-Tafel," an excursion that will terminate our visit to Orsova. The mist, which by this time has risen above the river, still hangs amongst the lofty crags of the Kasan Pass. and adds an indescribable gloom to the narrow, but majestic defile.

Just as we arrive at that portion of the Pass, where the tablet is situated, the mist ascending opens for an instant, and admits a shaft of sunlight, which, shining diagonally across the gorge, creates a beautiful effect of light and shade.

The form of the tablet has already been described in a previous chapter, and the following is an exact copy of the inscription :

IMP. CAESAR. DIVI. NERVAE. F.
NERVA TRAJANUS. AUG. GERM.
PONTIF. MAXIMUS TRIB. POT IIII.
PATER PATRIAE COS. III.
MONTIS L. | | AN BUS
SUP AT E.

the whole being perfectly legible when viewed closely, in

spite of the coating of smoke which for ages has been accumulating upon it in consequence of the Servian fishermen availing themselves of the shelter afforded by the overhanging rock to cook their food. Just as when we passed it in the steamer, a fire was still smouldering there on the

present occasion, some sacrilegious boatmen having as usual made the niche their place of bivouac.

On entering Orsova, after our interesting morning's excursion, we heard voices shouting lustily, and looking behind us descried a small group of people hastening in our direction with much brandishing of sticks, and waving of hats, of which we were apparently the object. What could it all mean? Had our guide again been committing some indiscretion, and getting us into trouble?

The mystery was speedily solved; for, on turning our backs upon our pursuers and hastening in the direction of the hotel, with the determination to ignore everything and everybody, the shouts were renewed with increased vigour, and some one overtaking us seized F. by the shoulder. This apparently formidable assault, however, was committed by no unfriendly hand, being none other than that of a Magyar, with whom, together with his three companions, we had travelled in the steamer from Pest. By this time all had reached us, and there was a general greeting.

"How glad we are to meet the *Ángolok* again! What joy," etc., etc.,—" Where have you been, since we parted on board the 'Szechenyi,' three days ago? Here? In Orsova? Is it possible, and so have we, and yet we have not met. How strange!—Well, you *must* come now we have found you, and dine with us at the König von Ungarn; we will take no denial," exclaimed they, all speaking at the same time.

Pleased as we should have been to accept their hospitable invitation we were obliged to decline it; for yonder, shading his eyes with his hand to ascertain whether it is his "sweet master and mistress" who are coming, is András standing by a vehicle to which three horses are harnessed abreast; whilst by its side is another in which the luggage is placed in readiness for our journey, on which we should have started an hour ago. We must, therefore, partake of a hasty lunch and be off.

We have only to bid adieu to our new acquaintances for the present, however, who are consoled on discovering that by a "happy coincidence," we are to be fellow-travellers to Temesvár, they leaving Orsova by the seven o'clock train that evening; and we joining it at Mehadia about twelve miles distant. Near it are the Hercules Baths, where we purpose spending the intervening hours, and it is a place which no one who comes to Orsova should fail to visit.

At two o'clock we mount our chariot, and off we start as if borne on the wings of the wind, the vehicle containing András and the luggage following slowly behind.

The first portion of our drive is most exciting: the pace at which the horses go, all of them keeping step; the fierce shouts of the Wallachian driver, who half stands up as he urges them into a gallop; the continual flourishes of his whip, which he invariably terminates with a loud crack that rends the air, the clatter of our bells, and the sight of the three horses abreast—wild-looking creatures, with neither collars nor blinkers—all impress us with the idea that we ourselves must be ancient Romans, driving in a triumphal car, until an instant's glance at the car in question dispels the illusion. It is not long, however, before the horses are permitted to assume the "regulation crawl." A hill has to be ascended, and then we reach the valley of the Czerna, enclosed on either side by wooded mountains, with their slopes cultivated with the vine. Snowing the summits, the wild cherry and pear are seen in full bloom, whilst plum-trees of immense size growing by the road-side, shower their petals on us as we pass.

The driver, now seated calmly on the box, sings a peaceful melody to encourage his steeds and accompany the plaintive music of their bells. The gurgle of the Czerna, as it winds along, sounds cool and pleasant. On the hill-sides women are hoeing the hard, sun-baked earth, or sowing seed for the late crops; and down by the river's bank are primitive water-mills, where the villagers grind their corn, and near which are huts surrounded by peach orchards, whose rich pink blossoms contrast gratefully with the green and brown of their immediate surroundings. By the roadside a flock of woolly long-horned sheep are browsing; and a group of peasants recline under the cool shadow of a tree. The horses' bells jingle in sweet harmony with the torrent at our feet; but the day is hot, the sun shines fiercely on the sandy road, and the driver, giving us the reins, goes down to slake his thirst. Then on we go again till we reach a village with its church and fresco-painted tower, near which stands a priest, surrounded by a number of Wallachian urchins just out of school, wearing white tunics, and lamb's wool caps, the very image of their elders. As at Orsova, the women here wear an outer skirt of thick fringe suspended from a broad girdle made to fit the figure, and richly woven in various colours, called an "*obreska*," the fringe, which generally consists of two colours only—scarlet and black arranged in stripes—extending to the hem of the white under-garment. It is a kind of dress which they must find very inconvenient I should imagine when working in the fields, yet all wear it without exception, old and young alike.

The huts we now pass are enclosed by stockades stronger far than even those I mentioned as having seen in the suburbs of Orsova, some being raised to a height of more than eight or ten feet, to protect the inhabitants and their kine from the attacks, not only of wolves, but of bears also, both of which abound in this locality—the latter often doing much harm to the crops of Indian corn.

Wherever we look now women are training the vines, their picturesque costumes gleaming in the sunlight, whilst their lords may generally be seen lying under the shadow of a tree, fast asleep, and the farther we proceed, the more Eastern vegetation becomes, parasite plants festooning many of the loftier trees, with long garlands that sway in the sultry air.

Coming towards us are three Wallachian women, trudging merrily along the road, and spinning as they go. How

graceful they are, and what lovely faces, half Roman, half Grecian, look up at us smiling, as they pass—their fringes flying out behind them like peacocks' fans!

Now and then we meet a whole family, consisting of two, and sometimes three generations, huddled together in one of the long country carts, from the open ladder-like sides of which hang just such gourds and leathern bottles as we read of in Scripture.

A picturesque wooden bridge crossing the Czerna now appears in sight; the valley contracts, and the mountains become more wild and precipitous. At length, nearing the village of Korabnek, we pass the ruins of a Roman aqueduct, said to have been in existence in the time of Hadrian, and believed to have originally extended from the baths of Mehadia to Orsova, in order to convey the healing waters to the latter place. There are evidences also of this aqueduct having been restored, and used by the Turks for the same purpose, a Pasha having for many years resided at Orsova, which at one period was an important Turkish citadel.

Vines now cluster close to the road-side, from the grapes of which Schiller is made—a delicate ruby-coloured wine, which, though exceedingly cheap, is good after it has been kept three years.

At last, after crossing a brand-new and gaudily painted iron bridge—so out of keeping with the ancient monuments we have passed, such a hideous deformity, so forbidding, ugly and out of tune with the poetry of its surroundings—that one marvels how it ever could have got there, we are greeted by the first glimpse of the little bathing establishment where the Romans, that bath-loving people, founded a colony, calling the place "*Ad aquas Herculi sacras,*" and its site "*ad mediam.*" From the latter, no doubt, the name of Mehadia originated.

A picturesque church, standing on an eminence at the entrance to the gorge, introduces us to this classic ground; and to our surprise, on turning a bend in the road, we find ourselves all at once surrounded by fair palaces and terraced gardens which remind us more of the "Arabian

Nights," than the ancient abode of Roman colonists. Grecian colonnades, fountains, statuary and exotic flowers and grasses, almost take our breath away, so sudden and unexpected is all this luxury in the midst of these lonely solitudes of nature.

These baths, whose discovery, as we have seen, is due to the Romans, are a very favourite resort of the Hungarians, as well as of the Serbs and Wallachians. Here, too, come the rich, luxurious, and pampered Boyards of Bucharest, who, to quote the words of one of our Hungarian friends, come annually to "boil their much-abused livers in the hot springs."

The *Kurhaus*, a splendid structure in the Roman style, the interior of which is adorned with frescoes, contains colonnades, and beneath their shade the visitors promenade during the scorching hours of day. The most beautiful building of all, however, is the *Elizabethen Bad*.

"Here," said our conductor, the manager of one of the bathing establishments—as he ushered us into a large apartment filled with steam, and smelling so horribly of sulphur that it might have been Tartarus itself—"Here the people step into the water, and *feel the evil being boiled out of them!*"

There are no fewer than twenty-four springs in this mountain gorge. The rocks, which, like all of this character, consist of limestone, are full of fissures from which water oozes, and beneath which singular rumbling noises are often heard. The springs are of two kinds, sulphur-thermal and alkali-saline, the former said to be the strongest in the world, the largest and hottest being that called by the Romans *Thermæ Herculis*, which bursts forth in a column half a yard in diameter, and produces no less than 5,000 cubic feet of water per hour, of the temperature of 131° Fahrenheit.

Having passed the military hospital, a large building to the left, near which is a fountain surmounted by a statue of Hercules, we ascend to the place containing the source of the spring, which bears the name of the heathen god.

Beneath an almost overhanging rock there exists what may be described as a small natural grotto or fissure, about eight feet high and three broad, on entering which, and descending a flight of rugged steps hewn in the solid rock, we reach an inner cleft filled with dense vapour, whence the stream issues forth and again disappears in the dark recesses of the earth. The air in this cavern is hot and stifling, and we are glad to emerge once more into the outer atmosphere.

Perfectly exhausted, we are endeavouring to cool ourselves on a slab of rock opposite, when the loud clatter of wheels is heard, and a carriage soon makes its appearance, in which are our Hungarian friends. Demonstrative as ever, off go the hats, accompanied by much waving of handkerchiefs and sticks so soon as they recognise us.

Unable to bear the absence of the " charming *Ángolok* " any longer, they had, they said, made up their minds to follow us here, and be our *ciceroni*. I am not at all sure we were as grateful for the attention as we ought to have been, but I trust at any rate that we looked so.

Sedate and melancholy as are the Magyars usually, they are given to great and sudden changes of temperament, their character being an admixture of habitual pensiveness and melancholy, mingled with the most child-like susceptibility to enjoyment. Like their national music, they are tender and passionate by turns, now plunged into a whirlpool of excited fury, and now into the lowest depths of melancholy and despair, but when out for a holiday they shake off dull care, and become as light-hearted as schoolboys. Knowing this locality well, they conducted us to many interesting spots, including a real robbers' cave, situated in a romantic nook in the wooded gorge, which we might otherwise have overlooked.

Higher up, on a rock about seven or eight feet above the roadway, and not far from the source of *Thermæ Herculis*, are two votive tablets of the Roman period, on which, carved in relief, are the busts of a male and female. The features of each are still quite distinct, but we could ascertain from no one, whom they were intended to represent.

In one of the chambers of the Hercules bath, which is still used, and which remains unaltered since it was built by the Romans—a small dark room a few feet below the entrance—is a large and almost life-size figure of the deity from whom the bath is named. It is carved in relief on an immense block of stone forming one of the walls of the chamber.

Nothing can be more romantic than the situation of this little watering place, where nature and art alike combine to render a summer's sojourn delightful. The pathways through the wooded gorge; the beautiful Czerna, which is here a foaming torrent clear as crystal; the hotels, with their terraced gardens bright with Grecian vases, statuary, and flowers; the gipsy-music, and interesting associations connected with the place itself; the variety of races; and above all the festivities that take place daily during the season—render it unrivalled as a resort for the idle or hypochondriac. I would, however, warn those of the stronger sex who may happen to be highly susceptible to the tender passion, to think twice ere they come, for the bewitching beauty of these daughters of Roumania and Transylvania is perfectly irresistible, and few there are, I suspect, who, after a sojourn here, could leave entirely heart-whole.

The season lasts from June till September, the one drawback being the cost of living, which, though less than that of most Hungarian baths, is nevertheless great, compared with anything of the kind in England, and I doubt if eight florins a day would cover the expenses of the visitor.

As we loiter in front of the hotel at which we have dined, waiting for our carriages to take us to the station, two miles distant, a young peasant comes to fill her pitcher at the fountain. Like the majority of Wallachian women she is very lovely, and there is a noble and unfettered grace in her dress and carriage. How well, too, her Juno-like head, adorned with gold coins, is set upon her shoulders! Standing beneath the ancient statue of the pagan god, what a model she would form for an artist!

At Mehadia station we almost lost our train, so silently did it glide up to the platform, whilst we were occupied outside the enclosure in endeavouring to effect the purchase of a very handsome "*obreska*," worn by a young girl. It was new, and its colours brilliant and unsullied, but by no offer could she be tempted to part with it, not even by a bank note for fifty florins, which, taking out his purse, one of our Magyar friends held up to her. She only shook her head in a dignified manner, smiled, and passed on.

"Suppose she had accepted your offer," I remarked to the Magyar who had tendered her the note.

"I knew I was safe," was his reply. "The poorer inhabitants of these wilds scarcely know the use of money. With their cow, pig, and little flock of sheep, whose wool furnishes the material for their clothing, which they spin, weave, and dye themselves, and their plot of ground on which they grow their daily bread, what can such persons want with money? Besides, their principal circulating medium is barter;" and I could not help thinking how favourably these Wallachian peasantry, as well as the Slovaks, contrast with our own poor—a supposition that was very soon confirmed.

Twilight's shadows had given place to night, when, after passing through a mountainous region, we entered another of those narrow gorges, so characteristic of the Carpathian chain, through the eastern portion of which we are now travelling. As we whirled along all was pitch dark; save here and there where a party of travellers, ten or twenty in number, clad in sheepskin cloaks, were bivouacking before a large fire, the flames of which, lighting up the rocky background, only made the darkness visible, and rendered the whole more weird.

This wild and rugged mountain district, however, introduces us to the fertile province of the Banát, one of the most productive districts in the world, and often spoken of as the "granary of Europe."

Three of our Hungarians having gone with F. into a smoking carriage to offer evening incense, I was left to the companionship of the eldest of the party, a dear old Magyar of about sixty years of age, but who looked much older, his wrinkled weather-beaten face and quivering voice bespeaking eighty rather than sixty winters. There is something infinitely pathetic, not only in the voices, but in the countenances of the aged Magyars, which seem charged as with a bitter memory. Is their habitual sadness caused by the union of the beloved Fatherland with a foreign power? In many instances I am inclined to think it is.

There are three political parties in Hungary: the Liberal party, founded by Deák in 1866; the Extreme Left, which demands disrupture with Austria, and rallies under the name of Kossuth, their great revolutionary leader; and the Opposition.

My *compagnon de voyage* belonged to the second, and, a patriot of the old school, he stigmatised the conciliatory policy of Deák as cowardly and unpatriotic. As he alluded to the political compromise of this Prime Minister the tears came into his eyes. To foreigners the Hungarians open their hearts freely, and as we were alone, he spoke without reserve. There are grumblers in every nation, but there is no doubt the Hungarians have good reason to complain.

CHAPTER XXXII.

THE FAMILY PEDIGREE.

THE town of Temesvár contains a population of 33,000 souls, and produces a medley that almost outdoes even Pest itself. Here are Greeks, Wallachs, Hebrews, Serbs, Croats, Bulgarians, a sprinkling of Turks, and a large proportion of Magyars. It consists of an inner town and an outer one, the former surrounded by strong fortifications. Wherever one looks there are bastions and ditches, and great guns and little guns menacing us in all directions, and seeming to dodge our movements continually. Never by any chance do we get out of the way of those guns. As we walk along the road by the side of the people's park, there is one facing us the whole way; as *we* turn to the left it seems to turn also. Never can I forget the expression of that one gun, which, for nearly half the day, fixed its hideous muzzle upon us like a great unblinking eye, and kept me in a state of nightmare throughout the live-long hours of slumber.

There has been good reason in the past, however, for all these hostile demonstrations; for Temesvár has twice played a very important *rôle* in Hungarian history. The town contains but few old buildings, having been nearly destroyed during the bombardment of 1849, when a thousand shells were sent into it, and nearly every house reduced to a heap of ruins. The greatest victory gained by the Imperial army over the Hungarians was fought here under General Haynau.

The Palace, built in 1443 by John Hunyad, one of Hungary's last kings, has been entirely restored, and is now used as a prison. At the present time Temesvár is one of the prettiest, cleanest, and brightest little towns in the whole of Hungary. The houses are new and lofty and have an Italian look, except beyond the gates where they are nearly all of one story.

The now smiling and beautiful plains surrounding Temesvár were once a huge morass infested with fevers of the most pestilential description, the whole district of the Banát at the close of the last century—up to which time it was the frequent theatre of Moslem incursion—being scarcely better than an uncultivated swamp. After the final expulsion of the Turks, however, foreigners were summoned to people this "luxuriant wilderness," and Greeks, Bulgarians, Servians, Germans, and even French and Italians availed themselves of the invitation, till the rich alluvial prairie, hitherto unturned by the plough, was soon converted into a fertile garden. The soil yielded the most extraordinary crops, fortunes were speedily made, and some of the wealthiest Hungarian families of the present day are said to be the descendants of poor adventurers in the Banát.

The climate of this region during the summer is all but tropical, and the rich, black, loamy soil capable of producing almost any crop. Besides Indian corn, tobacco, flax, hemp, and sunflowers—from which oil is made—rice also grows in the marshy districts. Nor is cotton missing, for in one district in the Banát we recognised the pretty serrated leaf, and white, fluffy balls of the useful plant.

At Temesvár we took the train to our next destination, our lumbering old carriage coming with us on a truck.

Leaving the old town we travelled through dense forests, and passed the castle where, as the Austrians say, Görgei capitulated, but where the Hungarians, on the contrary, declare that he turned traitor to his country.

In the plains the wheat and rye are being cut, and how many sweet pictures we see! Whole families in brilliant costumes grouped round their *széker*, or *Leiterwagen*, resting from their toil in the drowsy noontide, and some of them fast asleep. Presently we stop at a station close to a large and thickly populated village, inhabited exclusively by Bulgarian colonists. Their costume is not only distinct, but they retain their own language, and make themselves intelligible to the Hungarians by a smattering of Magyar. In a short time, arriving at Szaderlak, we find ourselves in a district peopled by a race who originally migrated from the Black Forest; almost every village we pass being denizened by a separate and distinct nationality, none of whom can understand the next. And now, leaving villages behind, we are again out on the rolling plains, with their immense herds of horses, cows, and swine. Although the various herds intermingle, they know their owners and their owners know them, and at the sound of the various horns at morn or eve, as at Füred, they all "sort themselves" and run off helter-skelter to their own villages, which are sometimes many miles away. If the traveller make any sojourn on the Alföld he will observe that every Sunday morning each peasant takes to his own particular quadrupeds a small quantity of salt and corn, and as soon as his form is seen approaching, when yet a mere speck in the distance, they race off to meet him, the pigs with loud and indignant squeak bringing up the rear.

As we approach the river Marós the plains are almost under water, and there are signs of inundation everywhere. How one pities the peaceful dwellers in the vicinity of these ungovernable rivers! A little further and we come to the Marós itself, winding over its shallow bed, a clear stream reflecting the sunlit sky, with the curious old boats carrying merchandise seen here and there floating calmly on its still and glassy surface. But leaving the plains behind we soon enter a beautiful valley hemmed in by lofty hills, one of which is crowned with an ancient Burg, the first of those many "peasant-fortresses" which, during the troublous times of Turkish invasion, formed a line of fortifications extending throughout this eastern portion of Hungary.

In four hours' time we reach the plains again and come to the end of our journey. Arriving at the station, we see beyond its enclosure a white carriage and four white horses driven by a white man, waiting to take us across the green and boundless wastes to the home of András's master, at which we are to stay some days. Casting our eyes round the whole circle of the horizon, however, we see no road whatever. Have we to cross these interminable plains hap-hazard, with nought but the sun to guide our wanderings? Nothing is visible but a long line of white cloud creeping along the ground. But leaving the station behind we soon enter the white cloud, and find that it covers a sandy track which itself forms the roadway, and before we have proceeded half a mile we feel we have swallowed a sand-bank, and, like the horses, the carriage, and the driver, become covered from head to foot with dust. There have been no inundations here at all events, for the ground is as parched as on the desert of Arabia, and instead of pitying the inhabitants of the district of the fertilising Marós, we almost envy them.

The horses gallop the whole way, and our seven miles of road are happily soon covered. In rather less than forty minutes we see through our sand-bedimmed eyes a group of *robinias* similarly powdered, and in their midst a large one-storied building. Passing through the open gates and a long sweeping carriage drive, we come to anchor at a broad flight of steps, where, seen through the dust that has followed us even here, stands a spectre in black, who, descending the steps in question with measured stately gait, welcomes the ghosts within the carriage and assists them to alight. And we soon hear the words, " My sweet servant," followed by " My sweet master," as the white form of András appears, who, stooping low, kisses with deepest reverence the black spectre's hand.

Other dark forms now appear, coming from the back premises, and there are loud acclamations at the sight of András, and a shower of *"per Kends"* ("your Graces") falls broad-cast, as these polite people greet each other according to the approved mode of salutation amongst servants in Hungary.

As usual the mansion consists of one story only, and covers a large area. There are no passages, and each room is approached through another. The living rooms form a cluster in the centre of the building, and are connected by lofty folding-doors, all of which being open, give an appearance of space and grandeur to the whole. Although of the very simplest order in architectural design, the mansion is luxuriously furnished, and seems strangely out of keeping with its surroundings. It is heated throughout by hot air, and none of the stoves, which form such an ugly feature in German houses, are visible.

It is only above the roads that the cloud of dust I have alluded to hovers, and, our rooms looking out upon the Alföld, we see before us a graceful landscape covered with vast stretches of Indian corn, the tall stems of which, already drooping with their ripening ears, are golden in the setting sun. Whilst dressing for dinner, which was at half-past seven, I watched from my window the great scarlet ball sink beneath the horizon, till the plains, drinking in the splendours of the sky, were as a crucible blending all the rainbow's tints into one delicious harmony.

We found a large family party assembled at dinner: the dowager, our host's mother, a widowed sister and her son and daughter, besides the young wife—a beautiful woman and a true specimen of Magyar, possessing those graceful and winning manners which are such a charm in all Hungarian society.

During dinner the conversation turned upon the Magyar language, and the obstacles to its acquisition which beset foreigners, the principal one arising from the fact that the prepositions and possessive pronouns instead of preceding are made to follow the noun, and become affixes to it. From this cause a whole sentence of six or seven words is sometimes capable of being expressed in one only; our hostess naïvely instancing two combinations illustrative of the lengths to which this peculiarity of the language may be carried, namely,—" *Hamegköpenyegesittelennittehhetnélek*," a word signifying " If I could deprive you of your clothes ! " and another — " *Legellenallhatlanabbaknak-bizonyultak* " — meaning " They have proved themselves the most irresistible; " and, as she did so, she uttered these to us unpronounceable syllables with so sweet an intonation that they made us in love with the language.

To render the above peculiarity, so aggravating to foreigners, intelligible to the reader, I will give one or two examples explanatory of the construction of the language in this respect. And first, when András addresses, in the words "my sweet master" and "my sweet mistress"—"*édes uram*" and "*édes asszonyom*"—the substantive nouns are *úr* and *asszony*, the final syllables, *am*, *om*, being merely the possessive affixes. Again, *anyá* (mother) becomes, with the possessive pronoun *my* affixed to it, *anyám;* whilst to instance an example in which both pronoun and preposition are used, we will take the word *haz* (a house). *Haz-am* (my house), followed by the preposition *ba* (*in*, which is affixed to the pronoun), becomes *hazamba* (in my house).

The construction of verbs too in Magyar differs so widely from that of any other European language that a perfect knowledge of it is extremely difficult to the foreigner, who seldom acquires it perfectly. The structure of the language in some measure resembles Turkish, Magyar, and Finnish, being connected with those of Mongolia and Turkestan just as English is with Persian and Sanscrit. The Magyar language is said to have undergone no changes whatever ; that spoken by the Hungarians of to-day being identical with that of the Magyars on their conquest of the country. A great many Turkish, Slavonian, as well as Greek, Italian, and German words have crept in; but all those essential to express common wants are the same as in the language of the Fins at the present time.

The drawing-room was full of English books, some of which were translated into the Magyar language. Hungarian literature is not as yet in a very advanced stage, neither, as a rule, are the Hungarians a very reading people. They have their own novelists, but greatly prefer English authors. They do not, however, care for the "sensational," preferring the sentimental and romantic.

In their cheap journalistic literature the kind of pabulum known as "penny dreadful" does not exist. The Hungarians of the lower class do not care to take their "horrors hot;" and such things as delight an Englishman of the same calibre fall flat upon the mental palate of a Hungarian.

There is nothing half so charming as a visit to a Magyar family. There is a well-bred ease and cordiality of manner about the Hungarians, that make the guest feel perfectly at home immediately he enters the house. There is no *gêne*, and the visitor becomes instantly as one of the family circle.

The following morning, whilst the lord of the domain was closeted with his *Ispán* (steward), we walked to some of the tenants' cottages, accompanied by his wife. Although we went into six, I do not think we saw as many children. The Magyars seldom have large families; and so often are they childless that it is a common thing for them to adopt the child of a wandering Slovak, and bring him up as their own. There is also a great mortality amongst children on the

Alföld, the chief reason assigned being the earthen floors; their aged also being said to suffer intensely from rheumatism, from the same cause.

Surrounding these dwellings was a small garden fenced in with the dried stalks of Indian corn, and nothing could have looked more comfortable than the interior of each one, which bespoke the existence of rude plenty. Yet the inhabitants were but the cultivators of the soil, synonymous with our English labourers. On our return we passed through the farm-buildings, and were shown the stud, consisting of about twenty horses. In the adjoining coach-house were carriages of all descriptions and of the most primitive design; whilst in the centre stood one the precise nature of which it was not easy to define.

"That," remarked our host, who had now joined us (pointing in the direction of the nondescript vehicle in question), "is the family pedigree." And its history, narrated by himself, showed how appropriate was its title. It had in fact begun its career by being a modest species of *britzska*, but ended in becoming a house on wheels, a veritable genealogical tree.

Our host, unlike his Magyar tenantry, was blessed with a "quiverful," having eight children, the eldest of whom numbered little more than as many years, all having arrived with the greatest punctuality like daisies and buttercups in May. When the third "hardy annual" was old enough to take his daily exercise with his parents, the *britzska* was converted into a *barouche*. On the death of our host's father, at which epoch the dowager took up her abode in the country château of her son, an excrescence was added to the back in the form of a "rumble," to which the "hardy annuals" were transferred in her favour; and when the sixth arrived, our pater-familias resorted to the ingenious expedient of having the carriage closed in after the manner of a *landau*, and the hood elevated to the top after the fashion of a *banquette* on the summit of a *diligence*. At last twins came; upon which happy occurrence two small seats were attached to the inside of the doors, which were ingeniously contrived to let up and down like a bracket.

"In this carriage," he remarked triumphantly, when he had finished its history, his whole countenance beaming with benevolence and paternal pride, "we all travel together to Pest, where we have our winter residence."

One can picture to one's self the start. The host and hostess, the dowager—our host's mother—his sister, the eight small blessings, the governess, the lady's maid, the footman, the postilion, the six horses and the dowager's lap-dog; in all a Noah's Ark of twenty-three bipeds and quadrupeds!

In the early evening our host took us for a long drive across his estate, and as our way was fortunately not confined to the sandy wastes we traversed yesterday, we were not smothered with dust as on our way from the station. Never can I forget that drive, or the railway speed at which we skimmed over the level surface of the *puszta*. Railway speed! It is nothing to it—not that of Hungarian railways, at any rate. We absolutely flew on the wings of the wind. The pace at which a good team of Hungarian horses go is the most madly exciting thing possible to conceive.

The domain of our host covered a large area of *puszta*; but it was small, he assured us, compared with many, which often cover from thirty to forty square miles; whilst formerly there were instances in which some were even seven and eight hundred miles in extent. It is difficult for us, who live in our "tight little island," to comprehend the existence of such vast estates belonging to one individual. Yet they were managed with great exactness under stewards, the labourers and their families sometimes consisting of an army of from a thousand to fifteen hundred souls. The word *puszta*, now so commonly and incorrectly applied to the great plains, originated in these estates; a nobleman's property, which was farmed by his own labourers—that is to say, where there were no peasants, and consequently no forced labour—having been called a *puszta*. The revenues are often as enormous as the domains themselves; and the flocks that graze the land not under cultivation numbering hundreds of thousands, remind one of patriarchal times; whilst the ingatherings of wheat, rye, rape, and other cereals grown on the estate each amount to hundreds of thousands of bushels annually.

Having dined before starting, the usual dinner hour in Hungary being two o'clock, we were enabled to prolong our drive, and did not return until a late hour in the evening.

"They are dancing the *csárdás*," exclaimed our host, as we approached a number of labourers' dwellings and saw the red petticoats spinning round and round. "Would you like to see it? They dance it every evening; but this is evidently one got up for a particular occasion, for the girls are in full fig, and I hear the clash of spurs as the Magyar dandies knock their heels together to keep time to the scraping of the gipsies' fiddles."

It was a pretty scene: the rapid movements of the dancers in their gay costumes, the picturesque background of low sheds covered with the large round leaves of the melon, its tendrils hanging in graceful festoons, and its golden fruit resting on the thatch. We might have been witnessing a Spanish saraband.

The Hungarians dance for their very lives. To them the practice of the Terpsichorean art is no mere languid and graceful undulation of the figure, but a perfect wild *abandon* of mirth; and they whirl, and spin, and gyrate with the velocity of dervishes, until their long black locks stand out straight, and their faces are ablaze with heat and excitement.

Watch them as they perform the *csárdás*—their national dance—to the strange wild harmony of the *Czigánok!* Watch them as they balance themselves backwards and forwards whilst adapting their subtle movements to the measure of its animating strains!

The *csárdás* is essentially pantomimic, and describes by mute action the unquiet "course of true love." The music is at first slow, and the couples walk up and down the room together in a stately manner; then, affecting to have made each other's acquaintance, and fallen victims to the tender passion, the music grows more lively, and the "courtship" begins in earnest.

The lover advances towards his *innamorata*, she coyly responds and they spin round together for a few seconds, when, as if thinking she has given him too much encouragement, the maiden retires pouting, whereupon he again approaches, but this time she turns her back upon him and dances off in a contrary direction. Following her, however, he overtakes and seizes her round the waist, and away they go again whirling deliriously, until she manages to extricate herself from his grasp. Shy and friendly by turns, now encouraging her partner, and now retreating with offended dignity, the lover at length becomes chagrined at her caprices turns his back upon her, and they dance *dos à dos* for a while with indignant gestures, till the maid with signs of repentance seeks reconciliation. The music grows faster and faster, the lovers, in the ecstasy of reunion, whirl and twirl madly, nor do they stop until both are quite giddy and out of breath, when, retiring from the scene, another couple takes their place, and the performance begins again.

The *csárdás*, of course, varies slightly in each instance, according to the locality and the spirit of the dancers, but the subject remains the same—love, courtship, jealousy, disappointment, reunion, and happiness "ever after." Sometimes, in the closing scene, it winds up by the lover throwing himself on his knees before his mistress, whilst she dances round him in token of her complete triumph. Several couples are always occupied at the same time in this dance, in one phase or other of the would-be courtship; whilst the men's hats, decorated with fresh flowers, the women got up in the most coquettish and picturesque costumes imaginable, the stamping of feet, clashing of spurs, and wildly exciting strains of the gipsies, as they saw away madly at their violins, all combine in rendering the *csárdás* a most interesting and animating spectacle. Nor is it danced only by the peasants: it is seen in the ball-rooms of the nobles even at the capital, where a gipsy-band is always summoned to accompany it.

The most interesting place in which to witness it is the harvest-field, where, laying down their sickles, half-a-dozen of them will often stand up, as if seized by some irresistible impulse, and begin dancing all amongst the sheaves of corn.

Besides the national *csárdás*, however, there is one called the *Loshau csárdás*, a very slow dance, but it is by no means a favourite with the Magyars, who, so calm and phlegmatic in their ordinary moments, are wont during recreation to give themselves up to the wildest excitement. A third is often seen in the east of Hungary, where a number of men, linking arms, form a ring and dance together, accompanying their gyrations with clapping of hands, shouts, and stamping of feet, whilst the fair ones remain outside the magic circle, till an intrepid Adonis, breaking from his companions, seizes one of them round the waist and waltzes with her for awhile, after which he returns to the ring, and another repeats the ceremony.

But whatever be the form which the Hungarian dance assumes, its constant theme is love, just as patriotism and the joys of home are the chief subjects of their song.

CHAPTER XXXIII.

GROSSWARDEIN.

IT is nightfall at Grosswardein and the fires of sunset have faded into cold grey ashes. All along the river Kőrös the stealthy vapours, following its leaden course, are slowly rising. Shadows deepen on the plains. The gilded steeples no longer glisten in the evening light, but stand out black and sullen, like huge sentinels, against the pale green sky. Everything in nature is sad and gloomy. Within the town, however, "high carnival" is nightly kept.

The Magyars, as we have seen, possess a tinge of melancholy even in their most joyous moments. This, however, cannot be said of the Wallachs. There surely never was such a gay and pleasure-loving people; whilst in their love of dancing they far exceed even the Magyars themselves.

Hark to the sound of music! the rhythmic beat accompanied by the rapid and hollow throb of steps. Let us follow its inviting strains, away through the broad streets to the great square.

Not only here, however, is there music and dancing, but in many of the one-storied houses also. In the cafés too the *Cziganok* are fiddling away for dear life. Inside, persons, sitting before small tables, sip their coffee and smoke like chimneys. They applaud and sip and smoke, and then smoke and sip and applaud again; whilst the streets are crowded with promenaders and cheerful with the laugh of girls.

Here and there, like moths amongst the butterflies, may be seen a group of middle-aged Wallachs or grave Magyars talking earnestly together, whispering of political complications between Russia and England, the result of the "Danube Commission," or the rising of the bed of the river Theiss. The beauty of the Wallachs is the same as when last we were here four years ago: the delicate and refined features, the pouting lips, the broad, low forehead, the lithe figures of the women, and the deeply sunken eyes, long hair, and aquiline noses of the male descendants of the Dacians, all are the same; but the ancient costumes of the people and their characteristic traits are fast departing under the facilities which, in these modern days, are afforded for travel. The railways, extending their iron arms into the very centre of Transylvania, are gradually weaving this former *terra incognita* into the duller web of Western civilisation, and the beautiful and graceful costumes, which so delighted us once, are day by day becoming absorbed and replaced by those Gallic abominations invented to conceal and render hideous the human form.

That monstrous article of female attire, the crinoline, which until recently was exploded by the fair sex of Western Europe, has been adopted by their Eastern sisters, and we recognise it not only beneath the skirts of the gaily dressed Jewess as her long train sweeps the streets, but under those of the Wallach lady also; whilst one peasant girl—though still dressed in her graceful, homespun garments—emulating her superiors—had her narrow but classical *katrincza* distended to the condition of a sausage by the adoption of this hideous contrivance. We saw, I am thankful to say, only one who had thus travestied the lovely and pictorial costume of her race, but it was sufficient to demonstrate the silent march of—in this case misnamed—" civilisation," which threatens ere long to obliterate all the distinctive external characteristics of nations and render every country alike.

Off the beaten track the Wallachs still retain the customs of their ancestors both in dress and manner of living, and after our visit to this place is ended we shall be travelling in the interior of Transylvania—of which Grosswardein is the frontier—where we shall see the Wallachs in all their delightful simplicity. It is here that the traveller is first introduced to this people in their own home, of whom, concentrated in the eastern portion of Hungary, there are almost two millions and a half. The Wallachs of Transylvania, however, must not be confounded with the dwellers in the Wallachian or Roumanian Principality, although they are offshoots of the same race, having been in olden times the overflow of the inhabitants occupying that province. Both races now form a distinct people, although they are alike descendants of the ancient Dacians, originally a Thracian people subjugated by Trajan in his conquests already alluded to in the chapters on the Lower Danube.

The term Wallach is said to be a German version of the appellations " *Welsh,*" " *Welsch,*" " *Wallon,*" etc., given by the Teutonic conquerors to the provincials or subjects of the Roman Empire, whether in Britain, Italy, or Gaul;

Welsh being the word still used by the Germans in the present day to denote strangers or foreigners of whatever nation.

Naturally preferring to trace their origin to the conquering, rather than to a vanquished people, the Wallachs affect to be the descendants of the Roman colonists introduced by Trajan after his subjugation of the province, and call themselves, though incorrectly, *Roumans*, or *Rummanyi*, and their country Roumania.

The language spoken by the Wallachs, which greatly resembles in its pronunciation the Italian of to-day, is soft, rich, and melodious, and composed chiefly of Latin, with a considerable admixture of Slav, Turkish, and Greek words. That there should be such a marked Latin element in their language is certainly a singular fact, seeing that the dominion of the Romans over the Dacians extended for a period of 170 years only; a circumstance tending to foster the idea that the Wallachs *have* some grounds for their pride of ancestry. There are, however, peculiarities about their language which prove that the origin of this people is more Dacian than Roman.

A considerable Roman element was doubtless imfused into the primitive inhabitants of Dacia by inter-marriage with the numerous Roman subjects who remained behind after the Emperor Aurelian relinquished Dacia in the middle of the third century, and this would account in a great measure for the resemblance between the Wallachian and Latin languages. Until the time of Alexander, the Dacians scarcely figured in history, and their original language is consequently not accurately determined. It is, however, believed to have been Slávic, not only from the number of Sláv words mingled with their corrupt Latin, but also from the number of Slávonic names given to the rivers and mountains of Wallachia and Transylvania.

In the fifth century the Wallachs peopled Thessaly, whilst the Thracian dialect of that period is said to have borne a strong resemblance to the Neo-Latin spoken alike by the Wallach tribes of the Pindus Mountains—the remnants of the former inhabitants of Thrace—and by the so-called Roumanian people at present occupying the province of ancient Dacia.

So much does their pronunciation resemble Italian that we experienced no difficulty in understanding, or even conversing with them, particularly after having ascertained that they place the definite article at the end of their nouns, joining in fact both noun and article together. This singular construction is also found in the Bulgarian language, but, strange to say, in no other Slavonic dialect whatever, from which circumstance it is supposed that both the Bulgarians and Wallachians—whose countries join each other—must have derived this peculiarity from the same source, viz., from their north-eastern neighbours, the Dacians, whose language is believed to have been neither Neo-latin nor strictly Slavonic.

In ancient time the province of Dacia comprised a district of 1300 miles in circumference, and was bounded on the north by the Niester, on the west by the Theiss or Tibiscus, and on the south and east by the Lower Danube and Black Sea; comprising not only the mountainous country of the Eastern Carpathians, but Bukovina and the district of Banát. The population of Moldavia and Bessarabia is likewise almost exclusively of Dacian origin.

On Trajan's Column in Rome is sculptured the history of

this first campaign of the young and ambitious Emperor, and the forms, cast of features, and dress of the Dacians. as there minutely represented, correspond, strange as it may seem after the lapse of sixteen centuries, in almost every particular with those of the Wallachs of the present day.

Grosswardein, or Nagy-varád, as it is called in Hungarian, is a fortified town of Bihar, the largest county in Hungary. It contains 36,000 inhabitants, the majority of whom are Wallachs, and is, in spite of its gaiety, one of the most ecclesiastical places in Hungary, full of churches and convents. At present there are thirty of the former, whilst at one period it boasted of no fewer than seventy. It is also the see, alike of a Catholic bishop and one of the Greek rite. The suburbs of the town are very pretty, each house being surrounded by a garden and orchard, and shut in behind high walls.

Like Temesvár, the town of Grosswardein is exceedingly pretty with long streets and numerous marketplaces.

From the bridge which crosses the Körös, a good view is obtained of the town with its glittering steeples of black and gold, together with that of the new Catholic Church which, standing by the dome of the Jewish Synagogue, looks like a huge coronet of gems. On the river long rafts of pine logs from the Transylvanian forests are leisurely floating down stream, whilst women with skirts tucked up wade in the water and wash their linen, thumping away at it with a big stone, and with a vigour and perseverance as if every blow were aimed at a Turk's or Austrian's head.

We were walking through one of the suburbs of the town when we heard the distant sounds of bitter wailing, and a little crowd of people soon approached, in the centre of which was an old Wallach woman who, with tears rolling down her shrivelled cheeks, was evidently telling her wrongs to the group of sympathisers following in her wake. On inquiring the cause of this unusual manifestation of grief, she clasped her hands and giving vent to renewed wailings cried,

"Only a Jew, gentle lady, only for killing a Jew."

The meaning of which unintelligible sentence the bystanders—who appeared to take no small interest in the case—explained by informing us that her husband had in a street quarrel accidentally killed one of those despised children of Israel, and that the Judge, having taken a somewhat different view from herself of the value of human life as exhibited in that particular type of humanity, had just sentenced him to condign punishment the extent of which however did not transpire.

As in all other towns in Hungary, Grosswardein is pervaded by the usual Hebrew element, and although Jews are no longer taxed as being such, but are permitted to enjoy all the rights and privileges common to the Gentile, they often find it difficult to hold their own even here against the antipathy so universally entertained against them.

All is bright and clean in this prettiest of towns save in the Hebraic quarter, which is full of marine stores where every kind of *bric-à-brac* is to be met with, even crucifixes, in dark dens which one would fear to enter. The Jew is the same here as elsewhere, the same miserable-looking, down-trodden outcast he has continued to be ever since Pompey the Great entered the Holy City and struck the first blow at the Israelitish nation. How, even to the letter, has the prophetic curse been fulfilled in this once "chosen people"!

The *spécialité* of the Hungarian Jew in this quarter, as in all others devoted entirely to the class, is "ole clo," and inside their hovels are found not only dirt and muddle, but pictorial rags, whilst over the doorways are seen such names as the following, Löwenstein Jukab, Kohn Mozesne, Füred József, and Szép Ábrahám, and on the walls sentences are written in Hebrew characters.

The type of Hebrew physiognomy is more marked here than in other parts of Hungary, a consequence possibly of there having been less intermarriage with the Christian community than elsewhere. Wherever we look we observe the long aquiline nose curving into the moustache, which only partially conceals the protruding lips. Now and then a fair young Miriam may be seen crossing the road and picking up a dirty little Moses who is wallowing in the mud; neither are Hagars and Ishmaels wanting, nor old Sarahs, fat, ugly, and repulsive-looking in their grease-begrimed garments.

Turning now to the Christian quarter, we see how the Gentiles flourish like a green bay-tree. Yonder stands the princely palace of the Roman Catholic bishop, whose income is 300,000 gulden, or £25,000 a year, whilst that of his Lordship of Erlan in the East of Hungary is twice that amount, and that of the Prince Primate £60,000, the revenues being derived in each case from landed estates. Surrounding the palace are beautiful gardens laid out in broad straight walks and long avenues of chestnuts, under the shade of which at eventide the Dom Herren may be seen sauntering in the cool still air. Near the palace are the houses of the residentiary canons, and opposite, the grand church built by Maria Theresa, a building so vast in its proportions that, as the doors are thrown open to admit us and we stand beneath its lofty roof, rising one hundred and twenty feet above, we almost lose our breath.

The church although built in the Doric style is cruciform, and its roof a succession of arches culminating in an immense central dome; the whole a gorgeous blaze of splendid colour, very rich and harmonious, but not adapted to inspire devotion. The Hungarian disposition is not suited to the "dim religious." They are a people who dislike mysticism of every sort, and with a very few exceptions their churches, garish and sensuous, are better fitted for the gorgeous worship of some heathen goddess or their Pagan *Magyarok Isten* (ancient Magyar deity) than for the pure and simple worship of Christians.

As we returned to our hotel, the sun just setting was gilding with impartial glory alike the temples of the Christian and the Jew.

CHAPTER XXXIV.

GOOD FRIDAY IN THE GREEK CHURCH.

A FEW miles from Grosswardein lies a valley, where, surrounded by undulating tertiary hills, is a mineral spring; and thither, a few days after our arrival, we made an excursion. Our way leads us through the market, where are milk-white oxen by the score, and hundreds of black swine with long noses and high backs, surrounded by swarms of piglings, the funniest little creatures imaginable, each with its back arched like a cat, and its tiny white legs and little black hoofs looking like shoes and stockings. In the centre of the square women are selling *tisch-wein* and hot soup thickened with macaroni, and wherever one turns there are gipsies selling baskets and wooden utensils.

Forcing our way through the vegetable baskets and the oxen and the pigs, we reach a broad road in which singular conveyances are jogging along. More strange by far than any we have yet seen in Hungary are the vehicles met with here, which, though apparently belonging to a class far above the ordinary peasant, are so different from any found in the rest of Europe, that we might have arrived at an altogether new world. Under the cool shadows of the *robinias*, which grow luxuriantly in the Alföld—a tree in

England erroneously called *acacia*, but which is the "locust tree" (*Robinia pseudacacie*) of the United States, so strongly advocated for English cultivation by Cobbet—the women stand and gossip, whilst resting their heavy burdens on the ground.

By the wayside are characteristic studies. A woman is making bricks, whilst standing beside her, smoking and languidly watching her movements, is her lord and master; for the male Wallach is a creature who loves to take life easily. A little farther on, and we see another woman hoeing away at the hard, sunbaked ground of her cottage garden, as her inferior half, sitting the while on the doorstep, nurses the baby.

In this country it would seem that "women must" not only "weep," but women must also work; whilst, by an inversion of the order of things, the men remain idle. But we are nearing our destination where there is a bathing establishment, for yonder is a broad still pool formed by the hot spring, in which, surrounded by clouds of vapour, washer-women are wading waist deep, as they hammer away at the visitors' clothes.

It was a pretty sight that at length greeted our arrival at the Bathing Establishment, and one that reminded us of *Fêtes Champêtres* in olden times. It is situated in the centre of large grounds, where, standing or sitting, were some two hundred people, with here and there knots of young men and maidens dancing to the inspiriting strains of a gipsy band. Beyond a number of chestnut trees, rises a densely forest-clad hill which birds make merry all day with song, and where numerous nightingales trill. There are so few woods in the Alföld that where they exist birds congregate in great numbers.

The hotel contains eighty rooms, and the people we here see disporting themselves so gaily, and who appear so completely the reverse of invalid, are but the ordinary visitors to the Baths. The Hungarians, like the Romans, are a bath-loving people, and resort during the hot summer season to places of this kind, just as we do in England to the sea-side.

The source of the hot spring lies at the bottom of a crater-like basin, from which the water comes bubbling to the surface as from a volcano, bringing with it a quantity of small shells of two kinds containing living creatures. Looking down into the water, which is clear as crystal, we see them not only being tossed up to the surface, but lying at the bottom of the crater, as well as round its sides.

The water here forms another broad pool, the surface of which is covered in many places with the *lotus* (*Nymphæa thermalis*) brought from the Nile and kept alive during the winter by the high temperature of the water. It begins to

ALL AMONG THE SHEAVES.

blossom in the beginning of April, and was in perfection at the time of our visit.

Besides the private baths attached to the hotel, there are large public ones also outside the grounds for the poorer classes, thousands of whom flock here during the season, and parboil themselves simply for the love of it. The charge for the use of these public baths is at the rate of thirty kreuzers (tenpence) for every twenty-four hours, so that the people who resort to them may be said at all events to have plenty for their money. They come hither from great distances. Slávs from Csaba, more than fifty miles away, and others from places equally remote, and simply divesting themselves of their top boots and fur jackets, plunge into the steaming tide, the men in their long-fringed *gatyák*, full white sleeves, and embroidered waistcoats, and the women in their gay bodices and coloured skirts. It is in fact an aquatic picnic, for they bring their provisions with them, and take their meals in the water, occasionally even dancing the *csárdás*, whilst some of the bathers, who possess a musical turn, sit on the edge of the bath with their feet and legs dangling in the water, and play their primitive instruments or keep time with the dance by clapping their hands, amidst the ringing and bewildering shouts of the dancers. They generally remain in the bath eighteen hours out of the twenty-four, and as our cicerone informed us, all for an "*ausflug*" (outing). Every now and then as they become faint and weak from the effects of the seething, they have recourse to the outer atmosphere for a while, where, lying down on the ground, wrapped in their bundas, they remain until the cool air has revived them, when they return and again join in the aquatic festivities.

Among the new arrivals we noticed two tall, fine-looking men wearing splendid lamb's wool cloaks, embroidered at the edges in gay colours, and others in curious blanket-cloaks like those worn by the Arabs.

It was late in the evening, and dark shadows were gathering over the plains when, leaving this singular locality behind, we directed our course homewards. From the cottages along the road now and then came the sound of the nervous little *telinka*, embroidering with fitful and fanciful variations, the hoarse snore of the bag-pipes as they droned out their wild, weird music to the night; whilst from a distance reached us the rich, deep throb of the cymbals. In many of the houses there is dancing and revelry, and accustomed as we are to the quiet and sullen habits of our own peasantry, we regard these pleasure-loving people with astonishment.

The Wallachs, like the Slovaks, belong chiefly to the Greek rite, of which there are two separate bodies, the non-united or "Oriental Greek Church," which acknowledges the Patriarch of Constantinople as its head, and the "United Greek," which recognises the supremacy of the Pope of Rome.

The recurrence of a high festival affords us an opportunity during the time we are here of witnessing one of the gorgeous services of the Greek Church, the splendid vestments and the imposing, and to us novel, ritual filling us with a new delight. The music was heavenly, the grand old Ambrosial chants, begun by a long-robed priest whose beard extended far below his chest, being taken up by the fresh young voices of the choir, which, welling upwards in a flood of melody, echoed through the vaulted roof.

It is impossible to give any adequate idea of the imposing ritual of the Greek Church to those who have not witnessed it, or of the apparent devotion and ecstatic adoration of the people as they prostrate themselves until their faces touch the marble floor, whilst the singing of the unseen choir seems to be that of a company of angels come down to earth to join in the Christian worship.

It was this music, the most beautiful and touching in the whole world, that melted the stern, cold heart of the Russian prince of old—the Great Vladimir himself—causing him to give up his Pagan gods, and was the indirect origin of the Greek rite becoming the national church of the northern branch of the Slavonian family.

Our visits to Grosswardein have been well-timed. On our last visit we happened to be here in the latter end of April and beginning of May, and were able to witness another, but a very different, ceremonial of these Eastern churches.

It was Good Friday. This day of penitence and fasting falls nearly a month later in the Greek calendar than in our own, and high up in the open towers of both the "United Greek" and "Oriental Greek" churches, instead of the sweet chiming of bells, men were busy with wooden clappers producing such unearthly sounds, as they kept hammering against a beam to call the faithful to worship, that, until undeceived by a friendly passer-by, we were under the full impression that giants with wooden legs were disporting themselves amongst the clock-work.

Inside the "Oriental Greek" churches the banners, together with the tables on which the sacred relics reposed, were draped with black. Tall tapers burned at sombre shrines erected for the occasion in the centre of the nave, and which were approached by a pathway of trees and flowers growing in large tubs—oleanders, geraniums, roses, lilies, and a variety of other plants, too numerous to mention, but all out of keeping to our thinking, for it was anything but a pathway of flowers which *He* trod, whose sufferings and death the people were commemorating. At the end of the long pathway was a canopy draped in violet, beneath which, on an altar, rested a silver crucifix and relics, and above a lifesize figure of the Saviour hanging on the cross. Towards this men and women, both young and old, pressed reverently, and approaching the table

on tiptoe lingered before it with sad faces and sometimes weeping eyes; they kissed the crucifix and relics, and dropped a coin into a bowl, and then stood and gazed again, as if reluctant to turn away; and when they did it was with steps soft and slow. Notwithstanding the immense crowd—for the great nave was as full as it could cram, there was perfect stillness and a hush almost supernatural, and our hearts were moved by the strong faith and love which the people evinced in and for the Holy Hero of the day, as they crossed themselves, and gently and sadly turned away to make room for other worshippers.

There was no sermon here to-day, for their bishop was dead; but crossing the marketplace, where men and women were sitting enveloped in black sheep-skin cloaks and jackets, we entered the cathedral of the "United" Greek Church, where one was being preached, and where the people were standing and listening attentively to the "old, old Story."

* * * * * *

I have travelled in many lands, but it is in Hungary alone that I have observed such intense devotion of the people. To them the religion they profess is no mere shadow, but a deep, great, and abiding reality. It is, however, principally amongst the Greek Catholics of both rites that this earnestness in devotion is seen. Although the Greek Church is in mourning and its devotees are fasting, it is the vigil of a high festival day in the Roman Catholic.

To-morrow is the first day of May, a month of rejoicing, so the churches are decorated with flowers, whilst in the streets young girls are carrying offerings to lay at the Virgin's shrine. Following them we enter the church of the San Franciscan Friars, a gorgeous edifice all tinsel and gold, with life-size, gaudily-painted figures of the twelve Apostles, the Virgin, and the Holy Women, all so natural that they seem endowed with sound and motion. Round the ledge of the pulpit are smaller ones in almost every attitude, some of which are poised on one leg, whilst others are hanging to the cornice, all of them so marvellously life-like that as we look at them we tremble lest they should break their little necks by toppling over on to the floor of the nave below. On the sounding-board there is another crowd of puppets, no less bewildering to the devout mind; but near the north entrance hangs a figure of our Saviour upon the cross, the blue lips, the livid face, and the expression of agony all so wonderfully depicted as to be painful to look at.

As we left the church the bells were chiming and the people flocking to the "Benediction;" whilst in another part of the town devout Jews were hastening to their synagogue, for it was the beginning of their Sabbath.

Not far from the hospital of "St. John of God" a funeral passed us. First came a small boy in a white surplice and black cassock bearing aloft a gilt cross veiled in white muslin, accompanied by other small boys; after whom came the priest, followed by several men in the ancient costume of the Magyars, in light blue embroidered *mentes* and caps of the same colour adorned with white feathers, the last of whom carried on a large white satin cushion a chaplet of flowers. Then came the bier, painted in blue and silver, and drawn by white horses draped in light blue cloth. Resting on the coffin, which was in the shape of a sarcophagus and looked as though it was made of silver, there lay at either end a beautiful wreath of flowers, the whole being covered with a white lace pall. Carriages followed, in which were ladies, but none of them were in mourning.

Meeting a gentleman we asked him whose funeral it was.

"Only that of some citizen," he replied, and without doing more than turn his head, went on his way.

I never saw such a place as Grosswardein for clocks:

almost every church steeple possesses four dials; but none of them agree as to the time, all maintaining a particular one of their own, and none of them being right!

May Day has come. We were awakened at five o'clock by the strains of a military band which according to ancient custom ushers in this golden morning by playing in front of the Palace of the Catholic Bishop, situated not very far from our own sylvan retreat. Everything wears a joyous appearance, even the trains, which are decked with robinia boughs, and full of holiday-makers on their way to a village a few miles from Grosswardein.

In the evening the *cafés* are full to overflowing, and the gipsies playing in one of them such an exquisite melody as we pass that, after listening outside, we enter softly and take our seat.

Like nearly all in Hungary the *café* in question was kept by a Jew; whose young and handsome wife sat beside us. So soon as she had ascertained that we were foreigners she sent for her four children and made them dance the *csárdás* to the music of the gipsies, who immediately began a lively air. The children were between the ages of four and nine, and it was the prettiest and most amusing sight possible to see the little creatures now advancing, now retiring coyly, then pouting with offended dignity as, pretending to make love, they went through all the phases of the dance.

* * * *

But to return after this digression to the period included in our present visit to Hungary. We get on "swimmingly" in our modest little quarters, and enjoying the quiet and repose which they temporarily afford us, regard them as an oasis in our travels—a brief rest in which to review our past experiences and make plans for the future. All is tranquillity until the fourth day of our residence in our little Wallach's rustic dwelling, when her husband, who had been absent on our arrival, returned. He was much older than his "better-half," and, were it not that the Wallachs never intermarry with the Jews, one would unquestionably have said from his general appearance that he belonged to the family of Israel.

From that moment our peace of mind grew less and less. It was quite astonishing the quantity of wine we managed to get through. Our tea also dwindled most unaccountably. I ventured to hint this to the little woman one morning, upon which, throwing her skirt over her head and bursting into tears, she exclaimed in broken accents, "*Es war immer so-o-o!*" and her sobs were quite overpowering.

What could we do but beg her to think no more about it? assuring her that it must be the cat, or the rats, or the mice, all of which are well known to have a weakness for such beverages. How could we bear to see her sweet face distorted by weeping? and peace was once more restored.

At length, our sojourn ended, the day of reckoning came. The bill, which was made out in German characters, was both exorbitant and a marvel of ingenuity. The number of eggs we managed to get through in one week would have sufficed for a banquet of Hannibal. It was surprising, too, the quantity of bread and butter we consumed; and as to our behaviour we must have been the most riotous of lodgers, for we broke three panes of glass, the backs of two chairs, and wrenched a castor off a leg of the sofa;

all of which misdemeanours were charged as separate items on the bill.

It was amusing to witness András's energy as he did battle with our miscreant host, whose wife did not appear upon the scene. It is only fair, however, to say that we saw her more than once during the stormy interview, standing behind the door bathed in tears. At length, after much expenditure of lungs, András came off victorious, the bill was settled to our entire satisfaction, and we were soon rattling over the uneven roads on our way to the station.

Here we were detained some considerable time whilst a train was leaving with a crowd of emigrants on their way to the United States. We had read that morning in a Wallach newspaper that 8000 Slovaks had also started from the north of Hungary for the same happy region, after having sold their property for a mere nothing. But our own train is ready at last, and entering the blazing Alföld, the heat becomes almost suffocating, the sun shining fiercely as it only does on plains. The sheep-dogs pant as they throw themselves down on the parched ground; in the distant horizon, however, long bands of dark cloud, extending perpendicularly to the thirsty earth, show that a gracious rain is falling. The cattle turn their heads to face the breeze which the storm brings with it. In the marshes the tall pampas canes bow their plumes and rock to and fro, and there is a grateful smell of earth refreshed by falling showers. The water ripples in the pools, and scuds before the wind, which soon increases to a gale. The storm overtakes us and the rain comes pattering down, but it is too fierce to last; in less than an hour it passes over, and the sun shines bright as ever, whilst to our left a rainbow embraces with its splendid arch half the circuit of the plains.

In the carriage with us was a gentleman, a native of Szegedin, returning to that ill-starred city, after having been to Pest on matters connected with its rebuilding.

A thriving place of seventy thousand inhabitants, it is difficult to realise that it has virtually passed away; that interesting city memorable as being near the spot where the first Hungarian Diet under Arpád was held, and which consequently received the name of "The district of organisation;" for here, on the establishment of the Magyar camp, a grand assembly was held, composed of heads of families and the chieftains of the various tribes, and at which the political affairs of the clans were discussed, and their relative positions determined; that strange city of pure Magyars, with its mixture of races; Germans, Christianised Jews, Nazarenes, and ennobled Greeks; above all, that city of Radicals, upon which Kossuth profanely declared he would build his dynasty; the words with which he ended his memorable speech, that was the immediate cause of the civil war of 1848, being, "*De én is mondom néked: Te Szeged vagy, és ezen a kősziklán épitem fel az én egyházamat: és a pokol kapui nem vehetnek azon diadalmat.*" ("And I say also unto thee that thou art Szegedin, and upon this rock I will build my church, and the gates of hell shall not prevail against it.")

But the foundations of that "rock" on which he was to build his dynasty—so much for the prophecies of the wisest of dictators—long undermined, have now crumbled to the dust, and Szegedin—the Szegedin that is that *he* knew, with its one-storied houses, white gables, and long wide streets, built, one would think, on the model of the camp of the Magyar's warlike ancestors—is now no more, and a new Szegedin is fast rising like a phœnix from its ashes, a finer and better city with nobler houses, but one that will lack much of the historical interest of the former. Active measures have already been taken for its complete restoration, and the Dual-Monarchy is endeavouring to raise a loan of ten millions of florins to be lent to the inhabitants to enable them to rebuild their unfortunate capital.

Not many years ago this ill-fated district, which has so often been the sport of nature, suffered fearfully from a severe drought which occasioned a terrible famine, and in 1863 from the ravages of cholera. In fact its dwellers have always existed on the confines of two impending calamities, which might occur at any moment—absence of rain, causing the destruction of their crops, and inundation, which might at any time not only overwhelm the surrounding country, but render their city a heap of ruins.

CHAPTER XXXV.

THE "QUEEN OF THE ALFÖLD."

THE terrible catastrophe which overtook Szegedin in the spring of 1879 must still be within the recollection of every English person. No surer destruction fell upon that other great City of the Plain than that which lately visited the "Queen of the Alföld,"—as Szegedin was called—by an element no less omnipotent, and through whose destructive power seven thousand houses were utterly destroyed, many more rendered uninhabitable, and seventy thousand persons —the whole once thriving population—rendered homeless.

The floods which converted no fewer than nine hundred English square miles of rich pasture, and tracts of land cultivated with maize, into a turbid ocean, were caused by the bursting of the dykes.

The position of Szegedin had always been a most perilous one. Situated in the centre of an alluvial plain, which lies even below the surface of the river, it was impossible not to foresee that a time might, and no doubt would, come, when the Theiss, no longer capable of being restrained by any human barrier, would gain the mastery, and the imprisoned waters by bursting through the artificial boundaries must render the condition, not only of Szegedin itself, but of all the towns and villages in its vicinity, one of extreme danger.

The greater number of the inhabitants of the unfortunate city, however, "laughed at the idea" of such a calamity befalling them, and pointed to the dykes of Percsora, which enclosed for thirty miles the windings of the river in a northerly direction, and also to that other means of defence, the dam of the Alföld railway, which likewise afforded the city protection from the north.

But whilst the majority of its dwellers denied the probability, like men who close their minds to a distant danger and will not allow it to take possession of their senses, there were others in whose hearts there always existed a latent dread that it would not be very long before a disaster of the kind would befal them. In the vain hope of averting the calamity, the dykes were raised to keep pace with the increase of the river's bed each year, but none—not even the most gloomy of Szegedin's prophets, anticipated how soon Nemesis would indeed descend upon them, or how terrible a catastrophe it would bring when it at length overtook the city.

The river Theiss—the Tibiscus of the ancients—a broad and navigable river, takes its rise in the Carpathian Mountains not far from the provinces of Gallicia and Bukovina; and the inundations, which in a greater or less degree are of annual occurrence in some part or other of the Alföld, are primarily due to the melting of the snow on the higher peaks, and the wearing away of the rocks through which the infant river passes, together with the sand it necessarily brings with it in its progress southwards, all of which cause its bed to rise slightly year by year. Flowing to meet the Theiss from the eastern frontier of Hungary come the waters of the Marös—the principal river in Transylvania, whose birthplace is in the Transylvanian Alps, and which empties itself into the Theiss at Szegedin. It was in the triangular space formed by the junction of these two great rivers, the Theiss flowing due south, and the Marös due west, that the fearful disaster occurred, the space in question being, as we have already shown, an immense alluvial plain.

Our fellow traveller, before alluded to as a native of Szegedin, spoke German fluently, and we had consequently no difficulty in conversing with him.

"Ah!" he exclaimed, referring to the fall of the city, "you see me an old man and my hair is grey, though before that time it was not so. Scarcely more than two years have passed since it happened, yet full twenty have been added to my life."

His appearance truly bore out his words; he was one who looked prematurely old, as those do on whom some overwhelming shock has passed, and whose nervous system has no strength to rally from the blow. He had somehow a kind of scared look, and as the harrowing memory of those long nights and days came over him his face grew inexpressibly sad.

"Did you lose any friend during the floods?" we asked, not liking to cause him pain, yet at the same time unwilling to appear unsympathising in forbearing to make the inquiry.

"Yes," he replied after a pause, sighing deeply, "yes, I lost—a *friend*,"—adding, "It was not only the loss of kith and kin—which, considering the colossal nature of the catastrophe, was comparatively small—that made shipwreck of the lives of so many of us big, strong fellows; it was the sight of the women and the children. Ah! there were scenes by the hundred occurring every day during that period that were dreadful enough to turn the hair of men far younger than I am as white as snow. Would you learn a little of the melancholy story from an eyewitness? It will make you sad, for you English have kind hearts as we in very truth experienced then."—"Yes."

"Well, it was on the fourth day of March that the danger began. The waters which had already inundated the surrounding country, impatient of restraint, made a wide breach in the dyke running to the north of the river, and rushed towards the one which extended to the eastern extremity of the town. From this moment the peril to the city became imminent, and measures were immediately taken to provide for the safety of other parts of the dykes, as well as to repair the ruptures already caused. Soldiers were summoned from Temesvár, and lifeboats from distant ports to rescue, in case of need, the threatened lives of the inhabitants. Every man in Szegedin worked night and day to barricade the dams, but all was vain, for after eight days' agonising suspense, during which the water like a greedy monster continued to rise and swallow up the land, a fearful tempest of wind and rain, like a visitation from the avenging powers of Heaven, broke over the condemned city, and added to the might of the rivers.

"In the darkness of the following night, just before dawn began to break, the Alföld dam, the very bulwark of Szegedin, gave way also, and the inundation of the town itself began. The waters burst in upon us with a roar, like that of a mighty cataract. Alarm-bells sounded to warn the citizens to flee the danger, and from that moment the scene was one of wild confusion, for all knew then that their beloved homes were doomed.

"As soon as daylight enabled those who manned the pontoons to see their way through the turbid, seething volume of water, which tore through the thoroughfares, many thousands were borne in comparative safety to New Szegedin on the opposite side of the river, but most of the poor, frightened, panic-stricken souls clung with tenacity to their homes in the vain hope that the tempest might abate and the waters subside, till they were compelled at length to take refuge on the house-tops from the cruel death that assailed them on every side. But even here they found no safety, for the foundations of their dwellings —sapped by the raging current which tore up everything before it—gave way one by one, and their houses, crumbling beneath their feet, fell with a dull crash.

"A boat having capsized, belonging to one of the rescuing parties, and all hands having perished, I volunteered to join the band. I had lost sight of my wife and children on that first terrible night, and knew not where they were, or if alive. Of the latter's safety, however, I learnt two days after; for they had been found, and carried to a village six miles distant. It was quite impossible in those awful days of confusion and turmoil for families to keep together. Some lost their reason from the fright, whilst others—children especially—got overwhelmed and separated from their parents by the very vehemence and pressure of the crowd.

"But as I have said I was alone, and having none to care for, I joined those who went to the rescue with an aching heart, yet hoping that in this way I might chance to light upon my dear ones, and maybe save them. The shrieks of women and children were dreadful to hear above the terrific roar of waters, the deafening noise of the falling buildings, and the shouts of the rescuing parties as they poled their way along. It needed a strong, clear head, and a steady hand to steer through the floating timber and avoid the numerous objects that, collecting as they went, heaped themselves one upon another, and formed eddies and whirlpools strong enough to suck us under if we had not taken care. The piteous cries for help, too, that greeted us on every side were bewildering; sometimes we knew not to whose rescue first to go. Nor only this. Often, when we had succeeded in getting the pontoon alongside, and were just about to take a family on board, the swift current bearing down upon us with tremendous force, bringing down with it a tangled heap of household goods, with now and then a human body in the midst, would come against it, and hurl us ten or twenty yards away. My God! to hear the shrieks of the women then, as we were borne thus irresistibly away, and they knew that with us their hopes of safety vanished! The men, though, uttered not a groan, but as we left them, folded their arms as if to confront the king of terrors with a steady gaze, whilst others took the swooning women in their arms, and gently laid them down beside them, and chafed their hands and feet, as if, poor souls, it were better to bring life to them again, than to leave them to die all unconscious as they were.

"Never can I forget one poor woman who was standing alone upon some scaffolding which, with a child in her arms, she had managed to climb. Carried along by the swift current we were passing down the middle of a broad thoroughfare with fearful speed, when looking up I saw her preparing to throw herself into the surging waters under the belief that we should be able to take her into the boat. We had lost our rope, however, the pontoon having been almost swamped a moment before, and without this it would have been impossible to save her.

"'Stay where you are,' I shouted, 'and wait for the next. It is your only chance of safety.'

"Tearing the child from her bosom and uttering a despairing cry she threw it down in the direction of the boat. 'Then, save my child,' she cried, 'or it will fall from my grasp, my strength is gone.'

"One of my comrades caught it in his arms, and taking off his jacket he wrapped the little creature in it—it was but a mere infant—and laid it in the bottom of the boat, half dead as it seemed from long exposure to the cold.

"As night wore on the horrors of the situation increased tenfold. Complete darkness reigned. There was no gas nor light of any kind to lessen the all-pervading gloom. The waters still rose, whilst, to add to our cup of misery already more than full, another hurricane more terrific than the first burst over us and ceased not to rage till morning broke. As I sit here and look back upon that awful night I wonder how any of us survived it, so exhausted were we by hunger and fatigue."

"But what of the child?" we enquired, interrupting him; for we were anxious to hear its fate.

"Washed away," was the reply. "Our pontoon struck against a raft that came bearing down upon us, and upon which we ourselves had to take refuge whilst we baled the water out, for we had again been well-nigh capsized, and when we had accomplished this we found the little bundle—*Häufchen*, as our narrator called it—*gone*, washed away, though we perceived it not in the din, confusion, and difficulty consequent upon righting ourselves, for we were this time nearly made a wreck.

"Hearing the following morning from the crew of a passing boat that numbers of persons had fled to the woods on the previous day, and knowing what their fate must be, we hastened to their rescue. As the waters rose they had climbed the trees, where, exhausted by fatigue and benumbed with cold, they were dropping off the branches one by one like flies. Some few poor creatures with a harrowing scream appeared to *throw* themselves in voluntarily to put an end to their misery, whilst others fell quietly with no sound beyond a dull, dull 'plash' which will haunt me to my dying day.

"We had managed to save several, and were just poling off with our human freight, when a woman floating in the water clutched violently at the boat.

"In an instant I realised the danger. She would drown us all, for we were so heavily laden that the boat was scarce above the surface of the water. Stooping I seized her hands and wrenching them off the boat I pushed her back with all my strength. She recognised and called me by my name, but it was *too late*, she sank, and was—may Heaven forgive me!—*my wife*."

He was, alas! but one out of many, who, during this our last visit to Hungary—when men's minds were still full of bitter recollections connected with the catastrophe—gave us a thrilling account of the fearful tragedies which occurred during that prolonged period of agony. Parents lost their children and husbands their wives, and in some instances were uncertain of their fate for weeks together, so great was the confusion that existed long after the source of the disaster had passed away.

As we listened to these sad tales, feeling thankful our own lot had been cast in a more favoured land, we were gradually nearing Arád, and it was not long ere we reached the station, when with a hearty shake of the hand the Hungarian left us for a train that would take him on to Szegedin.

A group of men were here engaged in the construction of a new line, and as we watched them we marvelled that anything was ever completed in this land of slow workers. Every man was smoking. Leisurely taking up a small shovel-full of earth he deposited it on the heap; then leaning on his implement he paused to take a whiff at his pipe to enable him to gather the needful strength to take up another shovel-full; after which followed another pause, and so on. These slow but strong, broad-shouldered, and muscular Hungarian navvies would soon drive an English engineer absolutely mad.

At Arád we stay to dine, and ere we journey on again, the shadows have begun to lengthen on the plains, and peasants are returning from their toil. The pastures, which an hour ago were full of life, are now almost deserted, and by the time we see the first dim outline of the Transylvanian Alps, the sky's deep orange has paled into citron, citron into faint green, green into pink and violet. Each moment the hills grow higher, bluer they rest their summits on the sky, and evening is falling fast. A long row of stately poplars rearing their heads aloft guard the entrance to a peaceful village, where women in short red petticoats and blue kerchiefs round their heads are driving home herds of long-haired goats. At the station men in large, high lamb's wool caps like mops come in groups to meet their friends, greeting them with words that sound like " *Sobosh ! sobosh !* " An aged " pilgrim father " descends from the train and walks across the platform leaning on his staff, his long white hair hanging in tangled masses over his shoulders. Girls bring water in classical-shaped pitchers, and hold up glasses of it to the thirsty passengers, crying " *Frisches Wasser !* " And again starting on our way we reach

the Marŏs, a beautiful stream, bounded on either side by lofty mountains. On the spur of a rocky promontory stands what appears to be an imposing castle, but which on nearer approach proves to be one of those fortified Burgher citadels of which we shall see so many in Transylvania and which add so great an interest to that land. The sun is setting behind the loftiest peak and casting its crimson reflection into the deep and winding river, on the margin of which some fishermen, having moored their boat, are cooking their evening meal. Away, beneath the mountain summits, and behind us out in the solitary plains, long belts of fires are gleaming red. Are the people burning down the precious forests as the Wallachs are known to do in the mountains of the Danube, or are they merely those of the thoughtful husbandmen burning the useless stubble of last year's maize?

In the marshes the frogs begin their concert, each tribe inhabiting one marsh doing its best to outdo their neighbours like "loud-contending factions;" whilst in the moist warm grasses of the surrounding plains the locusts do the same, and we are everywhere favoured with a deafening serenade.

About eight o'clock the following morning we reach Karlsburg, the fortress of which stands on a prominent hill surrounded by mountains of very singular and unquestionably volcanic origin. It is here that the gold found in the districts of Abrudbánya and Verespatak is sent to be coined. The mineral riches of Transylvania are both various and abundant, gold, silver, and nearly all the less precious metals being found in these mountains.

It is only 170 miles from Arád to Hermannstadt—our first stopping-place in Transylvania—but it takes eighteen hours to accomplish that distance, and we shall not reach the pleasant little capital till to-morrow morning if we ever do. Fortunately a gentleman with whom we travelled from a place called Radna-Lippa, and who alighted at a lonely little village containing nothing, so far as we could see in the moonlight, but a few wattled huts and a wayside shrine, bestowed upon us ere he left the carriage a bottle of old Tokay which he had brought with him for his own refection. How we blessed him afterwards for the generous gift which alone imparted the necessary strength to enable us to survive the tedium of the journey. Were I but a poet and a man I would write an ode to thee, oh, thou fragrant, topaz-coloured wine of wines, sweet, full-bodied, but never-cloying "pick-me-up," immortal Tokay!

At length dawn comes creeping over the mountain-tops, followed by little crimson cloudlets winging their messages to man that night is over, and the toils of day must soon begin. One by one the sleepy villages awake, smoke curls upwards through the roofs of the wattled huts, and we pass a crucifix beneath which two persons are already kneeling. It is only in "Christian England" where men are ashamed to be seen praying.

It is another saint's day. Every day would seem to be one in Hungary! "Tinkle, tinkle" go the cracked bells from the small steeples which rise above the melancholy cemeteries filled with large square ungainly mounds, one of the peculiarities of the Greek Church in this part of Hungary, for we have now entered Transylvania which constitutes its most eastern portion, "The land beyond the forest," as its name implies. On the low wall of a hut sits a youthful shepherd playing his pastoral pipe—a simple little instrument made of a piece of green stick, whilst his swine feed below on the hard dry stalks of last year's maize and the thistles which grow between.

Beyond all is a glorious background of snow-clad Alps; till, arriving at a junction, at which we learn we have to

wait two mortal hours for another train, we alight for breakfast, after which, lumbering on again, we enter a barren country surrounded by immense sand-hills, covered with stunted grass on which herds of buffalo are grazing.

The lowlands are white with deposits of salt, which

lying upon the soil greatly impairs its fertility. In some places the earth is honey-combed with salt mines, and we crawl along at the magnificent and exciting speed of four miles an hour. In other places the line has been artificially raised to admit of our passing over many miles of bog; the whole country consisting of a huge morass in which grow clumps of pampas-grass, ten and twelve feet high. In the carriage with us is an Austrian engineer on his way to a part of the line where attempts are being made to build a bridge, but which as yet have been unsuccessful on account of the difficulty experienced in laying the foundations, the bog in the majority of places proving almost fathomless. Although constructed by an English company, this railway is said to be the very slowest line in Europe; but after twenty-four hours' prolonged torture, for our train is of course two hours behind its time, our miseries are ended at last by its arrival at our destination.

CHAPTER XXXVI.

HERMANNSTADT.

WHAT a quaint, funny, mediæval old town Hermannstadt is, with its heavy stone archways and strong oaken doors leading to passages and *inner* archways far far beyond! Wherever we cast our eyes we see objects that remind us of pictures of Albert Dürer, and one seems here to be living in the times and place in which Hans Sachs composed his rhymes whilst hammering away at his boots and shoes. Many of the houses are built over archways which lead to sombre courtyards, round which are high wooden balconies, where youthful Juliets make love to Romeos in the region of the gutters below, and women sit and knit and gossip—yes, and quarrel too; for have I not heard the sweet rancour of their tongues, whilst watching them from my own particular balcony, within the courtyard of the hotel? Aye, and sketched them too.

Beneath these wooden balconies are stables and pumps and dark rooms, with walls so strongly built and doors so thick and massive that they might have been made to withstand a siege—as probably they were. Everything wears such an old-world look, that the brand-new houses which have managed to crop up here and there between the ancient ones appear so out-of-place, and altogether such anachronisms, that one feels inclined to request them to "move on," in default of which to burn them down or blow them up, in fact *anything* to get rid of them.

What a dear, ugly, hobgobliny old place the hotel is too, at which we are staying, with its heavy round buttresses bulging out far into the street, and deep-set windows with here and there a small room clinging to the walls, in the region of the upper story, like a convenient parasite. Our room, whose furniture takes us back to the middle ages, also juts out in the same way, and from the window we look down upon the heads of the passers-by. Nothing is new in the hotel but the waiting-maid, a rosy, fair-haired lass, with a pair of such ponderous "understandings" that we positively shudder as she walks across the room, everything is so old and shaky.

The hotel itself is ascended by a long flight of irregular stone steps walled in on either side with heavy masonry, in which are loopholes commanding an extensive view of the stables and the kitchen below—apartments which in Transylvania are usually contiguous. The *Speisesaal* is entered through a long dark room with a polished floor, and contains besides a mangle, two oak presses black with age, and a coffer large enough to have been the sarcophagus of Cheops. Groping our way along with many a slide—surely the house must have been built at a time when some stringent law existed for excluding the light of heaven—we reach the dining hall. Here we nightly consume our *Hammelsbraten* and *Kalbs-schnitzel*, and, I am afraid, grumble. Then making our way back again in fear and trembling to our own room, we pass a balcony so shaky in its entire constitution that, were we but to cough or sneeze at the moment of crossing it, we feel sure the whole crazy structure must topple over into the yard beneath.

Hermannstadt, although politically an important place, being the military capital of Transylvania, possesses nothing in its outward aspect to warrant the conclusion, its appearance differing little from a German town. Should, however, the proposed railway to Bucharest be carried into effect, Hermannstadt will be the shortest route to Constantinople, and, by becoming the connecting link between West and East, must greatly increase both in size and importance.

In no part of Hungary does there exist so great an anomaly as this district of Transylvania, which is peopled by a race calling themselves "Saxons," and their province "Saxon-land," although their ancestors emanated from a widely different quarter.

These colonists are in fact of Flemish origin, descendants of a people inhabiting Flanders, a district of the Upper Rhine, who, styling themselves Flandrenses, emigrated hither in 1141. Hungary, however, being a kingdom of anomalies, it is only natural and proper they should call themselves "Saxons," and their adopted country "Saxon-land," or anything else they choose.

At the period of their immigration, Transylvania—which even now forms the border-land separating civilisation from barbarism—so beautiful and peaceful in its outward aspect, was frequently the scene of bloodshed and devastation arising from the incursions of barbarian hordes from the East, who, entering through the passes of the Southern Carpathians, menaced it perpetually, until the fruitful land had well-nigh become a desert.

Transylvania was not wholly unknown to the ancient dwellers on the Western river; the Crusaders had passed through it on their way to and from the "Holy City," and had carried home with them wondrous tales of the fair and fertile country on the eastern borders of Europe. It was a land of green hills and vales, and fertilising streams like their own, a land literally flowing with milk and honey; in short a goodly land where men might plant and reap the fruits of the earth, and gather into barns in rich plenty. So it came to pass that when the Voivode, or Palatine of the province—who in those days held office under the King of Hungary—sent an invitation to the quiet and industrious inhabitants of Flanders to come over and re-people the beautiful but unfortunate country he ruled, and accompanied his invitation by a promise of grants of land to any that would avail themselves of it, not a few responded to the call, nor did they come alone, but brought over with them men of their own race, skilled in "divers curious arts of workmanship, and cunning artificers in precious metals," so that their fame soon spread abroad throughout the length and breadth, not only of Transylvania, but of the more eastern countries still, viz., Moldavia, Wallachia, and Bukovina. Their wares—the wonder and admiration of all—were sought after from every quarter, and the Flandrenses speedily became, not only a thriving, but even a wealthy, people.

The position which these early colonists held in the country of their adoption was assured to them by a kind of *Magna Charta* which, whilst defining their rights and privileges, constituted them an entirely free people, ruled by no Voivode—as were the other inhabitants of the land—but governed simply by their own laws.

It is both curious and interesting to read the history of this brave little band who ventured to roam thus far from their own kindred and people and tongue, to dwell in a strange and almost barbarian country ; and—following their fortunes through its pages—note how they managed to hold their own against all attempts at aggression, and how stern and unflinching was their determination to prevent all outsiders from gaining a footing in their newly-acquired territory, not excepting even the peaceful dwellers of other parts of the Hungarian Monarchy, some of whom would fain have cast in their lot with these thriving and more civilised people from the West, of whom all spoke well and whom all envied. But the Flandrenses, like the Scots of our own time, are said to have been a " canny " folk, exclusive and conservative to a degree. They would have no interlopers, "not they." None should be permitted directly or indirectly to share their new possessions, or who could tell but that such interlopers might increase and multiply, till, waxing bold in numbers, they might even intermeddle with their laws and manner of governing themselves, and if so there would be war and dissensions within their otherwise peaceful borders. No! they would crush at once and for ever such a possibility, and by excluding all outsiders, ensure peace and tranquillity to themselves and to their children for all generations. Nor were they firm adherents to their political institutions only, for they clung to the faith of their forefathers with the greatest tenacity and became the bulwark of Christianity in the east of Europe.

Of this so-called "Saxon-land," a district occupying the south-eastern portion of Transylvania, Hermannstadt, as we have seen, is the chief town. It is situated on a plain at the foot of the Fogaras Mountains—or Transylvanian Alps, as they are frequently designated—which for eight months in the year are covered with snow, and which, stretching a hundred miles in an easterly direction, embrace Kronstadt in their foldings.

Like all towns in Transylvania, which at one time were so frequently menaced by the Turks and other wild hordes from the East, Hermannstadt was once surrounded by a wall, the remains of which still exist. In consequence of being the military capital of the province, and only twelve miles from Roumania and Moldavia, it is strongly garrisoned, there never at any time being fewer than 8000 soldiers quartered here. In 1438 the Turks besieged the town with an army of 70,000 men headed by the Sultan Amurad himself, who however was killed by an arrow shot from the battlements by one of the brave little band of Flandrenses.

Times have changed since on taking up their dwelling in the land they enacted laws to exclude all neighbouring races from becoming residents in their midst—laws which, though rigidly maintained for centuries, proved not quite so unalterable as those of the Medes and Persians. By slow degrees, entering in the first instance either as labourers of the soil or domestic servants, the Wallachs have at length succeeded in gaining a permanent footing in "Saxon-land," till in the 19th century we find them forming large colonies in that portion of their country which long years ago was ceded to the stranger. Nor is this the strangest feature of the case. This industrious and prosperous "Saxon" folk are not only losing their political ascendency but are fast dying out, and the Wallachs will soon take their place as the dominant race even within the ancient Flandrenses' own borders; for the Wallach population is increasing in the same ratio as the "Saxon" is decreasing. In some of the villages in "Saxon-land" the population, without any emigration or other visible cause, has decreased to one half, and should the high rate of mortality which for the last century and a half has been steadily augmenting, continue to increase in future years in the same proportion, this Flemish people, who have done so much towards the civilisation of Transylvania, and aided so materially in the prosperity of the whole province, will soon cease to be lords of the soil which was given to their ancestors seven hundred years ago, and take a very secondary position.

Although they have been so prosperous a people, these honest Flandrenses would have been far happier had they remained in their own quiet little corner on the peaceful borders of the Rhine than in allying themselves to the fortunes of this fertile but hapless country; for until a century ago they were beset with foes, and the troubles they continually encountered make dark blots on the pages of history.

Like the rest of Hungary, Transylvania—which was annexed to the Kingdom of Hungary by St. Stephen in 1002 and governed by viceroys appointed by the king under the title of Voivode—has undergone manifold political changes as well as very painful vicissitudes. In the 14th and 15th centuries the Moslems, whose empire was then at its zenith, entering through the mountain passes, continued to menace this fair land with their wild hordes, until, like the waves of an advancing tide, they threatened to inundate the whole country.

During this time, so complete had been the victories

of the Turks that only a small portion of Hungary, and that a long thin strip of country, bounded on the north-west by Poland and on the west by the German Empire, remained in the possession of the Christian. At length Transylvania, which had always been considered an integral portion of Hungary, was again reunited to that kingdom during the revolutionary period of 1848.

It is mid-day and the stream of busy life is flowing steadily onwards to the market—Hermannstadt ladies, with small waists and fashionable, well-made garments, holding large fans to shield themselves from the sun, in lieu of parasols, and merry laughing "Saxon" girls in large straw hats, and Wallach matrons with their heads swathed in numberless yards of snow-white muslin folded turban-wise, a species of head-gear called a *volutura*. Besides these are grave, but pretty, little Wallach damsels. Oh, *how* pretty! with their sweet, smooth, oval faces, and slender figures robed in the home-made "*kathrincza*," an almost Roman dress, differing materially from that worn by the natives of Wallachia proper and far more classical. It consists of a long straight piece of cloth of many colours worn over the white under garment, the bodice and sleeves of the latter being embroidered in scarlet or black so as to bring out the graceful contour of the figure. Falling low over the neck and chest are endless rows of coral beads; whilst large silver ear-rings of an eastern pattern united to each other by a silver chain which hangs loosely under the chin complete the charming *tout ensemble*.

The "Saxons" differ from their Wallach sisters in face as well as figure, and even if they wore a similar costume it would be quite impossible not to recognise them. The

Wallachs are small and delicately formed, possessing features of a classic type and generally dark hair and eyes; the "Saxons," on the contrary, are of a heavier build, their complexion is fair, and they have blue eyes, but were it not for their frank and pleasing expression of countenance, their features would be almost plain.

There is no prettier sight in the whole of Hungary than that which Hermannstadt presents on the weekly market-day. The surroundings of the market-place itself; the quaint old steeples and metal cupolas of the cathedral and churches that form the background, the scores of milk-white oxen with their long horns; the bewitching costumes of the Wallach girls, and the bright faces and laughing eyes of the "Saxons" who look up at us archly, yet so innocently, from beneath the warm shadow of their large broad hats, all forming pictures for an artist. Look at that "Saxon" lass yonder, with her frank open face! See how her bosom throbs under her embroidered bodice, and the colour comes mantling to her brow as she sees she has attracted the attention of the two strangers, of whose nationality she is in doubt! Let us go across to that group of Madonna-like vegetable-sellers in their snowy "*voluturas*," squatting on the ground all amongst the hay-carts and the long-horned cattle, and watch the bargaining! Near them sit other women selling fowls and little families of chickens, and by them stand "Saxon" *Bürgers* and natty *cuisinières* haggling over their purchases as though the money they had to spend was the very last farthing they had in the world. A Bürger female comes stalking up and commences negotiations for a brood so extremely juvenile that they ought to have been safe at home under the maternal wing. The Wallach Frau asks four gulden for the lot, at which the Bürger female holds up her hands in astonishment and declares they are not worth two, and turns aside. Hitherto they have been peaceably huddled together in a long circular basket the shape of a cone. But on seeing her customer depart, the Wallach

Frau forces her hand through the small square hole in the side of the basket, and clutching hold of the chickens as though they had been a cluster of grapes, drags them forth, thrusts them into the hand of the Bürger, and asks her to name her own price. She offers two gulden, whereupon the Wallach Frau, with an air of offended dignity, uttering not a word, lays hold of the little brood of feathered bipeds and amidst their screams pushes them one after another into the basket, head first, legs first, just as it comes, and shuts down the cover. After a while the Bürger female returns to the charge, and peers at them again, upon which their possessor once more lugs them out of the basket in the same promiscuous fashion. The Bürger takes them in her hand and feels their weight—the whole ten of those little niggers together could not have weighed a pound—and this time offers two gulden twenty kreuzers, upon which the Wallach declares on the soul of her grandmother she will rather take them home than part with them at the price, and in they go again through the hole.

In a few minutes' time the sanguine little band, alike forgetful of their sorrows and their wrongs, and quite at home in their familiar prison-house, begin to chirp quite a merry gladsome little song. But the Wallach meanwhile is narrowly watching the movements of her customer just in the act of concluding a similar bargain with a broadfaced "Saxon" Frau opposite. Making a sudden grab at them, she this time drags the poor, ill-used little wretches out by their wings and eagerly rushing towards the Bürger female, declares she shall have them for the sum offered, whereupon, crying piteously, they are finally thrown head over heels into a sack which the purchaser's servant carries over his shoulder for the purpose, and are borne away to their premature doom.

"Who is that youth yonder with his hat adorned with gold tinsel and flowers?" we inquire of a "Saxon" lady.

"He is one who is just betrothed," was the reply.

"And those men standing in the centre of that group of people on the opposite side. Who can *they* be?"— we further ask on observing three men carrying white wands to which are attached bunches of flowers and long ribbons.

"There is evidently to be a marriage in the course of a few days in a village near Hermannstadt, and they are going about to invite the bride and bridegroom's friends. Such things are the custom here," replied the same lady.

From the market we stroll into the Cathedral, a very handsome edifice erected in 1440. Like every other Protestant church in Hungary it has suffered much from the "besom of reform," the beautiful pillars being smothered with whitewash. Service was taking place there, and the "Saxon" clergyman robed in a garb of the middle ages looked like a picture of a Puritan "roundhead" in the time of Cromwell.

At the conclusion of the service he offered to show us the sacred edifice, and conducted us to some vaulted chambers which no doubt originally constituted the cloisters, the walls of which were covered with interesting relics of a past age, consisting of life-size portraits graven in marble and stone of worthies who flourished long ago—the ancient Bürgers who held office in the town—all depicted in the costumes of the period, and telling of people and customs long since passed away, yet barbarously, like the pillars of the church, daubed with whitewash. Some of these tablets were dated 1300, the greater number being of the 14th and 15th centuries. To us there was a strange fascination about these old monuments so grim and silent, and we lingered gazing at them, till the Herr Pfarrer, taking off his black cocked hat, requested us to re-enter the church to see the Sacristy, where he would show us the ancient vestments and sacred vessels.

Returning to the market-place we find a momentary lull in the busy hum of voices, and all eyes are turned towards a distant street where a funeral procession is slowly wending its way along. At this moment also the bells from the various church-steeples begin to twang, each in a different key, and every one of them pulled so fast and loudly, that were it not for the din and discord, they would have sounded like a merry peal. In the direction of the garrison at the other end of the town come the strains of a military band, and amidst the inharmonious clamour the melancholy procession, with its flowers, white bows, and streamers, and delicate festoons of lace, crosses the market-place and disappears down an opposite street.

CHAPTER XXXVII.

" THE GOOD OLD TIMES."

THE country in the vicinity of Hermannstadt is very beautiful, and the villages in many of their characteristics wholly unlike those of any other country in the world. A few miles distant is the village of Hiltau, also a "Saxon" settlement, where the large straw hats are made which adorn the heads of the bonny "Saxon" lasses. At this place also the white frieze is manufactured of which the garments of both Saxon and Wallach men are composed, and which is exported in great quantities to Slavonia and Dalmatia.

Hiltau lies picturesquely embosomed in sheltering hills, whose slopes at this time of year are pink with the blossom of the peach. The village, as we approach it, forms a charming picture, the quaint stone houses with their curious roofs nestling round the old fortress-church, which stands on an eminence in the centre; the whole impressing the stranger with the notion that the site of the church must have been chosen before any of the houses were erected.

Exposed to the incursions of the Turk on one side and the Tartar on the other, these churches in Transylvania were complete fortresses in themselves, and, each possessing a moat, bastions, towers, and loop-holed walls of solid masonry, constituted the place of refuge to which the inhabitants fled when threatened by either foe. Within these consecrated strongholds the people also kept their corn, to the end that they might be ready at any moment to resist a siege. Thither the affrighted peasants repaired on the first approach of danger from the enemy, and whilst the women and children were well protected by the towers and battlements that surrounded the sacred edifice, the men, armed with matchlocks and rude arquebusses, defended them with soldier-like bravery. Within these fortresses the clergyman and schoolmaster invariably lived, and so accustomed were the people to these sieges that during the time they lasted there was no interruption whatever in the customary services of the church, and the children likewise attended school while their fathers fired upon the barbarian cavalry beneath.

The high walls and elevated position of these little citadels rendering them all but invulnerable, they generally held their own against the infidel hordes that so frequently assailed them, and upon their departure the peaceful peasantry, once more emerging from their stronghold, repaired their ruined dwellings, replanted their vineyards, and sowed their crops anew, all of which had been ruthlessly destroyed by the enemy. In those terrible times a loud curfew, called the "Turk's bell," rang daily at the hour of noon from the tower of every church throughout the land to summon the people not only in the towns and villages, but others engaged in the pursuits of husbandry in distant fields, to unite in prayer for protection from the Christian's foe.

The bells of these citadel-churches, which are very deep and sonorous, were also used for the purpose of apprising the people of the approaching foe as well as to bid them flee for refuge within the consecrated walls.

These "peasant garrisons," with their watch-towers, portcullises, and massive ramparts, are peculiarly interesting to the traveller, not only as bearing silent witness to the troublous times which we, in the peace of the nineteenth century, find hard to realise, but also to the bravery and heroism of the little bands who defended themselves so courageously against barbarian invasion; and there is something very beautiful in the sentiment that dictated the people's thus fortifying their churches and constituting them their "arks of safety" in the time of trouble.

Wandering round the ancient walls of the church in question with its many towers and turrets, we came to the church enclosure. Entering which we rang the bell of an inner door which we rightly conjectured to be that of the

Pfarrhaus. It was answered by a "Saxon" Mädchen, who, informing us the Herr Pfarrer was within, ushered us into a room containing numerous flower-stands, on which rested large pots of exotics in full bloom, all seeming strangely at variance with their austere surroundings.

These Lutheran pastors are always ready to welcome the stranger, and after pressing us to partake of refreshment, which in this instance we did not feel obliged to accept, he conducted us to the church, a singular old building, whose benches were full of black-letter prayer-books, and the pulpit surrounded by drapery of Turkish manufacture. After examining the interior of the building we walked round the enclosure, where, under arches built at regular intervals in the fortified walls, still stand the strong oaken coffers filled with corn as of yore; for the "Saxons," no less than the Magyars, are a conservative people, adhering tenaciously to the customs of their forefathers and slow to relinquish any that have once been adopted, even when— as in this case—the necessity for their existence has long passed away.

The sacred vessels belonging to the church—many of which were hidden in the ground during the stormy period of the Reformation—are of singular beauty and value, and consist of chalices and candlesticks of ancient workmanship, manufactured in silver-gilt by the early "Saxon" colonists, many of them containing enamelled tablets representing the various incidents in the life of our Lord. We were also shown a magnificent baptismal bowl of the 14th century, on which medallions of pure gold were laid in the form of anaglyps. But besides these relics already enumerated were two of still more ancient date, viz. a superb crucifix containing pearls and rubies, and an "*Ostensorium*," used for the purpose of exposing the consecrated host to the adoration of the " Faithful."

After leaving the church enclosure, the Pfarrer led us to the school, and showed us some specimens of free-hand drawing which would have done credit to any English seminary. To our surprise we also learnt that the higher branches of education were likewise taught, including botany and chemistry. Amongst the children we noticed many Wallachs, the Wallach peasantry liking of all things to send their children to the "Saxon" school, not that they appreciate the better education to be obtained there, but it gives them an opportunity of learning German, a language which they are quite as anxious to acquire as the Magyars to forget; one who can speak " High German " being regarded by the orthodox Wallach as a gentleman of distinction, and, in fact, quite a superior order of being.

The windows of the school-house commanded a view not only of the church with its moat and battlemented walls, but of the village also. How peaceful all looked from this eminence, and how difficult it was to believe that such times of war and terror ever existed! How wretched must have been the lives of the inhabitants in those days—not so very long ago either—when they were kept in daily fear of the enemy! How could they toil under such circumstances and persevere in cultivating the land which was so frequently converted into a desert by the Tartar or the Turk, to whom even the stony girdle of the Carpathians proved no barrier? We can imagine the honest peasant as he guided the plough listening for the alarm bell which might echo through the hills at any moment, and the affrighted inhabitants, with their children and aged, when it did so, hurrying for safety to the church citadel. To this day a Transylvanian mother is said to frighten her naughty child into obedience by threats of the Tartar's approach in the words—"*Jhon jönnek a Tatárok!*"

As we gazed at the picturesque old edifice beneath, which tells such a sad, sad history of the past, and whose pinnacles pointing to the peaceful sky have withstood so many sieges, a glory of sunlight bursting through the clouds shone upon them and kindled the metal balls that surmount each pointed turret into a bright and dazzling star.

In addition to the fortified churches before mentioned, perched here and there on the spur of contiguous mountains or hills are smaller ones, originally designed as supplementary defences to the former; one of which, erected between the years 1175 and 1223, exists at Michaelsburg, a short distance from Hiltau.

Beneath this ancient citadel lies a small hamlet, the houses of which are built entirely of wood, and whose picturesque chimneys, high palings, and beams supporting the walls, give to it a very romantic appearance.

Here we rest our horses, and climbing the staircase of a primitive little inn, find ourselves in a balcony covered in with freshly-cut boughs, whence we look down upon the village, almost deserted now, for most of its inhabitants, men, women, and children, alike have gone off to dig, hoe, or gather into barns the fruits of the fertile soil; for the women here take as active a part as their husbands in the pursuits of agriculture.

Beyond the narrow row of houses with their brown roofs and picturesque accessories, the great mountains capped with snow shine out of the liquid azure like domes of alabaster; whilst a Wallach woman and child walking down the road, the former spinning and clad in a rich mingling of orange, red, and violet, complete the scene and form one of the most beautiful "colour pictures" I almost ever beheld.

The people of these villages speak what is called *Platt Deutsch*, a dialect so singular that we found it quite impossible to understand them. It is, however, the language they brought with them to this alien land, and which they have managed to preserve intact throughout nearly eight centuries of absence from their country, precisely the same dialect being spoken by the dwellers in the district of the Lower Rhine at the present day.

Of all the "Saxon" settlements in Transylvania, the most interesting is perhaps Hamersdorf, also situated a few miles from Hermannstadt. It is here also that the singular costumes of the "Saxons" are seen in the greatest perfection.

It was on a sweet, calm Sunday evening that we visited it for the first time. Too late for Divine service, which took place at an earlier hour than we anticipated, we arrived just as the villagers were pouring out of church, the unmarried women wearing high black velvet hats, from which, reaching to the hem of their garments, countless ribbons of every hue were suspended, the heads of the young married women being covered with embroidered muslin veils. The dress of both is exceedingly elaborate, and preparation for church must, I should say, involve considerable expenditure of time. There surely never were people so hopelessly given over to the pomps and vanities of this wicked world as these "Saxon" maids and matrons. Their ornaments also are not only beautiful, but often of a very costly description, and consist of immense flat circular brooches, resembling breast shields, wrought in a species of filagree and inlaid with garnets, turquoises, pearls, and amethysts, their waists being encircled with belts of scarcely less value and richness of design, inlaid in like manner with precious stones, one and all specimens of an art now obsolete —heirlooms handed down to them by their ancestors; aye! and perhaps even brought with them from the *Vaterland* when they came over to settle in this far distant country.

"Where does the Herr Pfarrer live?" we inquired of three women whose heads we could just see peering through a number of flower-pots in a window high above us.

"He is at the school," replied a head enveloped in a blue kerchief, speaking with some difficulty in " High German,"·as the pure mother-tongue is called, adding—"If you will walk in we will fetch him."

The process of "walking in," however, was one of no small difficulty. First of all, to which flight of steps did the casement in question belong? was it the one round the corner, or that away to the right? or was the room approached through that quaint old doorway yonder leading to a small courtyard? We incline to the latter, but on entering the chamber find it occupied by three men. Meanwhile the owner of the head in blue had been searching for us, and coming to our rescue, just as we were beating a hasty retreat, conducted us through an archway, up six steps, along a passage, in which several immense oak coffers were reposing, across an open balcony and finally into the room itself, which proved to be quite full of womankind, two of whom, as we soon perceived by their dress and general appearance, were Wallachs.

Requesting us to be seated whilst some one fetched the Pfarrer, they subjected us to the usual cross-examination.

"Where do the strangers come from?" (a question interrogated in "High German" by a Saxon Frau).

"England."

(Chorus of "Saxons.") "*Ach, die guten Leute!*"—Then turning to the Wallachs and interpreting the interesting fact into Neo-latin, one and all exclaim, "The strangers are from England."

(Chorus of Wallachs.) *Englesca! Englesca! la—la—la!*"—the final syllable prolonged indefinitely—"that *is* a long way"—a journey that no doubt represented to their minds thousands of miles traversed by the slow medium of a *széker* or *Leiterwagen* filled with hay, the only modes of locomotion with which these simple folk are familiar, or, who knows! perhaps, even a ride on camels or elephants.

"Ah!" said another woman, looking very learned, and reminding us of our Gallician friend Martcha, "that is where the tea comes from and the sugar across the sea in big ships;" for in the uneducated Hungarian mind England and India are generally believed to be contiguous islands!

In a few minutes the Herr Pfarrer arrived, a benevolent-looking old man with grey hair, who, bearing us off at once to the Pfarrhof, conducted us to the room where the family were seated at *Abendessen* (supper). All rose at our entrance and shook us warmly by the hand, and the Pfarrer, placing chairs by the table, requested us to join them at their meal. Our arrival did not disconcert them in the least. There was no more bustle or fuss than if we had been expected guests, and, with that well-bred ease with which the stranger is everywhere greeted in Hungary, and that graceful inborn courtesy which characterises all classes, they bid us welcome to their frugal board.

The dwelling contained numerous rooms, all of which though carpetless were comfortably furnished, and, like the Pfarrhaus we had visited at Hiltau, there was throughout a fragrant odour of exotic flowers, emanating not only from the white clusters of the beautiful *Stephanotis* that was trained round the inside of more than one of the windows, but from other flowers blooming on stands in the greatest profusion.

Supper ended, they took us to the garden, a sun-dried plot on the slope of the hill, surrounded by lilacs, and in which lilies and hyacinths were doing their little best to grow; but where nothing seemed to luxuriate, save the vine, from which hung clusters of grapes. In the dustiest and driest portion of the whole garden was a bower of lilacs beneath which were a table and chairs.

"Oh, how pleasant it is on a summer evening to have such a place to sit in," exclaimed the Frau Pfarrer in gentle and grateful accents. "It is a large garden, is it not? and so full of fruit-trees; only look! Are things so *very* different in your country? Surely they must be, or you would not come so far. Have you a garden in your land where asparagus, and lilacs, and sweet hyacinths grow?"

It was pleasant to hear these dear people talk, and see how thoroughly contented they were with their simple idyllic lives. After showing us the dry little garden and dusty bower, they took us into the *hof* (yard), where the horses were being tended by an idyllic groom, dressed in a white leather jacket covered with embroidery, and a felt hat with a feather in it, who was talking to the idyllic Mädchen of the manse, a blue-eyed "Saxon" lass, attired in a short striped skirt of blue and red, violet bodice, and white embroidered chemisette covered with rows of coral beads.

"Do many English persons visit Transylvania?" we inquired.

"No! very few," was the reply. "Some years ago—ah, how time flies! it must be fifteen—twenty, an Englishman—Herr Bonar, whom everybody loved, stayed many months and wrote a book about our country. He visited us a fortnight, and after his departure we received one letter, but he never wrote again; it was so long, long ago, he must have forgotten us quite, or he would have written," continued the old Pfarrer with something like a sigh; adding after a few moments' pause, an expression of joy suffusing his whole countenance as a happy thought occurred to him, "You live in the same country and may see him; if so tell him how he lives in our memories still."

"We will," I replied, thinking that as England was such a *very* small place we should in all probability be able to deliver the message!

The dew was still lingering on the grass as we journeyed towards Hamelsdorf the following Sunday morning on our second visit. The sky was cloudless, and as we drove through the lanes, the villagers, Bible and nosegay in hand, were walking to their respective churches far away. There was a sweet Sabbath feeling in the air, and all nature seemed to have hushed itself in harmony with the day. We were determined not to be late again on this occasion, and as we reached the old pile, which, like all citadel churches in Transylvania, is built upon an eminence, the same friendly heads we saw last time peeped out of the little high casement and asked us to walk in and sit awhile, as it still lacked half an hour ere the bell would sound for *Gottesdienst* (service).

On entering the cottage an unexpected scene awaited us. Two young girls, one single, the other married, were being dressed in all their finery for church; and, oh! what a heap of pomps and vanities—exhumed weekly from the family locker—we saw lying on the table! Dressing for church in Hamelsdorf is an operation that cannot be accomplished by the individual herself, and is one invariably performed by the old married women who have relinquished such superfluities in favour of their daughters, who sit before a looking-glass whilst they are being attired.

As we stood watching the performance we thought it would never end. The young women, already clothed in their long white garments, the sleeves and bodices of which were beautifully embroidered in stripes of red and orange, were first arrayed in blue petticoats and large white net overskirts handsomely worked in "tambour" stitch, after which, a beautiful girdle studded with turquoises and garnets was fastened round the buxom waist, and a small white net cap put upon the head of the young wife, a girl of seventeen years, whose long hair had been cut off on the day of her marriage in token of subjection to her husband. The cap was bound tightly round the head with a scarlet ribbon four yards in length, which, fastened at the back, hung almost to the heels of the wearer. And now began the real vanities, for over this scarlet band a dozen ribbons of similar length were laid, each varying in colour as well as pattern, the upper one of which consisted of brocade. A thin muslin veil embroidered with gold was now thrown over the head, and secured by large silver pins inlaid with precious stones; and lastly a crimson satin handkerchief edged with fringe was placed at the side, and made to hang down over the dress diagonally by one corner being tucked under the belt. The object of this last article of attire is purely ornamental, but to my mind it injured the effect of an otherwise really pretty costume.

The head-dress of the unmarried girl differs materially from that of her married sister, and consists of a high cardboard hat covered with black velvet, those who are betrothed being distinguished by a band of ribbon worn round the top of the hat, as in the accompanying illustration, taken from a photograph; whilst, to complete the costume, a black garment resembling a clergyman's hood hangs down behind.

Top boots, which are *de rigueur* on week days, are not so, however, on Sundays, and the feet are often covered with  high-heeled patent leather boots open up the front, and laced so as to show the stocking beneath. But to-morrow these elaborately-dressed daughters of Eve will lay aside their finery, and be seen with bare feet working in the fields, if that term can be truthfully applied to places where no boundaries exist.

It was a pretty sight to see these "Saxon" maids and youthful matrons flocking to the church with their long, bright, many-coloured ribbons fluttering in the breeze, and the whole village looked *en fête*.

The interior of the church is very quaint and curious, and contains, in addition to the ordinary seats, several others high-backed, brightly surmounted with wooden canopies, where sit the deacons, severe-looking men in a costume of the Cromwell period. On each side of the chancel sit the unmarried girls in their high drum-shaped hats; whilst the young married women take their places in the body of the church with their elders, one side of which is set apart for the men, and the other for the women. The sermon, which appeared very earnest and was delivered with great impressiveness of manner, was in the ancient dialect. Every other Sunday, however, it is preached in the pure tongue, the *patois* being used for the sake of "*die alten Mütterchen*" (old grannies), to whom the former is an almost unintelligible language.

As we left the church with the Pfarrer, the young women of the congregation, who were evidently waiting for the purpose, pressed round him and either kissed his hand, or taking hold of a portion of his long black cassock raised it reverently to their lips. The scene took us back to the times of the early Christian Church, and we left the porch greatly impressed with the simplicity of the service and the patriarchal lives of the people.

All, however, is not "gold that glitters" in this seemingly happy "valley," for we saw, alas! more than one child-wife already separated from her husband at the age of seventeen. Here, as in France, marriages are those of *convenance*, and, if the Pfarrer spoke truly, they seldom turn out well. The suitor for a girl's hand, if not actually chosen, is at any rate accepted or refused by her father, totally without reference to her own personal feelings in the matter. If he hold a good position in the little commonwealth, and can give her a good home, he is accepted, the girl is told she is to marry him, and they are betrothed with much ceremony. In due course, when the harvest is over, with which no domestic occurrence is permitted to interfere, save the final and inevitable one over which finite man has no control, the marriage takes place, and the young wife is expected to be "happy ever after." But unfortunately for these "Saxon" women, they have hearts like those of other lands, and the tender passion is not always to be controlled. Previously to their marriage they are sometimes undutiful enough to set their affections upon some poorer lover, whom they cannot forget, and the marriage turns out ill. Occasionally, however, if she does not like the suitor chosen by her father, the girl refuses to submit to his authority, upon which commences a long-sustained war in the hitherto peaceful and happy family. Her mother, possibly influenced by the bitter remembrance of her own wrongs and heartbreak under similar circumstances—and entertaining, perhaps, in some hidden and secret corner of her heart a sneaking fondness even yet for the old, white-haired man over the way, whom she once loved dearly but was not allowed to marry, and who is now wedded to another buxom Hausfrau—sighs as she sees her pretty fair-haired lass, the reflection of her own girlhood, called upon to unite herself for aye to one she cannot love, and naturally takes her part against the father. Squabbles now take place between John and Joan, and the neighbours, together with the Pfarrer, are summoned to make peace between them, whilst the girl—seldom more than fifteen—mopes and makes her sweet blue eyes red with weeping. Sometimes, however, the father, under combined persuasion and the continuance of female agitation, is compelled to submit, but he does not forgive his daughter for her want of subjection to his rule, and the happiness of the little household is gone for many a day.

We return to Hermannstadt through the waving cornfields. As we approached the capital the sun was setting, and the porcelain tiles of the steeples and cupolas in the Haupt Platz glistening like liquid fire. How picturesque is the dear old place in the mellow evening light! and how pictorial is it in every line and curve! The streets are full of people in their "Sunday best:" Wallach peasant girls with arms entwined, their large silver earrings and coral beads jingling as they walk along; bonny fair-haired "Saxons," in large Hiltau hats with ribbons flying out behind, and spruce young soldiers in smart uniforms. As we rattle through the roughly-paved streets and shoot round the corners, heads crane out of windows all amongst the red tiles. A dandy Jew in canary-colour gloves, with a bouquet in his button-hole and a small cane in his hand, comes out of an archway as from a bandbox, and, swaggering down the street, is just about to make an elaborate bow to a group of Hermannstadt ladies coming from the opposite direction, when our droszky, dashing through the gutter that runs down the middle of the street, splashes him, alas! from head to foot, takes the starch out of him both physically and morally, and destroys the effect of the "occasion."

The bells from the steeples toll the hour of departing day, and at the entrance to the hotel we find András waiting to know our pleasure for the morrow.

CHAPTER XXXVIII.

WITH THE WALLACHS.

HEIGH-ho! Pretty little Wallach girl tripping along so gingerly over the muddy thoroughfares on thy way to the fountain opposite, and stooping to kiss—shall I say it—the dirty hand of the *Popa*, who just at this moment passes in his long black toga. Why does he linger so long speaking to thee, and why is thy head bent low, and thy sweet face, which until this moment was suffused with smiles, so downcast, whilst he addresses thee gravely in an undertone? Hast thou been remiss in thy observance of the thousand and one fasts of the Greek Church? Ah, no! The Popa points to the fountain, where, sitting in my projecting room, as in a martin's nest, I have often seen thee talking with a handsome "Saxon" lad, as he filled thy classical-shaped pitcher for thee and lingered in the doing of it as though he loved thy company; and here thou art again at the trysting place.

Steel thy heart, little Wallach, against that handsome "Saxon" lad, for thy spiritual father hath marked you both, and will not let thee wed a "Saxon" unbeliever. Think not harshly of him, for he means kindly. It is not well or customary for the Wallachs to intermarry with the "Saxon" folk; thy people are not their people, nor thy ways their ways. Forget this little bit of romance, and wait till some swain from amongst thine own people bestows his love upon thee.

How I feel for that pretty little maiden as the tears roll down her cheeks, and her full round lips tremble as she struggles with her sobs! What a pity there are hearts to break! for, love him as she may, she must not marry him. That a "Saxon" youth should wed even with a lass of the same kith from another village is regarded with the greatest disapprobation, and woe to the girl who is brought into one that is not hers by right of birth, for the whole female population rise up in dudgeon against the interloper. But —a Wallach!

"Mean, dirty, shabby, idle Wallachs!" are epithets often hurled at their unhappy heads—"A Wallach to intermarry with decent 'Saxon-folk,' who has scarce anything to her back, and washes her house-linen every week—Bah!"

In "Saxon-land," as in many parts of Germany, a bride's trousseau of under-linen is so enormous that the family washing is of scarcely more than annual occurrence, or at the very most quarterly; and as in England the respectability of a family is estimated according to the amount of its butcher's bill, so public opinion in "Saxon-land" is principally governed by the number of "washes" a family may have in the course of a year. The Wallach women, therefore, muddling in their weekly wash-tub, are held in great contempt by the thrifty "Saxon" dames, who possess clothes in their lockers they have never even worn. And, although tolerated as common citizens, the Wallachs are considered quite outside the pale of "Saxon" society. In fact there is no love lost between the two races. The Wallachs regard their "Saxon" neighbours as a "canny folk," prone to get rich too fast and sometimes by practices that are scarcely within the bounds of honesty; whilst the "Saxons" look down upon their Wallach brethren as idle, thriftless loons, possessing lax notions as to the respective merits of *meum* and *tuum*, and the exclusiveness of individual property.

During the war of Hungarian Independence, however, the canny "Saxons" curried favour with the Wallachs, and induced them to unite with them in siding with Austria against the Magyars. And fearful were the atrocities committed by the Wallachs on the defenceless Magyar residents and "Nobles" of Transylvania, many of whose children were carried round the villages spiked on the top of the Wallachs' bayonets, whilst women were cruelly tortured, and by a refinement of cruelty some of the men were buried up to their necks, and then mown down.

In this once exclusive "Saxon"-land there are at present large villages almost wholly inhabited by Wallachs, some of which contain a population of several thousand souls. The approach to these villages may invariably be recognised by the number of way-side crosses and little temples met with along the road; the latter crowded with statues and paintings in fresco, there being, as in Gallicia, no limit to the construction of saints, which are of every colour and material. These Wallach villages are far less clean, but they are more picturesque, than those of the "Saxons." Instead of stone, the houses are almost entirely built of wood, and their gables are surmounted by a cross. The streets are long and narrow; while each house has its own courtyard enclosed behind high wooden palings carved roughly but in beautiful designs, entered by a doorway covered with a small wooden roof.

The Wallach churches are very singular, and are often painted on the outside from top to bottom with grotesque figures. Inside they are invariably dark and gloomy, the walls being painted in sombre colours interspersed with gold. The small lancet windows begrimed with dust admit but little light, for the Wallachs, unlike the Magyars, indulge in the "dim religious" to such an extent that their churches resemble Buddhist temples far more than edifices dedicated to the worship of Christ. The roofs are dome-shaped, and the naves, which are paved with black marble, empty. There are no seats of any kind, and the people during the service either stand or kneel.

In these villages one sees no rags nor even mended garments, and if an "idle," the Wallachs would nevertheless seem to be a very thriving, people. Like the "gentle Slovaks," they have their cow, their poultry and little plot of land which their women sow with seed and hoe and cultivate, whilst the men guide the plough, or more frequently stay at home and look after the children. The Wallach woman is a most industrious creature, and much maligned by her "Saxon" sister, and if she does not possess a great store of ready-made linen in her locker, and washes once a week, she has at any rate large rolls of unbleached home-spun on her shelves. In the autumn she begins spinning vigorously for the winter's weaving, after which she makes the material into garments for her numerous progeny. Too much, however, cannot be said concerning the indolence of the male Wallach, whose prosperity is generally due to his wife's industry rather than to his own. More slow even than the Magyar, he works as though it were a matter of the most sublime indifference whether the occupation in which he is engaged be ever finished, and if he goes to market with farm-produce other than his own, he usually lies in the waggon fast asleep, and arrives at his destination just when the "Saxon-folk" are returning home.

He is in truth but too often a poor, feeble, and effeminate creature, greatly fallen from the courage and valour of his first estate. The form of Christianity taught him by the ignorant Popas, doubtless does much to foster this indolence and effeminacy, for the teaching of the Greek Church in these secluded villages is almost exclusively confined to the observance of its fasts.

"If God," so argues the Wallach peasant, "clothes the

lilies of the field and feeds the fowls of the air, who never go to church, how much more will He clothe and feed me, who go there every Sunday, and fast almost every alternate day in the week besides?"

The orthodox Wallach will do anything rather than violate these fasts, which occupy more than a third part of the entire year. He believes in ghosts, vampires, and changelings, and spends much of his time in inventing charms against the machinations of the Devil. The belief in witchcraft also is still prevalent in Transylvania, and more than one old woman was pointed out to us even by the enlightened "Saxons" as being gifted with that art.

Amongst other superstitions, the Wallachs entertain a strong objection to beginning anything either on Tuesday or Saturday; whilst the reverential awe in which they hold Friday may be evidenced by an amusing incident which has been related of two men who were committed to trial for having waylaid and murdered a traveller. When brought to justice they confessed the crime; but upon being asked by the magistrate what they had done with the plunder, they replied that they had only found upon their victim a few florins and a roasted fowl, the former they had divided between them, but the latter they had given to the dog, as, being Friday, they were afraid to eat it on account of committing a sin.

So ignorant are the priests of the Oriental branch of the Greek Church, that few can do more than read and write, whilst some are so miserably poor, that they are compelled to eke out their scanty subsistence by working as day-labourers. The priests of the "United Greek" and "Latin" Churches are, on the contrary, both better educated and better paid, their livings being largely endowed by the State.

Less picturesque in itself than some others, but beautifully situated, is the Wallach village of Czood, which lies at the foot of mountains that enclose it on all sides. In the centre of the village rises the metal cupola of the church, whilst nestling round it are the wooden houses with their heavy carved palings and doorways.

On first entering its cottages we were under the impression that they were shops for the sale of native manufacture, for the walls were covered, not only with rows of jugs and cups, but square pieces of striped drapery likewise. We soon found, however, that these articles were simply placed there to decorate the apartment, for, whereas the "Saxon" *Hausfrau* prides herself in her stock of linen, the glory of the Wallach matron, like that of her Magyar sister, consists in the number of articles of crockery she has hanging round her walls, much of the money received by the "gudewife" on market days for her butter, poultry, and eggs being spent, ere she returns, on these singular frivolities. Not only this, the Wallach woman covers her walls with useless square patches of woollen fabric, woven by herself in divers colours and patterns.

Wherever we go amongst the Wallachs, we are received with the utmost courtesy and kindness. They are adepts in the art of pleasing, and invariably meet us with a smile, addressing us in their corrupted Latin with such sweet, musical voices that they completely win our hearts. The men, too, doff their hats as we pass them on the road, and give us a word of greeting; but the less courteous "Saxons"—*never*.

We had travelled already more than ten days in Transylvania without having yet seen a Wallach baby, these little mortals seeming to be as scarce here as Slovak ones are numerous; but on entering another cottage we found, lying fast asleep in a cradle swathed *al bambino*, a funny stiff little atom of humanity that one could no more have bent than if it had been an idol made of wood or stone, whilst near it stood its mother, a child herself of sixteen years, scrubbing away vigorously at the weekly wash.

As is usually the case, the house formed the abode of several generations of the same family, and consisted of three apartments, the inner one being very prettily furnished, its tables covered with Oriental-looking cloths of home manufacture. Beneath the walls of the room were ranged benches with high backs, on which flowers were painted in a style that would have done for models of the so-called "high art" of the period. The Wallachs not only spin their wool and flax, and weave their own materials, but dye them also, and their arrangement of colours is always harmonious.

Great excitement prevailed in the cottage when it was discovered we were strangers from Ángol-land, and we felt pretty much as an illustrious couple from the Sandwich Islands might be supposed to feel on visiting our shores. What a lifting up of eyes and hands in astonishment, and cries of "La, la!"—the Wallach's favourite mode of expressing surprise. One ejaculated "*Intestate*," intimating thereby that she was bewildered at the very thought of it; whilst another, in adding gesture to her exclamation of astonishment, upset the washing-tub, and awoke the chrysalis in the cradle, which, beginning to cry, added its own small voice to the general tumult, in the middle of which in walked the village Popa.

A young man, with a soft expression of countenance, and with dark hair parted down the middle and hanging loosely over his shoulders, he might have sat for a picture of St. John. In intelligence he appeared far above the average of Popas of the Oriental Greek Church, and spoke German well. On ascertaining who the "illustrious strangers" were, he kissed our hands, and begged we would permit him to conduct us to his dwelling.

Passing under the massive wooden archway that led to the enclosure, we entered the house, which differed little from the one we had just quitted. His wife, to whom he introduced us in quite European fashion, was a sweet young woman dressed in the costume of the Wallach peasantry. We had scarcely seated ourselves, when, pattering about with her naked feet, she began to spread a white cloth on the table, and arrange upon it such things as their larder afforded, consisting of black bread, honey, butter, fruit, white wine, and Borszék—a mineral water with which wine is usually partaken of in Transylvania. We required nothing, but felt instinctively that by refusing to partake of the refreshment so gracefully offered, we should hurt their feelings. As soon, therefore, as we were bidden to the little feast, we took our seats as a matter of course and without demur.

According to the rules of their Church these Popas are obliged to be married men; but possessing in common with the Magyars somewhat Oriental ideas on many points, they regard their wives as slightly inferior in the scale of humanity to themselves. Whilst we partook of the simple repast prepared for us, the little wife sat at the other end of the room working, maintaining the while that respectful silence which she naturally would who felt she held an inferior position.

"My wife is always industrious," said the young Popa—calling our attention to her—"that is all her work"—pointing to a number of shelves on the opposite side of the apartment on which rested large rolls of unbleached linen. "At this time of year we have many out-of-door pursuits," he continued, "but in the winter days, when there is little to be done in the fields and there is no sowing or planting or ingathering of grain, our women work busily at their looms."

Going across the room to the bench where his demure little wife sat with her feet crossed one over the other, I looked at her work. She was embroidering, in scarlet and black silks, the bodices and sleeves of the white under-garment always worn by Wallach women, the stitch being that familiarly known as "sampler," two threads of the material being taken up on the needle diagonally, and then crossed: the effect of a broad stripe of embroidery in this stitch in a close Eastern pattern being very beautiful.

"*Quanto graziosa tu sei!*"—(How lovely you are!)— I exclaimed in Italian, as with her sweet, pensive, Madonna-like face she looked down on her work.

She understood me perfectly, and lifting her eyes to mine, regarded me with a frank, unconscious smile, for to the Hungarian women, wherever they are met with, vanity is a vice unknown.

Whilst F. and the Popa talked religion and politics, I lingered at her side examining her pretty bodice and sleeves, together with her large silver earrings, just for an excuse to look at and admire her.

Those of the Wallachs generally consist of a ring some three or four inches in diameter, from which hang loose pendants of rich design. They do not go through the ear, but are fastened round it; hence the necessity of the long, loose chain which crosses the neck and connects them for safety to each other. These circular earrings are very becoming to their Wallach wearers, who have oval faces, and possess, like the Magyars, bewitching beauty when young, but, alas! how soon their beauty fades.

Mr. Bonar was evidently well known here also, our host remarking that he remembered having seen him when a lad, and whenever he is alluded to it is invariably as "*the* Englishman."

CHAPTER XXXIX.

THE ROTHER THURM PASS.

PEOPLE never keep time in Transylvania, neither do the clocks. By the one ticking in our room it is just half-past four, whereas our watches, differing somewhat in opinion, point to a quarter to seven.

The previous evening a droszky had been ordered to be ready at six o'clock to take us on our proposed excursion to the Valley of the Aluta, but still it made no sign. At length, after sending András, two waiters, and the landlord himself to hasten its arrival, at half-past seven it came dashing under the old archway with " exemplary punctuality " according as that substantive is understood in Hungary.

Anxious to see some of the by-ways of Transylvania, and having left our own carriage at Pest on starting for the Danube, we hire one here for a week, together with a stout pair of horses, for which András agrees to pay eight gulden a day and the driver's expenses.

Some difficulty, however, was experienced in finding a driver, the landlord of the hotel being unable to spare his own for so long a period. There were plenty of Wallachs to be met with who could drive, but the difficulty was to find one of sufficiently lax morals to consent to start on the day we desired. To do so on a *fast* day would be out of the question, and as Tuesday and Saturday are *unlucky* days, and to start on a Friday would inevitably result in the most disastrous consequences, there were not many days left to choose from. Monday, however, fortunately happened to be an "off" day. True, it was the Vigil of St. Philomena, V.M., but on our proposal to start so early in the morning, that little obstacle was in some measure overcome.

Few arrangements were necessary for the journey. In a country where such Oriental hospitality exists, more than one day's provisions were unnecessary. Our programme in the first instance was to travel due south through the Valley of the Aluta into Roumania, and then, rejoining the highroad at Vestan, journey to Kronstadt, the latter being only two or at most three days' distance from Hermannstadt.

The morning is heavenly, and our hearts light as air, as, thundering through the archway, we emerge into a street and go rattling off towards the Fogaras Mountains. As we pass the barracks the cavalry are parading on the plain outside, and fifes and drums playing vigorously; but away we go into the open country between boundless stretches of yellowing corn. The road which is wide is crowded with vehicles on their way to market; waggons filled with hides, barrels of wine, and farm produce; pedestrians driving cows and calves, the latter so extremely juvenile that they cannot walk alone and require assistance, for infantine veal is much esteemed by the "natives." Other pedestrians are driving small colts—also weak on the legs—and carrying in their bosoms tenderly and lovingly wee, snow-white lambs.

Next comes a Transylvanian swine-herd driving his unsavoury flock of yellow pigs—lean as Pharaoh's kine—

and in form hyenas, with long, red-brown hair and high backs resembling those we saw when travelling amongst the Slovaks. All have come from distant villages, and who shall say how early in the dawn their owners started, for the Wallachs, whatever else may be laid to their charge, are at any rate no sluggards. Plenty of "Saxons," too, are hastening along the road clothed in white frieze jerkins and felt hats.

The two races are not easily distinguished by their dress, but we recognise them by a truer sign. The Wallachs as they pass us lift their hats, and in their soft and melodious tongue exclaim "*Bune deminiace!*" (good morning). A carriage passes us containing a Wallachian gentleman, who also takes his cigar from his lips and greets us with the word, "*Applecaciune!*" which also means "good morning," but a form of salutation used between equals, the former expression being invariably adopted by an inferior when addressing a superior. Even when lying down in their coats, the otherwise lazy Wallach, unless he happen to be fast asleep, will rise to perform this little act of civility, but the "Saxons" take no notice of us whatever, and go trudging on their way in dogged silence. Very pleasing is the courtesy of the Wallach, and we are careful to return it, upon which they lift their hats again and again and add something which we cannot understand.

Now and then a waggon covered with an awning of plaited reeds, and filled with peasant women and girls clad in holiday attire, comes lumbering along, and sometimes an old weather-beaten, time-worn *calèche* drawn by three horses abreast, with nodding hood, in which sit the squires and squireens of the neighbouring country, smoking long pipes, on their way to Hermannstadt to see the price at which the produce of their estates sells at the market.

Away right before us tower the Transylvanian Alps, their summits covered with snow. All the market people have passed by this time on their way—the last herd of swine; the last shaky little calves and long-legged, straddling colts; the last waggon-load of "Saxon" or Wallach girls; and the last family of unkempt, unwashed gipsies, their legs bound up in flannel *à la Wallach*, and tied round with leather thongs—all have passed, and we have the road to ourselves with the exception of a heavy bullock cart driven by a woman with a baby in her arms, and now and then a waggon driven lazily by a drowsy Wallach.

Already women from distant and unseen villages have begun their labours in the pastures, some guiding the rude plough, whilst others are sowing seed, grain by grain from their blue aprons, like people in the Bible. On the uplands, stretching across the mystery of blue mountains, stand the dead stalks of last year's corn; the brown of the untilled land, and the yellow lanceolate leaves upon which the sun is shining, forming just the golden tint the picture needed to rest against the azure background and render it complete. In other places oxen are turning up the soil that has been left fallow for three years; for land is so abundant here that it is only after that interval has elapsed that it is again cultivated. On these uplands sturdy "Saxon" matrons may be seen riding *en cavalière* the leading bullock which drags the heavy plough, maintaining to this day many of the characteristics of their Gothic ancestors, who associated themselves with the stronger sex, not only in the labours of the field, but also to a life of danger and glory, and whom we read of as "martial heroines," wearing "*braccæ*"—whatever those articles of attire may have been —and when taken captive in arms accompanying the triumphal processions of Aurelian on horseback.

The Rother Thurm Pass, to which we are bound on this loveliest of summer mornings, lies in a beautiful valley twelve English miles from Hermannstadt. Our driver, with a bunch of blue and pink hyacinths in his hat and another in his button-hole, keeps the horses well up to their pace. The road, which follows the river, is excellent the whole way, and we soon come in sight of the red tower which, standing to our right on the steep mountain side, has given the Pass its name. Behind its ramparts a soldier was patrolling, although there is little need of this guard-post now that nothing is to be dreaded from the Eastern tribes. In 1493 there was a terrible carnage in this peaceful pastoral valley, when its green hills echoed to the shrieks of the drowning and the slain, for the Turks, expecting to meet with no resistance, marched fearlessly over the border and entered the Pass on their way to the capital. Their intended foray, however, was happily discovered, and, under the prompt measures taken by the *Burgomeister* of Hermannstadt, speedily suppressed. Sending out secret emissaries to all parts of the district, he gathered together every male peasant in the borders, and causing them to lie in ambush, they awaited the coming of the unsuspecting foe, who as they advanced were routed and driven back with great slaughter. Half-way through the gorge in the very centre of the stream, a solitary tower is seen, which at one time no doubt also defended the Pass. It is in a state of ruin now, and, forming a very picturesque object, adds not a little to the beauty of its surroundings. At this point the Litriora meets the Aluta and both flow on side by side without mingling in the least, the one clear as crystal, reflecting the forest-clad mountains which rise above it, the other thick and sandy.

At noon we reach the Roumanian frontier, where, in the large kitchen which formed the entrance to the hostel, we found a number of footsore, weary-looking women resting whilst they ate their midday meal of black bread. They wore a very Oriental-looking costume, besides which their lips and finger-tips were dyed, but all looked dreadfully worn and exhausted.

"They have not yet recovered from their long *Fastenzeit*," exclaimed the landlord, a benevolent-looking man, on observing that we regarded them with pity. "It is wonderful how the poor creatures live, they eat so little food and do such hard work. They are on their way to Hermannstadt with fruit and honey, and will have to be back again tomorrow or they will be beaten by their idle husbands. They are good, quiet creatures, these Roumanian women; I know them well. The Popas keep them up to their weekly fasts, and during the forty days of Lent I have many a time seen them faint upon the road under their heavy burdens."

A tumbler of white wine, which we ordered to be given all round as an accompaniment to their black bread, soon brought light to their eyes and colour to their pallid cheeks, and we were much struck on observing that, ere tasting it, each woman stood up, turned her face to the wall, and uttered a prayer. If they had only known what they were about to partake of, it would not, I suspect, have been a very fervent one, for on tasting the wine afterwards we found it to be as sour as vinegar. So grateful were they, however, at the moment, and so much warmth did it bring to their hearts, that untying their bundles they withdrew from them handfuls of walnuts and forced them upon our acceptance, some even benevolently offering to crack them for our immediate refection in the most primitive of all methods. Several of these poor women I observed had *goitre*, that disease so prevalent in all mountainous districts.

This neighbourhood has an evil reputation for robbers. In an inner room, the door of which was open, we could see hanging to the wall a musket and two revolvers, but all were, I suspect, used more frequently for purposes of sport than as weapons of defence, for the forests in the vicinity are full of game. Deer abound in the wooded hills that enclose the Pass; whilst in the higher ridges beyond bears and even chamois are found; besides which a lynx is occasionally met with, together with wild-boars and wolves, the latter being the very terror of the shepherds. Bearing down in large packs they will often destroy a whole flock of sheep in a single night, killing even when they do not devour; bears, on the contrary, never attack, and have sometimes been known, as in the great Slavonian forests on the Lower Danube, to fraternise with the herds when led to the mountains for pasture.

Later in the day, walking further up the gorge, we crossed a bridge, and, passing the frontier with its custom-houses and guard-post, entered Roumania. The trees throwing cool shadows across the road rendered the walk delightful. How silent all was! not a sound was heard save the roar of the river, as it flowed beneath over its rocky bed; not a sign of human life was visible. How dreary must be the lives of these few soldiers who guard the frontier, completely shut out as they are from the world of men! To the right, high above us, on the steep slope of the mountain, were sad evidences, however, not only of their living, but also dying, here far away from their fellows. Climbing a rugged path, and looking over the high hurdles which protected it from the ravages of wolves, was a lonely little cemetery. In the corner lay the usual pathetic heap of battered wooden crosses—types of man's forgetfulness of those who lie in the domain of silence. Near the gates some gipsies or other travellers had evidently been bivouacking, for a fire was still smouldering, though all traces of themselves had fled.

Above, rose the summits of Surul and Negoi, the former, though completely covered with verdure, attaining an elevation of 8000 feet.

The mountains that enclose this valley are very beautiful, and form a succession of mighty buttresses, between every one of which is a leafy gorge whence issues a stream of water foaming down its rocky channel to swell the classic Aluta, which, taking its rise not far from Moldavia, wends its way southwards till it finally empties itself into the Danube.

Weary with our walk we throw ourselves down by the side of one of these streams, and watch it running in and out amongst the stones as it comes gurgling towards us with a pleasant dreamy sound. Presently, borne over the still air, comes the plaintive sound of a woman's voice singing a melancholy strophe, and looking over the crest of the opposite hill we descry a dark speck which, growing more definite as it comes zig-zagging down the path, turns out to be a young gipsy with a baby at her back. She was singing one of those Roumanian *doïne* or ballads which, like those of the ancient troubadour, are full of tenderness and love, the one in question ending each verse with the words *Yuchza! Yuchza!* which sounded like a call.

Like nearly all the Transylvanian and Roumanian gipsies she was exceedingly pretty, with small features, full lips, and large lustrous eyes, her complexion as dark as that of an Asiatic, whilst her hands were of that peculiar shade of blue black one often sees in the Indians of the south. We spoke to her in German, but she could not understand us, the only word she herself seemed capable of speaking in that language being *Deutsch*, which she uttered interrogatively as though wishing to know to what nation we belonged.

"*No!*" we replied, in Italian—"*Inglese!*"

"*Englesca! Ah! Dei pace! Dei pace!*" was the rejoinder, in that sad intonation in which every gipsy speaks.

"Where are you going to take those?" we inquired in

the same language, pointing to a number of new baskets she carried on her arm, and which appeared to be for sale.

"To Hermannstadt, *buona Signora*."

"To Hermannstadt? But where will you sleep? You cannot reach that town to-night."

"There!" was the laconic reply, motioning in the direction of the woods opposite.

The bestowal of ten kreuzers brought upon our heads a shower of gipsy blessings, and as she kissed our hands and went wandering on her way, we watched the blue mist rising from the valley and shuddered as we pictured to our minds the young creature lying with her baby in the lonely woods through the hours of darkness. To the free, unfettered, true-born gipsy, however, the canopy of heaven is her roof, the horizon the boundary of her habitation, the stars her companions, and grim night itself the kind and gentle mother soothing her to sleep, for familiarity with nature has made her one with it, and it with her.

As we recross the Roumanian frontier, and once more plant our feet on Hungarian soil we see approaching in picturesque procession a large herd of long-haired goats accompanied by a man playing the bag-pipes, the harsh strains of which he seems to be thoroughly enjoying as he slowly heads his woolly charge. He is a wild-looking fellow, clad from head to foot in sheep-skin, but we address him also in Italian, and he understands our simple questions perfectly, and tells us he is leading his flock over into Turkey for pasture. On observing that we take an interest in his rude instrument, he takes from the capacious pocket of his loose jacket another consisting of a long horn made from the bark of a tree, through which he blows lustily, waking the echoes along the valley for many a mile. He is followed by two lovely Roumanian girls, of whom it is said there are many in the Sultan's Harem, who have been stolen from this district from their parents and carried back captive to Turkey.

The natives of Roumania or Wallachia proper have a very Grecian type of feature, and seem to possess even yet the reflection of the Thracian blood of their ancestors.

CHAPTER XL.

THE GREEK HERMITAGE OF BUCSECS.

IN consequence of its proximity to Turkey, Kronstadt wears an almost Eastern look, while, lying as it does between mountains that separate Transylvania from Wallachia, its position is exceedingly picturesque, its walls and towers and bristling spires standing out against a background of green. It is a bustling town, full of life and animation, a considerable trade being carried on between it and Moldavia and Wallachia in articles manufactured in the district, from which cause Kronstadt is frequently called the "Transylvanian Manchester."

Its population, which consists of about 50,000 souls, is, like that of many other parts of Hungary, "mixed," and the stranger, as he walks the streets, is jostled, not only by the canny "Saxon" and wily Székler, the cunning Jew, and the polished Greek, but by the demure and smooth-faced Armenian, likewise the "Quaker of the East."

If everything in Hermannstadt reminds one of the "life and times" of Albert Dürer, how much more does Kronstadt, in spite of its polyglot population and Eastern habits. What curious old passages, staircases, and galleries are there, and strong buttresses, gateways, and towers which seem to be enclosing prison walls!

In the old quarter no two houses are alike. There are high ones against which small "leans-to" are clinging like barnacles against a ship's side, whilst others seem to have thrown out bulbs and bulbous protuberances like miniature reproductions of themselves, and there is a hopeless and bewildering medley of masonry everywhere.

In this neighbourhood, as in Hermannstadt, the churches are surrounded by high battlemented walls and other means of defence against the wild Moslem hordes, which, pouring in through the passes of the south-east Carpathians, once swept over the smiling plains of Kronstadt. In the quaint little suburban villages we are reminded of those of the Sieben Gebirge on the Rhine, their heavy stillness being full of the poetry of the middle ages.

In one of these villages it was also our fate to spend Sunday. As the great bell began to toll for *Gottesdienst*, the people pour out of the massive oak doorways of the houses as from old picture-frames, the women in their high, drum-shaped, black velvet hats, and the men in quaint leathern sleeveless jerkins and small clothes precisely like those worn in England in the 17th century.

On many of the houses in these villages, painted in large German characters above the doors or windows, and sometimes stretching across the whole length of the house, are appropriate verses of Scripture, such as the following: "The Lord bless thy going out and thy coming in." "Except the Lord build the house, they labour in vain who build it;" whilst on a barn where corn was housed, we read the words, "The earth is the Lord's, and the fulness thereof," and on a house at the entrance to the village were the words, "Except the Lord keep the city, the watchman waketh but in vain,"—all testifying to the devout minds of the inhabitants. But let us follow them into the old church, and taking our seats on the benches that are arranged, one side for the men, the other for women, await the commencement of the Lutheran service. The sermon, happily for us, on this occasion is in "High German." The preacher, a funny little man of unusual volubility of speech for one of the Teuton race, takes for his subject the "Peace of Heaven." No sooner had the hymn ceased and the sermon begun, than, with one accord, the old men and women deliberately folded their arms and went off into a comfortable doze!

Within the pulpit, as in many old Roman Catholic churches, were several steps, and the preacher, beginning his sermon on the lowest, mounts one by one as he warms to his subject. In olden times it would seem to have been the custom for these "Saxon" grandsires and grandams to fall victims to slumber, for in the ancient archives of their church are rules framed when they first settled in the land, one of which imposes a penalty of eight kreuzers—a large sum in those days—on any one who should fall asleep during Divine service—a rule that would, however, seem to be relaxed in these degenerate days.

Presently, whilst the other sleepers maintained rigid silence, an old goody clad in a black cloth cloak of mediæval pattern, and sitting on a bench immediately before me, began to snore, an occasion which was "improved" by a younger woman, who, by a series of strong-minded and well-directed pokes with her elbow, endeavoured to keep the offender awake. These demonstrations, however, had no effect, beyond that of arousing her for the moment. Raising her heavy eyelids and fixing them upon the region of the pulpit, her head soon drooped upon her chest again.

The preacher, as he advanced in his discourse, grew more eloquent. He stood on the topmost step, and leaning over the side looked down upon the sleepers. "The peace of Heaven? Ah, yes! But not for you who slander and defraud your neighbour"—turning his head in the direction of the high-backed canopied seats, where sat the lay dignitaries of the church;—"not for you who spend your time in idle talk, in dancing and at *Fests*," regarding this time the young girls seated demurely in the chancel with their floating ribbons and drum-shaped hats;—"not for you—a-a-ah! not for you, and you, and you, and you,"—pointing each time to an individual still in a state of somnolency, "who waste the golden moments in this sacred place by yielding to slumber."

This homethrust was evidently more than the strong-minded female could endure; for, giving her neighbour an indignant protest with her elbow, she exclaimed in no gentle tone—

"*Erwachet!* (Awake!) The Herr Pfarrer is talking to you."

Thus aroused, the sleepers—accustomed only to the sonorous ejaculations of the preacher—suddenly awake, and there is a general stir throughout the little congregation, during which the sermon happily draws to a close.

The following morning, bidding adieu to Kronstadt, we started for the Castle of Terzburg and the Greek Hermitage of Bucsecs, situated in the most south-eastern portion of Transylvania. We are now so near the Fogaras

Mountains that they appear within a stone's throw, their noble buttresses and steep sides scoured by a thousand watercourses, showing rugged in the sunlit portions, and blue, deep, and mysterious in the shadows.

Towards noon, passing through a forest, a family of gipsies pounce out upon us unexpectedly, and follow our carriage, turning somersaults, hopping on one leg, and performing other gymnastic exercises, with the view to attract our attention whilst keeping pace with us, one and all looking so inhuman with their dark skin and matted hair that they might have been demons of the woods. As we near a village, others come pouring out of a nest of huts on its outskirts, who, joining the first company, hold out their little hands for kreuzers, and clutch them when bestowed with a greed as if each had been an infant miser and every coin had been of sterling gold.

The whole of the plains here are cultivated with hemp, flax, poppies, buckwheat, and tobacco, and seem a beauteous garden; the deep crimson and purple of the poppies, tender blue of the flax, delicate pink of the buckwheat, and yellow flower of the colza forming a wonderful harmony of colour in the brilliant atmosphere; whilst here and there in the uncultivated portions a herd of black buffaloes idly browsing give quite an Eastern appearance to the scene.

Here, as in the Tátra, Slavonia, and other parts of Hungary, many of the forests have been either cut or burnt down, but nowhere could we detect signs of replanting, and the romantic name of this beautiful country—Transylvania—will soon cease to be appropriate unless some counteracting influences are brought to bear against such reckless spoliation.

The castles in Hungary are very interesting, and, like those of the Robber Knights of old, are almost invariably perched on the summit of some inaccessible mountain or high pinnacle of rock, where the dwellers could defy all foes. The village of Terzburg, situated on the extreme confines of Transylvania, is of the most barbarous description, inhabited solely by herdsmen and their families, who graze their cattle on the mountains. The castle or fortress, which, with its many turrets and towers, is a mixture of the Byzantine and Gothic architecture, stands on the topmost ridge of an isolated rock commanding the pass into Wallachia, and was originally garrisoned by a military religious Order of Teutonic Knights. It is approached by a steep pathway,

the interior of the castle being entered by a small postern under the tower now reached by a wooden staircase, but in ancient time by a movable ladder.

Anything more wild and romantic than the position of the castle cannot be conceived, its accessories reminding the spectator of the nursery tales of his childhood—of Bluebeard and Giant Despair. Inside there are grim passages, trap-doors, and yawning depths, all bearing silent witness to the troublous times when these borders were invaded by the Tartar and the Turk.

In order to make the excursion to and from the Greek Hermitage in one day, it was necessary we should sleep at Terzburg this and the following night; but to bivouac in the "open" with so barbarous and formidable a folk as the Terzburger herdsmen was a thing we had by no means bargained for in our travels; András, however, apostrophising his favourite deity—assured us, "*der Teufel!*" that they were not a bad "*Herrschaft,*" if we only knew how to take them; and at once made friends with them by enlisting their services in procuring wood for our camp-fire, after which, having learnt many useful lessons from the gipsies, we soon erected the orthodox tripod, and cooked our evening meal whilst the setting sun was blazing on the castle walls.

Although the day had been extremely hot and sultry the evening air was chill, and crouching round our cheery camp-fire we watch the night creeping silently over the hills and upon the castle walls till they stand out black against the sky. Then, wrapping ourselves in our *bundas*, we follow with our gaze the stars on their silent track through space, and note how some burn red to the very verge of the horizon, while others rise above it but to set again, like those dear ones who come on earth to bless us for awhile, and then leave us with nought but their shining pathway to tell us whither they are gone. Suddenly out of the deep blue zenith shines forth one of those strange visitants of our firmament, a shooting-star. With inconceivable velocity the fiery traveller took its course from east to west and then vanished into space.

Night had far advanced ere we laid our weary limbs to rest within the shelter of the carriage, which, like our own old friend, was constructed to permit of our lying in it at full length. How strange it was to be listening to the soft and gentle noises outside, the mysterious rustlings of insects in the grass, and the muffled sound of voices proceeding from the huts, in which lights are flickering here and there, but we slept soundly and did not awake till a loud *Alpenhorn* blown by some muscular herdsman aroused the echoes of the dawn.

András was already up, and had not only made a fire but was preparing breakfast for us on the dewy greensward, his figure, weird and mysterious in the dim light, looking like some *Erd-Männchen* as it moved about. From out the veil above the stars were shining feebly, and blinking like the weary eyes of persons who have been keeping vigil all the night. The air which fans our cheeks comes fresh and moist from its bath of dew, and there is everywhere around a succession of small, tremulous, and intermittent sounds like those of living creatures roused from a state of inaction into new life.

The sun was rising, and, like a row of mighty altar-fires, glowed the snowy pinnacles of the Transylvanian Alps, as, mounting our mules, we started on our journey, one of the Terzburg herdsmen accompanying us in the capacity of guide.

Like the Northern Carpathians, those of the south also are characterised by dense forests and narrow gorges. Our path, formed by the dry bed of a watercourse, was stony and difficult, but we soon entered a forest of pines, through whose tall straight stems the snowy peaks could here and there be seen glistening like silver. At length, making our way along the rocky sides of a mountain—our path often scarcely more than two feet wide—we looked down upon a dark and narrow valley filled with black pines, from which wreaths of vapour were ascending as from a huge cauldron.

Reaching the Wallachian frontier-post on the edge of the mountain, we have a splendid panorama, and look down not only upon Burzen-land—as the country round Kronstadt is called, on account of the river Burzen which flows through it—but likewise on a portion of Szeklerland with its sombre pine-clad mountains.

In an hour's time, and after a most fatiguing ride, far exceeding in difficulty any of our equestrian experiences in the Snowy Tátra, we find ourselves at the bottom of a valley terminating in a narrow gorge, the rocks of which assume all the appearance of cliffs. On the highest pinnacle of one of the rocks stands a wooden cross, whilst another erected a little above the pathway indicates the approach to the cave. Entering the gate of a small enclosure surrounded by a paling of pine-logs, we ascended the narrow zigzag path, and soon caught sight of one of the hermits in his long loose toga and high cap, who, having heard our voices, had wandered out to see who could be coming to profane these sacred solitudes.

Greeting us in Wallachian, he conducted us to a small door in a wall built to enclose the entrance to the cave, passing which we found ourselves standing in the gloomy recesses where, screened from the light of day, these poor hermits spend their lives.

The cave, which is between sixty and seventy feet high and three hundred long, contains a small Greek church and two rows of buildings divided into cells, eight being the full number of the little band when all are there. At the time of our visit two were "itinerising" in the neighbouring districts in quest of food—for these brethren of the Holy Cross live entirely on charity.

Though the cavern is large, the atmosphere, from the absence of ventilation, was exceedingly damp, the walls in many were dripping, and we were soon glad to return to the open air.

How suitable is the spot chosen by these hermits for their seclusion! Shut in on all sides by lofty cliffs and pine-clad mountains which almost shut out the sky, they are indeed separated from the outer world; whilst the complete stillness and gloom of their surroundings naturally favour contemplation. No sound is heard save the murmur of a waterfall plashing from rock to rock as it comes foaming and tumbling down a narrow gorge, and now and then the scream of an eagle as circling over head it settles on some lofty crag.

After wandering about in the vicinity of the cavern for half an hour, sounds reach us, the meaning of which we had previously been taught, and, hastily returning to the little community, we find one of the hermits striking a wooden hammer against a board to announce to the brethren the hour of worship. Occasionally, facing the east, he prostrated himself to the earth, and then, walking round and round the church, continued his hammering, while repeating some prayer in an undertone as though he had been uttering an incantation or weaving a mystic spell.

Entering the dark little edifice, which contained anything but the odour of sanctity, we stood awaiting the commencement of the service. There were the usual genuflexions and painful bowings to the earth that are invariably seen in Greek churches, but the chanting of those holy men was the most barbarous thing I ever heard or could have imagined possible even in my wildest dreams. Two were exceedingly decrepit, with long white hair and flowing beards. These hermits belong to the Order of St. Basil and follow the rules of that fraternity, and it was very painful to witness the evident difficulty with which they accommodated their enfeebled and stiffened limbs to the various postures imposed by the Greek rite.

After leaving the church we were conducted to one of the cells in which a small oil-lamp was burning, but so feebly that it did little else than render its immediate surroundings dimly visible—a small brown and well-worn crucifix standing on a bracket against the wall, a few dark-coloured pictures of saints, the narrow pallet at the side, and a gourd and leathern bottle hanging from a nail being all the furniture it possessed.

In the centre of the cavern a fire was burning on the ground, over which was an iron pot, suspended from a tripod, containing a kind of porridge made of Indian corn; whilst in a little three-legged earthen pot, here called a *labos*, which stood on the red-hot ashes, some edible fungus was being cooked.

The hermits were very hospitable, and produced from their larder wild cherries, strawberries, and a kind of sloe, pressing us to partake with them their homely fare. We had brought provisions with us, however, and amongst other things a roasted chicken, which we offered them in return, and which was not only gratefully received but eagerly

devoured in our presence. It is seldom these poor monks get anything better to eat than *mamaliga*, black-bread— which they make themselves—together with the roots, fruit, and wild honey which in summer they manage to find on the surrounding hills; their drink the milk of goats. Occasionally the Wallachian shepherds bring them fresh food, but only during a few months in summer, as, during two-thirds of the year, these exiles from humanity are cut off from all communication with their fellows, the passes being blocked by snow. There was something very sad not only in the thought of the complete isolation of these poor men and their self-imposed exile, but in the uselessness of their lives and the mistaken zeal which prompts them to renounce the world and their share in its cares and toils for the love of Him who " *went about* doing good."

A *douceur* of five gulden being put into the unwashed palm of a grey-headed old hermit, and our animals sufficiently rested, we take our leave of the brethren, and, ascending the valley, are glad to feel once more the warmth of the blessed sun, which seldom or never visits the lonely hermits' caves.

Though the days were long, the sun had set upon the castle walls, and the last golden gleam had faded in the west, ere we again neared the village of Terzburg, the distant smoke of fires where the ruthless Wallachs were burning down the forest trees showing against the purple ridges of the hills like that from burning craters.

The herdsmen, who by this time had begun to take quite a proprietory interest in us all, turned out *en masse* to welcome our return. A large fire was blazing near our carriage, and during our absence they had made for us a *Laubhütte*, or hut of boughs, in the construction of which these hill Wallachs, who are essentially a nomad people, are great adepts; whilst some fish caught in a neighbouring stream, eggs, buffalo cream, and delicious honey were also provided for our repast by these hospitable but uncanny-looking herdsmen.

In these Transylvanian streams and rivers fish abounds, not only salmon-trout of enormous size, but grayling also, and the angler would here find ample food for his rod.

As night wears on clouds dim the empyrean, and in addition to their fires some of the herdsmen—possibly in our honour—light torches made of resinous pine-wood, which add not a little to the wildness of the scene, as, with curious lamb's wool caps and knives stuck in their belts, they flit to and fro, now standing out black against the fires, and now disappearing again into the mysterious outer circle of darkness like demons of unrest rather than peaceful shepherds guarding their flocks.

A soft bed of leaves with which the Wallachs had lined

our hut rendered it a very dry and comfortable abode for the night. Throwing one glance around us through the impromptu doorway of freshly-cut branches, we see that our neighbours, the herdsmen, have already delivered themselves up to the slumber-god. All have retired within their dwelling, and the fires themselves, sending up a blaze now and then by way of expiring effort, are fast dying out. Our wild *entourage*, however, is anything but provocative of sleep, and the great silence, broken only now and again by the harsh scream of a night-bird, becomes eloquent, as the "voices of the night," now that human speech is hushed, come whispering on the air like dim echoes from the far-off unknown land. At midnight the wind rises high and threatens the stability of our little habitation; whilst a ladder placed against one of the herdsmen's huts falls with a loud clatter and awakens all the sleepers.

The morning broke amidst heavy clouds and threatening rain, but at seven o'clock, our camp-breakfast partaken of and our coachman punctual for once, we are once more bowling along towards Western Transylvania.

CHAPTER XLI.

WESTWARD.

KOLOSZVÁR, situated in the valley of the Szamos, and surrounded by hills on every side, contains 25,000 inhabitants. Although enclosed on all sides by a Wallach population, that of the town itself is principally Magyar, with the exception, however, of one portion of it, which contains a little colony of "Saxons."

Was there ever such a clatter as we made driving down the streets of this little Magyar capital of Transylvania? If the four hoofs of every horse had each been a vigorously played castanet, and each paving stone a cracker, I doubt whether we could have made more noise. If the railway locomotives take their time in Hungary, the horses make up for it by the pace they take the traveller—at any rate on starting. As they gallop through the streets we startle the whole neighbourhood. Waggoners, who, Hungarian-like, have left their teams in the middle of the road, come rushing out of wine-shops where they are leisurely sipping their morning's *glässchen* of *Slivovitz*. Frantic mothers are seen issuing from dark doorways, gazing distractedly up and down, in quest of their small "blessings," who, as a rule, are squatting quite composedly in a nice cool puddle in the centre of the road. Pigs grunt and use unparliamentary language; whilst the genius of a group of youthful engineers, engaged in the erection of earthworks and fortifications at the side, is very nearly nipped for ever in the bud by the wheels of our chariot, as, deviating slightly to the left, we make room for a timber-waggon coming down the street.

As the four capital little horses which we have brought with us from the "Saxon" town of Shässburg, a place midway between this and Kronstadt, and the most spruce and *betyár* of coachmen, pull up at the hotel archway, a crowd of spectators gathers to see the turn-out, and we once more hear the words "*Ángolok*" and "*Ángolorszag*," spoken in an undertone—which have not greeted our ears since leaving the plains of the Magyars—proceeding from mouth to mouth in a "stage whisper."

It is market-day, too, and in the square opposite the hotel and beneath the shadow of the fine old cathedral is a kaleidoscope of perpetually shifting colour. Unlike the market at Hermannstadt, the space devoted to the purpose is filled with booths and covered stalls, whilst to the left is a gipsy's tent, close to which, squatting on the ground, are its owners, their simple wares of home manufacture displayed before them on a piece of matting.

Bäuerinnen, too, in scarlet top-boots, black skirts lined with yellow and looped up over scarlet petticoats, sit also by *their* wares, whilst Koloszvár Bürger ladies, in black silk shawls worn cross-ways over the head, stand over them and haggle, as usual, for salads, flowers, vegetables, infantine chicken—yes! and *snails*—the large wood species being regarded by Hungarian epicures as an *objet de luxe* in the gastronomic line. A Hungarian housewife's ordinary winter

supply of these little animals is several thousand. Here and there boys are carrying coloured candles for sale, and two Hungarian peasants with long corkscrew curls are bargaining for a long string of garlic, for which they eventually pay five kreuzers—a cheap luxury! On the ground are little islands of Transylvanian pottery and classical-shaped bowls and pitchers, resembling a coarse kind of Majolica. There is a penny theatre, also, the audience of which is principally composed of men; and booths innumerable for the sale of ready-made clothes and vestments of Hiltan frieze beautifully embroidered in green and red. We pass one in which hang hundreds of embroidered waistcoats of the cut, colour, and material of the costume of each neighbouring village.

How amusing it is to stand and watch the purchasers try them on, and see how vain mankind is even when exhibited in the "Saxon" or Wallach peasant, and how difficult to please. Here is one negotiating for a baggy coat with large sleeves and a hood—an out-of-doors, red-letter-day garment that would fit anybody; but he tries it on notwithstanding, and views himself up and down to see how it hangs, then looks over his shoulder to judge of its effect behind, and finally regards himself intently in a glass provided for the purpose by the seller. He has already tried on eight or nine, when he fixes at last upon one which he thinks will do. The material is white frieze embroidered in black, and its price—fourteen gulden—is marked on the article, but he beats the seller down to thirteen gulden forty-seven kreuzers, and has almost decided to buy it, when the owner of the booth takes from his store one lined with scarlet and embroidered in green, the price of which is thirty-three gulden. The purchaser's spirits sink. He is now quite put out of conceit with the unpretending black-embroidered garment and is caught in the trap. The seller, a wily "Saxon," induces him to put it on, and, drawing the hood over his head, bids him look in the glass to see how it becomes him and judge of the charming effect. Passing on to other booths we have quite forgotten all about our Wallach purchaser, when, returning that way in half an hour's time, we still witnessed the same little scene being enacted, at that moment, however, drawing to a conclusion. Slowly taking from his purse thirty gulden which, together with his pipe and tobacco-pouch, he kept in his topboot, the bargain was struck, and with a somewhat dejected air, for the Wallach loves not to part with his money, away he goes with his splendid garment tucked under his arm.

There are booths, too, where "*Kipfer*" and delicious Hungarian bread are sold, and gilded sweetmeats; and stalls pervaded by a strong odour of turpentine, where repose piles of Szekler cheese, the flavour of turpentine being imparted to it by the bark of the pine-wood in which it is packed. These stalls are presided over by Szeklers, a people occupying a large tract of country in the extreme east of Transylvania on the borders of Moldavia, and whose origin for a long time was one of the historical puzzles with which Hungary abounds. But they are now believed to be the remnant of the Huns of Attila, who, after the Romans in the time of Aurelian had retired from Dacia and left the country defenceless, perpetually menaced it from the north, and finally formed a colony where they now exist.

How it came to pass that this remnant of the great people, the Huns, who subjugated Pannonia, got left behind, does not appear, but it is determined beyond all controversy, that when the third Turanian horde—the Magyars—bore down upon the country in 886, they found a people settled in an eastern corner of Transylvania calling themselves Szeklers, who not only spoke their own language, but possessed the same characteristics.

Koloszvár possesses the honour of having given birth to the great Matthias, "Matthias the Good" as he is called by the grateful Hungarians. It was also on a mountain near here, overlooking the valley of the Szamos, where poor Rákótzy II., the last of Transylvania's native princes, witnessed the defeat of his army under the overwhelming forces of Austria. Brought up as a Jesuit, he notwithstanding fought for religious freedom, but, on being defeated, he fled to Turkey, a country which has afforded an asylum to so many of Hungary's patriots, where he died.

The Cathedral dates from the 13th century, but since its completion it has passed through many vicissitudes and into various hands, its chancel having been sadly mutilated and altered, to suit the requirements of the various forms of worship which have been celebrated within its walls. Originally Roman Catholic, it subsequently fell into the hands of the Lutherans, who discarded its statues, pictures, and shrines. In the 15th century its walls echoed to the doctrines of Unitarianism under the teaching of Francis David, after which it was given over to the Jesuits, but was soon regained by the Unitarians, who continued to hold it until 1716, when the altar was once more adorned with the great crucifix which had been strangely preserved through all its varied fortunes, and the church passed into the hands of its original possessors, the Roman Catholics, who retain it to the present day.

There are no fewer than 50,000 Unitarians in Transylvania, and they have erected a large brand-new church here, on which is inscribed in imposing letters their distinctive motto, "*Soli Deo Gloria*." The doctrines of this sect were introduced into the country by Isabella, daughter of the King of Poland and wife of Zápolya I., and they are doing their utmost to extend their influence here, a deputation from England visiting both Koloszvár and Hermannstadt every year for this purpose. During the time we were at the former place we found it difficult to persuade its inhabitants that the English National Church was otherwise than " Unitarian."

" What," said they, " the English not ' Unitarian ' ? Why, you send money to help to support them."

The Transylvanian capital does small credit to the province, and the hotel at which we have put up is by far the worst we have encountered in our travels. How many a time as I walked up and down its stairs I wished that I wore top-boots and short petticoats like the *Bäuerinnen*.

Not far from the hotel, and just round the corner where women sit at stalls and sell parched Indian corn and "gipsy-roasts," is a shop where ready-made coffins are sold, and where a woman, standing within, looks through the window and over her grim wares invitingly at the bystanders, and appears quite disappointed when they do not turn in.

In the winter season many of the "magnates" reside here, and their splendid equipages enliven the little city; but it is so dull during our present visit, that we have no inducement to prolong our stay. Summer is passing, and autumn, when heavy rains will render the roads almost impassable, is stealing upon us with noiseless wheels. The following morning, therefore, we bid adieu to the mountains, the domain of the Wallach, the "Saxon," and the Szekler, and journey towards Debreczin, the very centre of Hungary, and the most Magyar portion of all Magyarland, and the exclusive realm of the Magyar.

Once more reaching the plains, we are seized with a sort of poetic enthusiasm akin to that which inspired Petöfi and Eötvös and Vorösmartz in their great love for their Mother Alföld. Again beholding its immense breadth and length, and enwrapped in its wondrous repose, we no longer marvel at the affection entertained for it by its people—an affection which must grow upon all who travel long over its boundless tracts.

There again in the horizon is the Alföld's faithful daughter, "Deli-báb," beguiling the traveller with her shifting slides of mystic pictures, now of pale and hazy lakes, as of those from which the morning mists are rising to greet the god of day; anon, of fair green islands surrounded by a golden shore—silent and majestic ever. Oh! immortal daughter of a mythic past!

There are some who call these plains monotonous. Monotonous! *That* they are only to those who are blind to the ever-varying effects of light and shade; but to those who are alive to the Alföld's ever-changeful moods, "day unto day uttereth speech," and each hour brings a new revelation.

Those who travel across the great Alföld by the iron roads which, linking places together, follow only that portion of it where towns and villages are most frequent, can form no conception of the thinness of the population nor of the infinite vastness of the plains; but as we are borne onwards in our own carriage over these almost trackless wastes, we realise why this region, not only in ancient times, but even up to the seventeenth century, has been so peculiarly the theatre of barbarian incursion. It is no doubt due in a great measure to the geographical position of the country, but chiefly to its physical characteristics. These vast plains watered by the great rivers, the Danube, the Marós, and the Theiss, offered great attractions to the pastoral nomads of the north and north-east.

No associations such as those which attend the cultivation of the ground amongst Aryan nations, bound them to their native soil. Freed from all the labours of husbandry, and living either by the chase or on the flocks and herds which grazed these steppes or prairies, they never attached themselves to any place in particular, but roamed from one to another as, the herbage around them exhausted, they were compelled to migrate to other pastures. The same may to some extent be said of the Osmanlis, to whom these plains with their rich pasture offered every facility for camping out.

Journeying steadily onwards we pass salt marshes, with which this part of the Alföld abounds, with their tall, dark-green reeds, concealing snow-white waterfowl and endless peewits, and a little farther on an *ágas* with the usual accompaniment of a shepherd's hut. It is noon and the shepherd lies fast asleep. The sheep are likewise taking their noon-tide siesta. Another mile or so and we come upon a group of happy peasants surrounded by their "*jószag*"—a few goats, sheep, and cows, their sole possessions—dining like kings on black bread and bacon, and drinking water from a large gourd like the people in the Bible. Then we pass a village and drive out again into the great, silent, solitary plains, with nothing between us and the flickering horizon—which seems to melt into the sky—but a clump of trees. The plains are streaked here and there with golden stretches of sand and rich brown soil, and in other places with long miles of vivid green showing where the husbandman has sown his grain, now rapidly ripening unto harvest.

At two o'clock, beneath the very clump of trees we had seen from a distance, we come to a halt for lunch, and whilst absorbed in all the intricacies of a truffled chicken, which had been provided for us at Koloszvár, we hear a slight rustle in the grass behind us, and looking round see a poor, lean, and apparently half-starved dog, which might easily have been mistaken for a wolf, had we made his acquaintance in the dusk of evening instead of in broad day. Dogs are so officious in Hungary and so much in the habit, as I have said, of considering themselves in the light of "rural police," that we regarded this one as a member of that canine body simply come to request us to "move on." F. consequently, by way of returning the compliment, threw his stick at him. He was not to be daunted long, however, for, emboldened by the sight of food, he soon made another advance, and this time it was evident that his feelings were those of friendship. Whether his instinct enabled him to detect in the expression of my face a feeling of sympathy towards him, I cannot tell, but as he stealthily approached us he wheedled round to my side; and there was something so human in the beseeching way he looked, first at us and then at the viands, that we could no longer find it in our hearts to repulse him and he was consequently allowed to share our repast. The poor creature must have come from a long distance too; for, look where we would, there was no sign either of habitation or of flocks grazing, the pastures all around us being one great and absolute void. Perhaps he had fled from the tyranny of an unkind master; for there were scars upon his body and his lean limbs bore witness to long fasting.

Quite at home by the time we had completed our meal, he attempted after canine fashion to assist in the process of "washing up," and was so pressing in his offers of assistance that András was at length obliged to have recourse to the driver's long whip.

The horses harnessed, and the pic-nic hamper safely

deposited in the rumble—for we are again in our own carriage which was sent to await our arrival at Koloszvár—we take our seats, and move on again. But here we are beset by an unexpected difficulty. The dog follows us, and that notwithstanding the most strenuous efforts to send him away. We console ourselves however by the pleasing assurance that in all probability he will leave us at the next village, which we now descry resting on the remote horizon. Having arrived at which comforting conclusion we one and all subside into the usual half-somnolent state produced by the heat and drowsy motion of the carriage as the horses drag it slowly along, and scarcely open our eyes again for another hour or two, when we see before us the same village in precisely the same position, the only difference being that its houses have grown larger and its steeples higher. At length we approach its outskirts, and a large straggling place it is.

We had by this time forgotten all about the dog which had been the source of so much annoyance to us on starting from our last place of bivouac; but happening to look over the side of the carriage, there we see him, no longer following as before at a becoming and respectful distance, but limping along on three legs close to the very wheels. Passing the village at last, which has been in sight for so many hours, with its one-storied houses and gables facing the same direction; passing its Magyar girls, with their long, many-coloured ribbons flying out behind, on whom the incorrigible András—sitting demurely, so far as bodily attitude is concerned, with his arms folded—smiles sweetly from his lofty eminence on the box, we shudder as we picture to ourselves our entry into Debreczin, accompanied by this disreputable "hanger-on." Once there, however, we could give him in charge of András, and possibly by stealing away without his seeing us, we might get rid of him altogether; with which ungenerous and inhospitable intention, we take no further notice of him for the present.

CHAPTER XLII.

DEBRECZIN.

IT has been aptly observed that no country in the world presents such a number of paradoxes as Hungary, and this statement is perhaps in no instance more marked than in the terms applied to its towns and villages, which are designated in exactly the opposite way to those in other parts of Europe. The towns (*mezővárosok*) contain an exclusively agricultural population ; whereas, the villages (*falluk*) are very large, and often possess many thousand inhabitants, an example of which may be given in Orosháza, " a village " in the neighbourhood of the Theiss, which contains no fewer than 13,000 souls.

Having arrived at another *mezőváros*, we find a tolerable inn, and decide to anchor for the night.

In a few moments the usual scuffle takes place in the *basse-cour*, and the shrieks of feathered bipeds announce the fact that *paprika hendl* is about to be prepared for our benefit. The cook, a lusty female in top-boots and white petticoat and black bodice, is seen in hot pursuit of a victim, which, once captured, she summarily dismisses from this world by twisting its neck. Then plunging it bodily into a pot of boiling water which is standing on the stove in the kitchen, she allows it to remain for a few seconds, when it is again dragged out minus its feathers and skin, all of which it has lost by the process. It is forthwith cleansed,

cut into small pieces, and thrown into another pot containing cream, butter, flour, and a quantity of red pepper, and served—the whole accomplished in the brief space of twenty-five minutes. It is, however, a national dish to which, from the precipitate nature of its manufacture, we do not take kindly, and throw out a gentle hint to the landlady, through the medium of András, that some other kind would be more acceptable, whereupon one passing under the euphonious name of *gulyás húz* is presented to us—a kind of stew, also swimming in a sauce thickened with red pepper. It must not be supposed, however, that this condiment at all corresponds with cayenne. It is made from the long red pods of a plant called in France *poivreon*, which, though a species of chilli, is not very pungent.

As in other provincial towns and villages on the Alföld

the cottages are here unpoetically neat and uniform, and one looks everywhere in vain for a bit of pictorial dilapidation. No starling ventures to burrow its nest in the warm thatch of a Hungarian cottage nor martin build beneath its eaves; the outer walls are pink as sea-shells, and the casements, painted bright green, with their flower-pots arranged in a row, look like those of Dutch toys.

The tobacco-harvest has begun, and all around the cottages are festoons of leaves hanging up to dry. The leaves are gathered as they become "ripe," and not all at once, the lowest being taken first and then the higher. The harvest consequently occupies a considerable time, occasionally lasting a month, and depending greatly on the season.

As we take a stroll into the suburbs of the village we see the people coming in from the fields in merry groups, bringing with them the peace-inspiring weed, the men carrying it in large bundles on their shoulders, and the women in the ample folds of their up-turned skirts, followed by *székers* laden with the same. The peasants' horses appear dreadfully ill-used in this district; their downcast, abject look bearing testimony to years of oppression and wrong. How sad it was to see them dragging their heavy loads, and as I look at them how sure I feel that some "happy hunting-grounds" await these patient servants of man which receive his cruel kicks and cuffs so uncomplainingly and do his work so nobly. God bless a thousand times the patient worker who died a year ago, and left the savings of her own hardly-earned wages to the cause of London horses, and who each morning for many a year in frosty weather might be seen in the heart of the great city with her heavy load of sand, scattering it over the slippery thoroughfares ere she went forth to her daily toil. Some men called thee mad; but, mad or sane, God give thee rest and peace and "keep thy memory green!"

At the extreme end of the village were three gipsy-tents, and near them a camp fire, round which sat smoking a ragged, bronze-faced *Zingary*. At his side stood one of those ancient silver goblets, for the possession of which the gipsies are so noted. A little distance off sat others of both sexes, and the ruddy glow of the fire lighting up their many-coloured rags and creating a zone of darkness beyond, contrasted oddly with the pale, cold grey of the surrounding twilight, and produced weird alternations of glow and gloom. They are a wild uncanny-looking people, very unlike the ordinary itinerant gipsy. As we went across to them they seemed to regard our presence in their midst as a decided intrusion, and several withdrew from the fire and hid themselves in the surrounding darkness.

Tethered a short distance beyond the camp, but hidden by the surrounding darkness, were several horses, and from the frequent neighing and pawing of the ground that proceeded from that direction, we were led to imagine them to belong to a type of animal vastly different from the poor, miserable *Rosinantes*—the beasts of burden which had dragged the heavily-laden carts over the rough roads, and were now left to graze and roam at will on the opposite side of the camp.

"*Bitang!*" exclaimed F. at my elbow in an undertone, throwing away the end of his cigar—"bitang" being a term applied to strayed or stolen cattle.

Possibly the term was correctly applied in this instance,

but horse-stealing is by no means "made easy" in this country, and the stringent laws regarding the possession of horses bear evidence to the low state of morals of one or more sections of the community at any rate; no one being permitted to sell a horse without previously presenting to a member of the constabulary, or some other official appointed by Government for the purpose, a paper duly signed by the magistrate of the town or village at which the purchase has been made, and in which a full description is given, not only of the animal itself but of the manner in which its possession has been acquired. Without such a document no horse is admitted for sale at any fair, at which small offices are invariably erected and presided over by officers of the constabulary, whose duty it is to inspect these forms, and where both the sellers and purchasers of horses have to repair before either transaction is completed. Here the seller has to deliver up his "pass," when another is made out and placed in the hands of the purchaser, giving a full description of the animal and its antecedents.

There are no doubt many instances in which even these preventive measures have proved unavailing, and ways have been found of ingeniously evading the law, but the precautions that are taken must still be a great check on the proverbial cupidity of the "wandering tribe." Should a horse awaken the suspicion of the *pandurok*, and its pedigree seem of doubtful origin, it is impounded for a year, during which time it is advertised in every police-station throughout the country, or at all events until the true owner comes forward to claim the "*bitang*" as his long-lost steed, or the person whose ownership was doubted can prove beyond all question that he obtained it by lawful means.

Whilst the suspected animal is kept by the police in durance vile, it is let out on hire by the authorities; but whether, in the case of the suspicions of the *pandurok* having been incorrect, any compensation is made to the unfortunate individual who has lost the use of his beast during the period it was kept in "*bitangság*," I cannot say. Probably he has to rest satisfied with the ultimate restitution of his rightful property, and like persons in our own land who, when they have been falsely accused of some crime, have been tried for it and found innocent, he will be consoled by receiving a "full and free pardon" at the hands of a benevolent and magnanimous Government.

Familiarity having by this time rendered the gipsies far less formidable, we seat ourselves by their fire, the warmth of which is pleasant, for the nights already begin to be frosty, although we have only arrived at the end of August. The dog had followed us, and was crouching at my side. The gipsies both understood and spoke German, and as we were explaining how we came by him, he looked up sharply, his ears well pointed, and regarded us inquiringly, looking first at one and then at the other. The gipsies, to whom a dog more or less never comes amiss, will, they say, take him off our hands, and we tip them a gulden to confirm the bargain; but on casting our eyes towards the spot where he had been lying, we find he had silently slunk away and hidden himself in the darkness, as though he had heard all we had been saying. Well is it, my *bánya* (dog), that thou didst so, or thy fate would surely have been decided there and then.

It was not till the following evening, just as the sun was closing his great scorching eye, that we drove through the broad streets of the ancient and "Royal Free City" of Debreczin, and found ourselves not only in the very heart of Hungary, but in the very centre of the most exclusive and rigid Protestantism.

The territory of Debreczin in its capacity of "Royal Free City"—a privilege which it has enjoyed since the middle ages—covers an area of no less extent than 378 English square miles, and as the meaning of that term has already been described, the flourishing state of the municipality can easily be imagined. The city contains between sixty and seventy thousand inhabitants, but, in driving through it— unless he has been previously undeceived—the traveller will imagine it to be scarcely more than a large village. Like every other place on the Alföld, where land is so abundant, the houses are nearly all built of one storey. There have been great improvements, however, since we were last here, particularly in the paving of the streets. In the place of a mere plank which formerly kept the foot-passengers out of the sea of mud that constituted the road in rainy weather, there now exists a broad and even pavement in all the chief thoroughfares, a fact which does credit to the enterprise of the municipality, who must have accomplished the undertaking at immense cost, every stone having been brought at least a hundred miles. There is a tradition of no very remote date to the effect that at a period anterior to the improvement of the roads a cow had sunk into the "Slough of Despond," and having been swallowed up in it, was no more seen. But whether this is a mere fable or not, it is quite true that officers quartered on one side of the street formerly were often obliged to mount their chargers to cross over to the other. At that time the "pavements" consisted of merely a single plank, and it is said to have been a great amusement to the inhabitants, whenever they met a soldier of the Imperial Army—whom they cordially hate—to push him off the narrow path into the sea of liquid mud below.

Having brought with us a letter of introduction to one of the Professors of the College, we hasten to deliver it in person. Reaching the edifice in question, we see standing in the square that encloses it a number of students, of whom we inquire the way to the Professor's quarters, addressing them in German. Great is our surprise, however, to find they cannot understand a word of what we say. Failing to make ourselves intelligible in that tongue, we try in turn French, Italian, Spanish, Latin, and Greek, putting the question in each of these languages in the most simple form possible, with the same result, and, for anything they appeared to comprehend of the European languages, either living or dead, we might have arrived in the very heart of the Chinese Empire. With a look of extreme mystification, and a shrug of the shoulders, they raised their hats, and, passing on, left us to our fate.

At length, spurred on by defeat and waxing bold, F. ascends the broad flight of steps leading to the College, and soon returns, accompanied by two students whose rooms he had invaded, the trio laughing heartily on finding they were unable to understand each other. The letter of introduction, however, bearing the name of the Professor furnished a clue to our inquiries, and beckoning us to follow them across the College garden, the taller of the two students ran to announce our arrival, doing so, as we afterwards learnt, in the following words:—

"Some foreigners have arrived with a letter for you. They speak every language under the sun, and have tried to make themselves intelligible; but to what nation they belong we cannot tell, but think they may be *Angolok*."

Following our conductor across a road ankle-deep in dry sand, we reach a wooden archway leading to a porch, where we find the astonished Professor, and standing behind him our pioneer, looking very happy in having at last succeeded in bringing us to the right place. A few words addressed to the former in English accorded us in broken accents a warm greeting in the same tongue. The Professor was a very handsome and distinguished-looking man, dressed in the Hungarian costume, consisting of Hessian boots and braided *attila*.

Knowing we were anxious above all things to see the College, he at once proposed accompanying us.

"Every square yard of this paving," remarked the Professor, "cost us twenty florins; the stones were brought by railway from Tokay. And is not this nice and soft to the feet?" he continued, as we stepped off the pavement into the dust of the road, which was at least eight inches deep, and which, though doubtless very delightful to a Hungarian, had scarcely suggested itself to *us* in that light.

We soon again reach the College, which is a large and very imposing structure, where two thousand students are educated. At present there are three hundred studying Theology, one hundred and fifty Law and Philosophy, upwards of one hundred in the Normal Department, and seven hundred in the so-called gymnasium; but we were *not* informed of the number who were studying as a necessary branch of education any of the modern or ancient languages!

Besides the students who form the academical portion of the College, there are six hundred boys in the elementary school. Within the last three years two new wings have been added where three hundred of the *togati* (students) are lodged.

In the Hungarian kingdom there are three universities, one at Buda-Pest, one at Koloszvár, and one at Agram, the capital of Croatia. There are also schools of Law and Jurisprudence at Pressburg, Kashau, and Grosswardein, besides the *Collegii* of Debreczin, Eperies, Raab, and others; that of Debreczin being exclusively Protestant and Calvinistic.

Attached to the College is an immense church in the *Renaissance* style, capable of containing 2,000 people. There is also a smaller private chapel *within* the College, which is interesting as having been used by Kossuth for the assembling of his Diets in the memorable year of 1849, and in which he announced the independence of Hungary and the downfall of the Hapsburg Dynasty. To add to the solemnity of this latter occasion, preceded by the great agitator himself, the members of the Diet adjourned to the large Calvinistic church above alluded to, where, standing beneath the pulpit, he read the proclamation which sent such joy into every Hungarian home, but which was destined, alas! to be of such short duration. The windows of the College look out upon the battle-field so memorable in Hungarian history, where Austria, with Russia as her ally, crushed the national independence of the

Hungarians which they had only recently regained, and on which occasion so much Magyar blood was shed.

The oldest part of the building is devoted to the Library, which contains many ancient and valuable manuscripts, together with two original copies of the tenets of the Hungarian Calvinistic faith.

Notwithstanding the silence and solemnity which pervade the place, Debreczin is the most commercial town in Hungary, a brisk trade being carried on not only in the manufacture of meerschaum pipes, but of *bundas* also, between two and three thousand of these splendid garments being exported annually.

It would have been impossible to leave without carrying home as souvenirs to our friends—who are victims to the vice of which pipes are the medium—some of these interesting articles which are displayed so temptingly and in such endless variety in the windows.

Going into a shop to make some purchases on our way from the College the Professor exclaimed to the woman in attendance:—

" I have brought you a lady and gentleman who have come all the way from England."

"Merciful Heaven!" she replied, " is it possible ? And they are not Hungarians ? What a pity ! " regarding us as she uttered this pious ejaculation with a look in which not only the deepest compassion, but contemptuousness also was mingled.

The Magyars are passionately attached to their country —" *Aldott Magyarorsag* " (Blessed Hungary), as they call it, the half-educated looking upon the subjects of all other countries with the greatest pity and contempt. The following mediæval rhyme in confirmation of this fact is still quoted :—

> "Extra Hungariam non est vita,
> Et si est vita, non est ita."

Whilst the greatest toleration exists in other parts of Hungary amongst all classes of society, the Debrecziners form an exception to the rule, and are exceedingly exclusive in matters of religion.

In the estimation of the Debrecziner, there is only one true faith, which he calls the "*Magyar vallás*," and which he believes he alone of all others has preserved in its completeness. There may be other forms of religion by the observance of which men may scramble into heaven, but the one true and narrow road is that which was instituted by their apostle Calvin. In consequence of its being the headquarters of this faith, Debreczin is often spoken of as the "Calvinistic Rome," and its inhabitants, with their plain attire, their simple deportment, and the stillness of the place itself, as well as the earnestness that sits on every countenance, give to it a character wholly different from that met with elsewhere in Hungary; and as we walked through the town pervaded by this deep Calvinistic gloom, and noted the stern and rigid countenances of the people, we felt thankful we were not compelled to cast in our lot with them "for aye."

Every three months an immense fair is held in the great plains in the vicinity of Debreczin, when an enormous space of ground which the eye can scarce command is covered with tents, booths, and immense flocks and herds. At one time no fewer than 20,000 fairs were held each year in Hungary, their number, however, as well as their importance have lessened considerably since the opening of the Alföld Railway, before which time the dwellers of the plains were completely locked in from all communication with distant towns.

At the time of our visit to Debreczin, the municipality, or whatever form the governing body takes in these "Royal Free Cities," was carrying on an anxious debate on the subject of the supply of fuel for its 50,000 inhabitants. Plenty of coal is found in the country, and the prejudice once existing against its use—to which the Hungarians attributed the "pulmonary complaints of the English, their *melancholy disposition, and frequent felo-de-se*"—has partially subsided, but the expense of transport would be enormous. At the same time the forests in the neighbourhood are fast becoming exhausted. The construction of a canal between Debreczin and Tisza-lök—about thirty-five miles distant—has consequently been decided on, by which timber may be floated down from the forests of the north-east Carpathians.

CHAPTER XLIII.

THE WINE DISTRICTS OF TOKAY.

FROM earliest dawn a throng of human life has been pouring into the Square outside the hotel, and the ceaseless hum beneath our window of female voices, the quacking of geese, gobbling of turkeys, and agonising cry of smaller birds whose legs are tied too tightly, assail our ears in a perpetual din and confusion, very hard upon tired pilgrims, to whom, for once, morning sleep might have been sweet.

Looking down upon that busy, hurrying hive who would think it is Sunday?

At ten o'clock the "Big Ben" of the College church begins solemnly to toll for service, which is the signal for the bells of other churches to do likewise, but still the people buy and sell and haggle and bargain and depreciate. The buyer saith, " it is naught, it is naught," and then going his way, vaunteth himself, just as men did in the days of Solomon; and altogether the Debreczin "*civis*," * stern Protestant though he be, manages to combine the worship of God and Mammon on the Sabbath-day in a way that would do credit to any Roman Catholic country on the face of the globe.

But now the bells stop, and entering the church in the market-place we find that a few stragglers are already there,

* A term used to denote a Debrecziner citizen.

whilst a man standing behind a small desk is singing lustily for his own honour and glory to a small congregation of admirers. Presently he mounts the pulpit—his hair is unkempt, and his dress proclaims him one of the lower orders—and begins reading the lessons, during which people one by one come straggling in till the church is full, and the clergyman, robed in a costume of the Vandyck period, makes his appearance, when the real service begins by the singing of another hymn, accompanied this time by a rather fine organ. Singing forms a very important part of the worship of the National Church of the Magyars, and the people sing with their whole heart and lungs, pausing momentarily after each line to take breath, and then beginning again with renewed vigour, embroidering the "Plain Psalm" with little turns and quivers.

Many of the hymns sung in these Calvinistic churches were composed by Bethlen Gábor, one of the governing princes of Transylvania, a firm adherent to the doctrine of Calvin, who flourished about 1620, and whose memory is much cherished by the Magyars.

It was a curious sight, and somehow took one back to the times of the "Covenanters"— the plain building, the men wearing large cloaks fastened loosely across the chest with heavy clasps, their long white hair hanging over their shoulders. Wonderful to look at are these earnest, almost scowling, old Debrecziner "*cives*," there being scarcely one of Rembrandt's studies which does not possess its perfect counterpart in the assembly. What fine old pilgrim fathers leaning on their staffs, as they sit and listen to the clergyman now lifting up his voice in prayer to the great *Isten*—the hearer of all prayer!

The women, on the contrary, their heads and faces wrapped in large woollen kerchiefs, are anything but picturesque. The greater number wear handsome and very full cloaks, richly embroidered in silk of every shade *originally*, but now assuming, by reason of many years' wear and tear, a rich mingling of mellow tints, delightful only to the eyes of an artist. The men sit in one part of the church and the women in the other, and thus clothed, the latter form a very dismal assemblage. There are some men whose long hair is held back over the forehead by a large circular comb, and others with ringlets all round the head like women; but these are principally men of middle age.

The Magyar, for oratorical purposes, is a most telling language, clear sounding, rich, and melodious. Though understanding little, I enjoyed listening to the fine enunciation of the preacher, whose manner was very earnest and impressive.

On the conclusion of the sermon the organ pealed forth, and the congregation, one and all lifting up their voices, united in singing the grand old hymn—

"Ein' feste Burg ist unser Gott."

But the sound was deafening. In vain the organist pulled out his *bourbon* stop and tried hard to hold his own; the voices so completely drowned him, that he might have been a tuning fork in the midst of a full orchestral band, for anything we could hear of him or his noble instrument. But the singing, though loud, was at any rate harmonious, and in all their hymns there was a grandeur and solemnity as well as heartiness that made one feel there must be, notwithstanding their apparent coldness in externals, a real depth in their religion after all.

Just as I was leaving the porch I was joined by F., who had been to the large church attached to the College, and had likewise been greatly impressed with the quiet and deep solemnity of the service.

Later in the day a heavy shower of rain, accompanied by thunder and lightning, broke over the town and kept us prisoners to our rooms till the evening, when thinking a walk in the suburbs might be pleasant, we happened to mention our intention in passing to an old woman—a servant of the hotel—who was standing on the staircase; whereupon, lifting up her eyes she exclaimed—

"What! The lady is going out in those boots? *Bóldog Ister!*"

Hereupon Julinka, the chamber-maid, runs off to her own apartment, and brings thence her own Sunday "tops," entreating me to wear them—a twofold hint so eloquent of the state of the Debreczin roads in rainy weather that we determined to defer our acquaintance with the *rus in urbe* of the " Royal Free City " until the morrow, when we should be driving through it on our way to the wine districts. We therefore visited instead several Calvinist places of worship in the town itself, all of which exhibited the same baldness as those we had seen previously, the walls being covered with whitewash, and the arches and original character of the structures completely destroyed by these Magyar Calvinists in their puritanical horror of anything that savoured of the Gothic in their style of architecture.

On arrival here, our intention had been to travel hence to the bright little city of Kashau, but meeting by accident an old Magyar acquaintance who lived half-way between that place and Debreczin, and who, hearing us express a desire to see one of the wine-growing districts of Hungary, hospitably proposed to conduct us to his home not many miles from Tokay, a proposition that was far too tempting to be declined. A direct line of railway is now open between Debreczin and Kashau, but as we had our own carriage, and he assured us it would only be a day's journey with four horses, we decided to post as usual, our friend promising to accompany us.

The following morning, in spite of the earliness of the hour, the usual crowd assembled at the archway of the hotel to witness our departure. The sky, cleared by the rain of yesterday, was brilliant, the sun just risen in all his glory from out the mist that still hovered above the warm moist plains. The coachman, in his heavily frogged jacket, small felt cap adorned with an eagle's feather, and with his moustaches twisted into a stiff curl at each end, was making, as we emerged from the hotel, the demonstrations customary with such functionaries, and, flogging the air with his long whip, pretended to be dispersing the little knot of anxious spectators, who, determined to see the last of the *Ángolok*, returned each time to the charge shrieking with laughter.

András had evidently made great friends with the servants of the hotel; the old woman comes out and almost weeps over him; the chambermaid, standing shyly behind, wipes a tear from her eye with the corner of her apron; the waiters throw themselves upon him and call him "Brother." Sundry nondescript menials from the back premises also present themselves and affectionately embrace his legs as he mounts the box. Finally, the landlady comes out, and with the prettiest speech possible places a bouquet in the hands of the "*tekintetes asszony*" (worshipful lady), and expresses the hope she may see her again. And thus, our coachman gathering up the ribbons, we bid adieu to the "Royal Free City," and with the usual clatter tear madly through the streets into the open country—the dog following us.

Whilst at Debreczin, András had done his best to dispose of this miserable hanger-on, but failed in finding a home for him. He was a sheep-dog, and as such no one seemed inclined to accept him here; but as András assured us that, being a valuable kind of animal, we should have no difficulty in getting rid of him as soon as we should again find ourselves in the agricultural districts, we gave him permission to retain him pending that happy moment.

By this time, under the nourishing influence of hotel bones and possibly something else to boot, the poor creature wears a far less miserable appearance. He still limps occasionally on three legs, but is evidently fast getting the better of his injuries, from whatever cause they may have arisen, and no longer creeps along by the side of the carriage, but runs on in advance as our pioneer, making incursionary forays now and then into huts by the wayside, and beginning to look as though he thought life, after all, was not half so bad as he had hitherto imagined. At one moment he nearly got himself into serious trouble with other sheep-dogs whose territory he invaded, and us also with the shepherd, whose flock he chased for fully half a mile.

The districts surrounding Debreczin are much better wooded than in other parts of the Alföld, there being large forests of robinia, the sandy nature of the soil favouring the production and growth of these graceful trees.

Our friend the Magyar who accompanied us, although living in the very centre of Hungary, and a Hungarian to the backbone, was not above speaking German fluently. He had travelled a good deal in other countries besides his own, and was in all respects a highly educated and enlightened man. In asking him how it came to pass that, notwithstanding the acquirement of foreign languages was frequently pursued amongst the upper classes at Pest to an extent which sometimes excluded the study of other and more necessary branches of education, yet at Debreczin—one of the chief seats of learning—the Magyars spoke nothing but their own language, he replied—

"Our brave Queen Maria Theresa did her utmost to extinguish the Magyar language by introducing German in its stead, hoping thereby to blend all the nationalities into one. At the present time, however, the effort of our people is to stamp out the German tongue, and cause the Hungarian to be the only one spoken throughout the country. Debreczin may be called with truth the seat of patriotism and Magyarism, as well as one of learning, and there is no place in the whole country where such strong prejudices exist. Just as the people here are exclusive in matters of religion, so are they in language. In fact, their speaking nothing but Magyar may be said to be in effect a mild form of political demonstration.

"I dare say you have long ago discovered," he continued, "whilst travelling in my country, that we Magyars are the proudest race living, and likewise I fear the most prejudiced. A Magyar who has not travelled beyond his own country is deeply imbued with two ideas, one being that the world was created for his express benefit, the other that his is the only language that ought to be spoken. Another characteristic trait is his dislike of all foreigners with the exception of the English, whom he condescends to regard as an enlightened and advanced people, who have a right to a share of his natural inheritance, and from whom something is to be learnt. You may also have observed that the Hungarians often speak of themselves as the 'English of the East!'"

It was a delightful day that we spent in this Hungarian's society. We have had the privilege of knowing many, and our impression has always been that a travelled, well-born, and well-educated Hungarian is one of the most polished and perfect gentlemen in the world.

It was a splendid day, too, so far as the weather was concerned. The rain had cooled the atmosphere, and instead of the fierce, dry heat, which at this season of the year generally envelopes the whole region of the Alföld, a balmy breeze was blowing, and, reclining in the languid luxury of our comfortable old carriage, we drank it in, and felt strengthened and invigorated. It was like the climate of Italy without its summer heat.

Long before the sun began to sink and throw long shadows on the plains, we came in sight of the volcanic hill of Tokay, rising out of them like a promontory from a vast expanse of ocean, and ere it set we had reached our friend's dwelling. He was expected to arrive by the 6.25 train, and his carriage had been sent to meet him at the Tokay station five miles distant. Great, therefore, was the surprise of his wife and daughter, who came running out at the sound of wheels, to find he had arrived not only an hour earlier than they had anticipated, but in the company of strangers and in a strange carriage. There was a great barking of dogs in the great courtyard behind the house, and a general buzz of welcome, in which we could perceive that we also were included.

A brief introduction soon made us feel perfectly at ease, and, as on similar occasions, our arrival created no more confusion than if we had been expected guests. Ascending the steps we entered the large, one-storied building, and were at once ushered into the drawing-room. A burst of joy and gladness followed our immediate entry, proceeding from the younger members of the family, who came trooping in to welcome their father. All kissed our hands, and then, without the slightest appearance of forwardness, endeavoured to satisfy their very natural curiosity as to who we were and whence we had come.

"And have you come from very far away?" inquired, in French, a fair-haired child of about eight years old, wishing to elicit, but not liking to ask, the direct question as to what nationality we belonged to.

"The strangers are from *Angol-orság!*" replied the father, in the same language.

"*Angol-orság!*" repeated a chorus of little voices. Oh, how glad I am you have come, it is always nice to have *les étrangers* staying with us, but *les Anglais* we have never before seen. *Oh! quelle joie!*"

"Come, let me show you to your rooms," exclaimed the lady of the house presently. after we had partaken of coffee.

Like so many houses in the plains, one room opened into another, and we had consequently to pass through several, including the library and a lady's boudoir, before reaching those to which our hostess now conducted us.

They were pretty rooms with cool pink and white hangings, the floor covered with Indian matting; the open windows, which were shaded by Venetian blinds, looking out into a garden where there were vines and melons growing in wild luxuriance, and crowds of heartsease holding up their expressive little faces to the light and straggling flowers in sweet disorder, reminding one of Lothair and Lady Corisande's garden. To the left was a long range of stables and out-offices, rendered picturesque by vines and other climbers which covered their walls completely. Beyond all were the plains lying in the crimson sunset. immersed in their drowsy peace and breadth of calm, while the air was filled with a pleasant odour of flowers mingled with ripe fruit.

The Hungarians, particularly those who live in the country, dine early and take supper at eight o'clock, but that meal is, however, quite synonymous with "dinner," and includes not only soup, but a variety of courses. The table was laid very prettily, and adorned with flowers and old-fashioned plate. After supper, which lasted more than an hour, we went out into the garden at the front of the house, where was a table on which wine and glasses were set, our host declaring we must not be longer under his roof without tasting "Imperial Tokay."

As we sat in the warm star-lit alley of robinias, we could see into the drawing-room, where on a centre table a large lamp was burning. Round it fluttered insects, and near it sat two of the elder children reading. In a distant part of the room was the eldest daughter playing the piano—a fragile, pensive girl with blue eyes, dressed in a cloud of white, her hair tied back with a cherry-coloured ribbon, and looking, as she sat with the light falling full upon her, almost spiritual in her pale prettiness.

We soon found that our host's family was not so numerous as we previously imagined. He had three children only, the eldest daughter, Örzse, a son at school in Pest, and Irma, the little girl who had spoken to us on our arrival. The others were nephews and nieces, who, with their governess, were merely on a visit.

On going into the breakfast-room the following morning we find the whole family already assembled. As we make our appearance the children cluster round us and silently kiss our hands, a universal custom in Hungary, where children in greeting do not kiss the cheeks, even of their parents, but their hand, in token of deference and submission.

Our hosts were Lutherans, and the meal was preluded by those beautiful lines from the 145th Psalm: "The eyes of all wait upon Thee and Thou givest them their meat in due season. Thou openest Thine hand and satisfiest the desire of every living thing."

"I purpose driving you to one of the Hegyalia, to-day," exclaimed our host, as we rose from his hospitable board, at the same time interpreting that Magyar word into French, and informing us that it means literally "mountain slopes," a term that is invariably used in reference to the vine-clad hills in the neighbourhood of Tokay.

At eleven o'clock a splendid pair of horses appeared at the door; the carriage, however, was an ordinary one of the country, with open sides, and but a refined and improved species of the genus *Leiterwagen*.

"You have grown used to our style of locomotion by this time, I trust," exclaimed our host, after we had mounted, and he had taken the reins. "This sort of thing is lighter and better suited to our country roads, which can scarcely be dignified by the name, and that you will speedily discover for yourselves, I fear, when we have proceeded a short distance on our way."

Striking off the main road, we now pass through plantations of tobacco and buckwheat; the various shades of green as we look across the plains being exceedingly beautiful as well as refreshing to the eye. Yonder, in graceful outline, rise the hills, that of Tokay assuming the appearance of a cone. This, however, we leave to the left, and gradually near another hill, like all the rest, vine-clad from its base to its summit, every tree and shrub having been eradicated to make room for the cultivation of the grape.

These Hegyalia are said to have been similarly planted, even before the Magyars entered Pannonia; but the cultivation of the vine was subsequently greatly promoted by Hungary's mediæval kings, who seem to have been no less capable than other crowned heads of appreciating that which "maketh glad the heart of man."

During the dominion, however, in this country of the Moslem hordes—against whose creed it is to drink any fermented liquors—the whole district was laid waste and almost every plant uprooted; but after their expulsion a number of Italians were called in by King Bela IV., who not only restored the former cultivation, but improved the species of vine, causing the wine made here to attain its present celebrity.

We had lunch, or rather what they call dinner here, at one of the vine-growers' houses, and then walked up the zigzag paths through the vineyards. The slopes of the hills, where they are steep, are cut up into terraces. The soil is exceedingly light, and it is to this peculiar character that the excellence and distinct quality of the Tokay wine is attributed.

The vintage in this district does not commence until the 26th of October, by which time it is over in other parts of Hungary. The season is ushered in with great festivity; all the noble families of the neighbourhood gather together, when there is a succession of balls and fêtes which last for a fortnight.

There are three kinds of Tokay so called, the most luscious and costly being *Essenz*, which is, however, seldom used except to give "bouquet" to other wines. It consists entirely of juice extracted without the agency of any external force, and simply pressed out by the weight of the fruit itself, and also from grapes that have been allowed to shrivel and dry upon the stalk. *Ausbruch*—by which name the kind of Tokay best known is designated—is made by mixing the juice of ripe grapes, which have been pressed by the ordinary mechanical process, with a certain quantity of thick pulp, formed of the dried fruit. The third kind—*Mászlás*, being similar to the former, the only difference consisting in its possessing less of the flavour of the dried fruit, a smaller quantity of pulp having been added to the juice.

In consequence of the grapes being allowed to hang so long upon the tree, they naturally lose a great deal of their juice, and in withering become exceedingly sweet; but the particular kind called Essenz, though luscious, is not sickly.

The very finest of all the wines made in the districts of the Hegyalia is manufactured at Tokay itself, and at a small place named *Mézes-Mále*. The vineyards of these mountain slopes are said to cover an area of 68,000 acres, and produce annually from nine to twelve million gallons of the precious beverage; the most ready purchasers being merchants from North Germany and Scandinavia. During our visit, however, an American arrived and purchased 300 hogsheads.

Some of the fruit, already ripe, was hanging in rich clusters, and, sauntering up the sunny slopes, how many we plucked and ate as we forced our way through the narrow paths!

On our return, the gentleman at whose house we dined, insisted on our tasting some of the vintages. The first was only three years old, the last twenty, but one and all had a delicious bouquet. "Imperial Tokay" is a most fascinating wine, but inclined to make one "joyful," and it was perhaps well that the carriage was at the door, and the horses too impatient to be kept standing any longer, or the consequences might have been serious.

It was evening by the time we again reached our friend's hospitable mansion. An early supper had been ordered, which gave us a long evening afterwards to wander about the sweet, flower-scented alleys in the garden, and after darkness had set in we sat in the porch listening to music within, Örzse being a brilliant musician, having studied for three years at the *Conservatoire* at Paris.

Whilst here we were surprised to find how much our English literature is appreciated and read. On the table I noticed a Magyar translation of "Adam Bede," and other English authors, amongst whom, by the way, Bulwer is almost invariably the favourite with the Hungarians.

Our host and hostess were most earnest in their efforts to induce us to prolong our visit to an indefinite period, and the time we had already spent in this delightful home had been so full of sunshine, that we would gladly have availed ourselves of their proffered hospitality had we been able.

During our stay in this charming and well-appointed household, we were made aware of the fact that it was customary for a gipsy to form one of the regular staff of servants in a Hungarian family. The one in question was a pretty young woman with masses of raven hair and a clear skin; but notwithstanding her neat dress and civilised surroundings, we recognised her immediately. It is in truth not until one sees the *Czigánok* translated to an entirely new form of existence, and under circumstances inconsistent with their ordinary lives, that one realises how completely different they are from the rest of mankind in form and feature. Instead of disguising, the garb of civilisation only enhances the type and renders it the more apparent. No matter what dress they may assume, no matter what may be their calling, no matter whether they are dwellers in tents or houses, it is impossible for gipsies to disguise their origin. Taken from their customary surroundings, they become at once such an anomaly and anachronism, and present such an instance of the absurdity of attempting to invert the order of nature, that we feel more than ever how utterly different they are from the rest of the human race, that there is a key to their strange life which we do not possess—a secret freemasonry that renders them more isolated than the veriest savages dwelling in the African wilds—and a hidden mystery hanging over them and their origin that we shall never comprehend. They are, indeed, a people so entirely separate and distinct that in whatever clime or quarter of the globe they may be met with, they are instantly recognised, for with them nearly forty centuries of association with civilised races have not succeeded in obliterating one single sign.

Old Cronies.

CHAPTER XLIV.

TEMPLES OF THE NIGHT.

KASHAU—the winter residence of many of the "Nobles" —is an exceedingly nice little city, and, after Pest, by far the most pleasant in Hungary. The houses are irregular and picturesque, and the cathedral, erected in 1300, is a splendid Gothic structure with five naves, and contains rich fret-work of great elegance and purity of style. The whole, however, is spoilt, in a great measure, by the gilded and gaudily painted altars, which, resting against the beautiful groups of pillars, greatly detract from the harmony and size of the building.

The best time to see this splendid edifice is at the hour of "Benediction," when the shades of evening are gathering beneath the lofty arches of the central nave, and the setting sun, glistening through the painted windows, shoots soft arrows of gold and blue and crimson, which fall upon the pavement and the white kerchiefs of the women kneeling below the altar in the western transept.

It was pleasant to linger in the cathedral whilst the evening service was taking place, listening to the heavenly voices of the choir singing high up over the western porch, and hearkening with bated breath to the sounds which, travelling along the Gothic roof and in and out amongst the arches and side chapels, seemed not to come from human lips, but through the painted windows; as though angels had brought it on their wings.

On our second visit, one of the *Dom Herren* (canons of the cathedral) observing we were foreigners, showed us several costly chalices, libariums, ancient missals and vestments, all of which were well worth seeing. He also caused to be uncovered the forty-eight pictures over the high altar illustrative of incidents in the lives of Jesus and Mary, twelve only of which are exhibited save on high festivals.

To the south of the cathedral is the little mediæval church dedicated to St. Michael, and further still, opposite the Promenade, that of the Jesuits.

As at Koloszvár, one of the first things that arrests the stranger as he walks along the streets of Kashau, and looks into the shop windows, is the conspicuous display of coffins of all shapes and sizes, some of very elaborate designs, the most common being a sarcophagus in white enamel, with gilt cornices, standing on lion's claws. There are, however, others to suit all comers and all tastes. One of these shops is situated close to a grocer's, and hard by a Jew of elastic conscience sells crucifixes.

In spite of all its gaiety there was something very sad to us in Kashau after all.

Close to the hotel at which we were staying, a large building was being erected, upon which prisoners were employed in such numbers that they swarmed about the scaffolding, and in and out of the windows and doorways, like a lot of busy ants. They were all young men, and it was painful to watch them working under the vigilant eyes of the guards who stood over them with their bayonets, and to notice how they toiled hour after hour without pausing for an instant—working on with a perpetual motion that made one weary and wretched to witness.

It is in the hilly country, the Felföld of Kashau, that are found the mines from which the precious opal is taken, a gem that is alleged to exist in no other part of the world, for the species called "Oriental" is in reality brought from these mines, which also contain jasper, agate, and chalcedony of great brilliancy.

Anxious as we were to see these celebrated and interesting mines, we had no time to visit both these and the caves of Agtalek. We therefore decided to accomplish the latter, for which purpose we requested András to be ready with the carriage and four horses at five o'clock the following morning, the distance being considerable. The hotel bill was accordingly paid over night, our luggage packed even to the rugs, and we retired to our "*napi*" with the uncomfortable sensation all travellers have who know they must be up in the morning before the world is awake. Since leaving Debreczin, we have been spoiled for early rising and got into bad habits in this respect, taking our coffee in our own room, and coming down to breakfast at the sluggard hour of ten.

On the following morning at dawn, we were awakened by a loud pattering against the window panes. It was raining heavily. At half-past five, the inevitable porter comes, "rapping, tapping, at my chamber door." But so strongly do we object to starting on a journey in wet weather, unless obliged, that we send a message to András and inform him that we shall not leave Kashau till the morrow.

The morn had indeed broken drearily. On the rigid leaves of the oleander trees in the balcony outside, doing their best to grow in tubs much too small for them, the rain drips from the roof in heavy drops. An hour later, and chamber-maids with skirts held tightly round them, and heads bent low, dodge in and out of doorways, and waiters, carrying steaming coffee and other creature-comforts to the gentlemen guests, likewise pass and re-pass on their errands of mercy, holding dripping umbrellas. Dark clouds hang over head; there is a steady and calm determination about the rain as it comes pattering down perpendicularly, and falls from the roof through a shoot outside, with a swish, swash, and gurgle, that seems to say it is not going to cease yet awhile now it has come at last. A little half-drowned bird perches on the window-sill, and shakes itself, and then looks in pathetically with its head on one side. More little birds do likewise, and trim their dripping feathers, and then go hopping amongst the oleander branches, carolling as sweetly as if they had been in their native woods. How much they must have " made believe " those happy little birds, and what an example of contentment under difficulties did they not preach to us who were grumbling within. But it was such a dreary sight looking down upon the dingy streets—the draggle-tailed Hungarians with their white-fringed *gatyák* dangling against their muddy top-boots as they walked along, and the poor ants opposite still toiling in their " daily round and common task " —that after breakfast we hailed a *droszky* and drove to the station. A train happened to be just leaving for Abos, by which we could also return early in the evening, and jumping into a coupé, we soon felt glad we had come, for the scenery in the neighbourhood of Kashau is exceedingly beautiful; our route takes us through a narrow gorge along which winds the Hernat, changing its fitful course from right to left and left to right continually. The mountains, scarcely less than 4000 feet in height, which enclose the gorge on either side, consist of rugged limestone, and the further we go, the more sublime the scenery becomes— mountain rising above mountain, and crag above crag, foaming torrents, and pyramids of rock jutting out here and there, over which the birch droops its slender and silvery stems. At length we come to the region of dark pines, which, spreading their branches, almost span the gorge. At long distances apart are little hamlets, whose cottages are built on the extreme edge of rocks. What fairy glens we pass, filled with lovely wild flowers, lilies of the valley, Alpine anemones, and the *Polygada amara* with its purple spikes! And wherever we turn our eyes we see a bewildering prodigality of beauty and luxuriance.

In an hour's time we reach our destination. There had been no rain here, which had evidently been confined to the region of the Plains; and we spent a most delightful day in wandering about amongst the woods, entering some of the little cottages and making friends with their simple dwellers. The peasantry in this locality eke out their livelihood by keeping bees, which they guard in little sheds, built high up the mountain slopes. The honey is delicious, perfectly clear, and much esteemed by people of other countries whither it is sent for sale.

On our returning to the Abos station to take the down train for Kashau, we found it crowded with emigrants on their way to America, viâ Hamburg; and as there was not sufficient room in the train to contain them, a delay was occasioned on account of more carriages having to be attached. A crowd of persons—men, women, and children—had come to see them off. The Hungarians are a warm-hearted people, deeply attached to their kindred, and it was almost more than we could witness unmoved—the fine, stalwart young fellows sobbing on the necks of aged parents, and bidding adieus to wives, children, and sweethearts, whom they might never again behold on earth.

It is a singular fact that, notwithstanding the superabundance of land and the thinness of the population, the Hungarians are every day leaving their country in vast numbers. There surely must be something radically wrong in the system of a Government which does not offer inducements to the labouring classes under these circumstances to remain in their own country.

In the same carriage with us was a gentleman on his way to Debreczin, who, in course of conversation, imformed us he was a tobacco planter, having an estate of 3000 *jochs*—a *joch* being, I believe, rather less than an acre—for which he had paid at the rate of £15 per *joch*. With land, then, not only so cheap, but so abundant everywhere, we again wonder what is the reason for these people emigrating?

It had evidently been raining all day at Kashau, but as we arrive, the leaden clouds, gathering themselves together, are sailing away from the golden west, where the sun, setting gloriously, promises better things for the morrow.

Sitting at dinner in the hotel restaurant we were taken aback by a person at an opposite table accosting us in English in the following words, which were uttered in the most unmistakable Transatlantic brogue, and with a fine, bold, nasal twang that would have done credit to the oldest inhabitant of that quarter of the globe:

"How long since you left England, sir, and what have ye come here for? I guess there isn't much in Hungary that you have found to your liking."

"Where do *you* come from?" was the reply that followed his questions, which seemed slightly to savour of impertinence.

"I've jest come from Amurica, sir. I've been there ten years."

"But you are surely an American yourself?"

"Wall, sir, I guess I'm a Hungarian. I went to the U-nited States to make my fortune, but instead of that I lost one."

"What do your countrymen do when they get there—such men, for instance, as we saw leaving to-day?" inquired F.

"They die by a fence," was the laconic reply.

"What do you mean?"

"Why, jest this. When they get out there, they can't speak any language the Amuricans know, and so no one will employ them. They go around from place to place in search of work, but find none; then, having spent the few florins they had in their pockets when they landed, they starve right away."

"Who induces them to emigrate? Surely some prospect must be held out to them of doing better there than in their own country, or they would not go in such numbers."

"It's the newspapers that does it," continued he, with the same brogue, in which he was evidently an apt scholar, "the *Government* newspapers, I mean. They are always telling our chaps the wonderful things they will do if they go there, and how that in a few years' time they will come home rich, and be able to settle down in the old country and be landowners; and they know it is a wicked lie they are telling all the while, and that there is nothing good to be gained there by our poor fellows. But what do they care *what* happens to them? they only want to get them out of the way that they may *Austrianise* our country the easier by colonising it with their own people."

Whether the above statement is correct or not I cannot say; I only repeat exactly what we heard. It is quite possible, and would doubtless be in the interest of Austria to induce Hungary's oft-times too patriotic sons to emigrate, that she might be enabled by degrees to colonise it with her own; but this, of course, is one of those matters which can never be more than mere conjecture.

At five o'clock A.M. we took our leave of this pleasant little city. Notwithstanding the matutinal hour, a crowd of attendants benevolently presented themselves to bid us adieu, possibly remembering that it is the early bird that catches the worm. "Worms" we were on that occasion at any rate, as well as on most others of the like nature, but a small *douceur* goes a long way with Hungarian servants, who are often ill-paid. Passing other hotels we see similar little performances being enacted, where more disinterested menials are assembled to speed the parting guest.

The Magyars are by no means a grasping people, and are always satisfied with whatever is given them, returning a hearty "Thank you," no matter how small the gift, which, by the way, they have the good taste never to look at in your presence.

About noon, arriving at a village, we found some difficulty in procuring a relay of horses, and whilst strolling about its labyrinths to pass away the time, we saw before us a church, and were just about to enter it, when a woman, who had evidently witnessed our approach, and who was standing at the door, closed it abruptly on the outside to prevent our doing so. Upon our asking her the reason in German, she replied, somewhat uncivilly, in her own tongue, that as we spoke an *idegen nyelv* (foreign language), we could not belong to the Magyar religion, and therefore it could afford us neither pleasure nor profit to see her church. " The national religion of the noble Magyar," I regret to say, does not " light up well." Its people are, for the most part, stern, demure, and exclusive—a fact even more apparent on our journey from Debreczin to Kashau than in the capital of the " *Magyar vallas* " itself, and of which the above little episode is an example. It was an amusing instance of bigotry, but I felt sorry it should have been from a Protestant that for the first time throughout the whole of our previous and present travels amongst Gallicians, Rusniaks, Slovaks, Wallachs, and even Croat-Serbs, we received any incivility. In the minds of the ignorant, the Magyar language and Protestantism are inseparable, whilst the Magyar language is, they believe, the only one known in heaven.

It is related of an old Magyar nurse attending a sick lady, that on hearing her make use of the common German exclamation, addressed to the Deity, she cried, "Ah, my lady, forgive me! but how can you expect the good God to listen to you if you speak to Him in a language He does not understand?"

At nine o'clock at night we reach Rosenau, a mining town situated on the river Sajó. The roads were execrable the whole way, but the scenery was both varied and beautiful. Our fatigue, however, had not been great, and the mountain air infused such new life into us that the next day we felt equal to anything; even to the announcement which greeted us on descending to the little restaurant of the inn for breakfast, that we should have to proceed to Agtalek by "*shaker*," the roads being, as we were assured, too bad for anything else on wheels.

We had already passed over so many hundred miles of Hungarian roads, that we scarcely believed there could be anything in store for us of a worse nature than we had hitherto experienced. Our ardour was consequently not in the least degree damped by the above announcement, and we set out with light hearts, András and *the dog* accompanying us. *A propos* of the latter, we had found a home for him at our friend's with whom we stayed, near Tokay, who assured us he was in need of just such a quadruped, but who advised us to keep him with us until we should be returning to Tokay, when we could leave him behind as we passed through the district.

As this waif was now a respectable member of society, and belonged to "the quality," it was necessary to give him some name. We therefore bestowed upon him that of *Essek* —the Magyar signification for Archbishop—on account of his resemblance to that ecclesiastical dignitary; his long black hair, and white front, giving him the appearance, when assuming a sitting posture, of a person in a black robe and lawn sleeves. We are once more in the land of gipsies, whom we have not met with on our travels for some time, but who now greet us at the entrance to every village, and exhibit, as elsewhere, the old Roman contempt for the superfluous.

Essek—a name which for the sake of brevity soon resolved itself into Esk—was at first a dog of somewhat low proclivities, much given to fraternise with gipsy children; but he already begins to turn up his episcopal nose whenever we now happen to fall in with a party of *Cziganok*, and is wont to pass by proudly on the other side.

Arrived at the village of Agtalek, after many a jolt and bump—our *shaker* true to its appellation to the last—we are met by guides who accompany us to the caverns situated a short distance above the village.

Like all others of the kind they are formed in the limestone rock, and extend a distance of many miles into the heart of the mountains. On entering, the *Tanz-saal* is the first great cavern we see, a vast hall where the peasants of the neighbourhood often resort on festivals, and dance by torch-light, arrayed in their pretty costumes.

Magnificent, however, as is the *Tanz-saal* in its vast proportions, we do not linger here, our desire being to penetrate farther into this marvellous region by one or more of its intricate windings.

Leading from the "great dome" is a narrow passage, through which a brook forces its way. Following it we reach, in a quarter of an hour's time, what is called the *Paradiesgarten*, a name given to this part of the cavern on account of the resemblance which the objects it contains bear to those which are supposed to have existed in the garden of Eden, and certainly the exquisite beauty and elegance of form which the stalactite and stalagmite matter here assume, far exceeds anything of the kind we ever beheld. Trees, fruits, and even the serpent—a good likeness of him too—were severally pointed out to us, nothing being absent, in fact, but Adam and Eve to complete the guide's *epitome!*

How those guides wearied us! In vain we besought them to be still, and leave us to our own imaginings; they continued to point out first this object and then that, and talked so perpetually, whilst we desired nothing so much as complete silence, in which to admire in awe and wonder, these great mysteries of nature, that, maddened at last by their persistence, F. let off, like a succession of pistol-shots, a string of telling Magyar expletives which he had previously learnt by diligent study, and which so astonished the guides by the fervour with which they were administered, that we heard nothing afterwards but the beating of our own hearts.

As we henceforth pursue our way, we do so almost with bated breath, for the farther we wander through these labyrinths the more the feeling of awe grows upon us; and as the guides precede us with their torches, the giant fragments of dripping stalagmite gleam grimly in the fitful light and take shape of living things, which seem to move, or stand spectral, and colourless before us. Sometimes these passages lead to small side chambers, hewn out roughly and majestically by nature in the solid rock, like ancient funereal vaults, in which lie rude *sarcophagi* and dead men's bones, guarded by wan figures, standing enveloped in half transparent drapery which covers them from head to foot. Anon we come upon shattered and ruined temples with Gothic arches, and fonts, and windows, and the

Hand that formed these objects of weird and fantastic beauty is still at work upon them, for we hear, above the muffled sound of our foot-fall, the steady "drip, drip" of the water in near and far-off passages.

Whilst examining a beautiful little grotto enclosed on all sides by slender pillars and drooping garlands, and in which were ferns and mosses and a net-work of fanciful leaves engraved on a mass of stalagmite, I suddenly found myself in darkness. F. and the guides had all passed on, and I was alone. It was useless to attempt to follow, I could only shout to them to return, and as I did so, how my own voice frightened me, as it echoed above, below, around, and then went rolling off into distant passages till it seemed to die away in boundless space!

They soon responded to my call and came tramping back with all speed, and then we reached the brook again flowing on through its lonely prison-house, the torches reflecting themselves strangely in its black waters.

We could not ascertain whether this subterranean stream contained the little animal, half-fish half-lizard—the *Proteus Auquinus*—found in the river Poik in the caverns of Adelsberg near Triste; those poor little eyeless creatures which, born in darkness, have—when taken by the curious from their native solitudes—to be shielded from the light of heaven in order to be kept alive.

The temperature of the caverns was so low that on returning to the hot outer atmosphere I nearly fainted. We were in fact both exhausted by fatigue and fasting; but found on reaching the village inn, where we had left András, that but for his exertions we must have lunched off honey, milk, and rye bread. There was in fact literally nothing else to be had. The brave little man, however, during our absence had again gone to the priest and obtained from him a fat pullet which had been already trussed for his Reverence's own dinner; and which, stewed and served with cranberry sauce, quite set us up for the day, and sent us on our way rejoicing.

CHAPTER XLV.

DICKENS *alias* " BOSH."

NOTHING can be more charming than the town of Tokay from a distance. Lying snugly at the foot of the Hegyalia with its picturesque wooden roofs peeping above the forest of willows which here grow luxuriantly, it looks like an ideal spot where one might spend one's days in pastoral tranquillity, a happy valley in which even Rasselas himself might have been contented to remain for ever.

Tokay is surrounded on one side by what appears to be a series of small lakes; they are, however, but the inundations of the Theiss, which here joins the Bodrog; and Tokay, notwithstanding its appearance from a distance, is a delusion and a snare, a long and inexpressibly dirty town whose houses are little better than hovels.

Besides the ordinary population of Hungary, Tokay is inhabited by an ethnological medley composed of Armenians, Greeks, and Jews, the latter being the "middle men" between the manufacturers of the wine and the merchants who purchase it. They consequently congregate in numbers at this place, and the Israelitish element is perhaps stronger here than elsewhere.

Although containing a population of five thousand souls, Tokay boasts of only one hotel—a straggling barrack-like building, with long, dark, cut-throat passages.

"Alas!" exclaimed András as he carried our portmanteaus up to our room—"to think that my sweet master and mistress should have to sleep in such a den, and that in my country too. It is a bad place, full of thieves and Jews; but they shall come to no harm, their faithful András will watch all night. Let not my master and mistress fear."

We have reason at any rate to thank the kind priest at our last resting place for his present of the fowl, for the only thing we could meet with on arrival here was *halázz lé* or "fisherman's soup," a dish consisting of various kinds of fish stewed together in a gravy, thickened with red pepper, a celebrated Szegedin dish, at which place we had eaten it with relish two years previously; but we do not feel inclined to partake of it here, and having ordered a small bottle of Tokay, for which the charge was five gulden, we sallied forth to the town, staggering under the old archway and over the rough stones like drunken folk, not from the effects of our libations, but from the road being full of deep holes which were hidden in sand, and of which we did not know the existence till we found ourselves plunging headlong into them. Crossing the street and passing at length under another old archway that must have been built in the time of Moses, we found ourselves standing on the banks of the river.

The Theiss here, as elsewhere, is a muddy and sluggish stream, but there is a great deal of navigation on its waters. It contains fish in great variety, and the sturgeon caught in this neighbourhood, whether from the superior muddiness of the water, or from whatever cause, is said to exceed in richness of flavour that found even in the Danube. So great is the quantity of fish left behind on the subsiding of the waters after an inundation, that the people of the town collect it to feed their numerous pigs, and to manure their land.

This now wretched and mean little place has had, however, a glorious past, and was in olden time the site of one of Attila's royal camps, who, barbarian though he was, united the splendour and magnificence of the East with the luxury and licentiousness of Rome. We are told by an ancient historian that his table was covered with goblets of silver and gold, wrought in divers rich devices, the dress of his warriors being embroidered with the same, whilst portions of their attire were studded with precious stones, as also were their sandals and the trappings of their horses. The entrance of the great chief to Tokay—then called "the royal village"—was celebrated with great solemnity and pomp. A numerous company of women, going forth to welcome their hero and their king, formed themselves into long and regular files, and held aloft a canopy of thin white muslin veils for him to pass under, whilst a number of maidens marched before him, chanting hymns in the Scythian language.

As we wander along the willow-fringed banks of the river, the basaltic Hegyalia with their vine-clad slopes, against which the town is built, rise above us.

These mountains extend for twenty miles in a northerly direction, and are separated from the plains by the river Bodrog, which, as I have said, falls into the Theiss at this spot.

Sauntering along, we were giving vent to our impressions of the place and its inhabitants in the most unguarded English, when a young man, the only respectable individual, by-the-way, we had yet seen in Tokay, whom we observed standing on the banks of the river as we passed, came toward us, and, taking off his hat, remarked abruptly—

"I sch-peak English."

He wore some kind of uniform, and we began to fear we might have offended the sensitive ear of an Austrian spy who might possibly get us into trouble, but our minds were soon relieved by his informing us that he liked our English literature, from which fact we judged him to be a man of peace rather than of war.

"I like your *Boulvair*," he continued, "but I cannot always understand your *Bosh*."

This seemingly uncomplimentary statement was, at first, not a little astounding, until we remembered that Dickens is always spoken of in Germany—and that therefore he would most probably be so in Hungary likewise—by his *nom de plume* of "Boz," and that that word on the lips of a Hungarian, if he happened to mistake the final letter and substitute "s" for "z"—which in the Magyar language is invariably pronounced like "sh"—would result in "Bosh."

"I hope we have not hurt your mind by anything we have spoken about this place and its inhabitants," broke in F., wishing to be gracious. "If we have I trust you will forgive us; you must have heard much that we said."

"You need not apologise," he replied. "I am not a native of Tokay,"—speaking partly in English and partly in

German—"and fully sympathise with your feelings concerning the place. There is some excuse for its inhabitants, however; Government, which takes care to receive the revenues, does nothing towards helping them to improve the condition of the town, a circumstance which naturally engenders apathy in the minds of the people themselves on the matter."

"Probably," we replied. "Yet it would cost them nothing to be clean ; there is plenty of water in the river here, such as it is."

"Eh!" rejoined he, after a pause, during which he was searching in the tablets of his memory for an English adjective, "the people are *faul* (idle),"—a word which, being pronounced *foul* in its own vernacular, was a much more suitable one in its present application than than of "idle," which he was desirous of expressing in English.

As we were returning to the inn, the church nearest to it rang out the "Ave Maria," and climbing the hill we entered the building by a side door. All was quiet and dark inside, for the evening light came feebly through the dusty windows. There were tapers on the altar, and a little lamp was glimmering here and there before some shrine. Few of us can go out of the daylight into a dimly lighted church without feeling subdued and solemnised, whatever creed be taught within its walls; and it was all very simple and impressive, and the contrast very great between its hush and peace and the noise and turmoil of busy life outside, which reached us in muffled tones, as though the sounds of earth were not permitted to enter the abode of peace and rest, save softly and subdued.

The door opens, and an old woman comes hobbling in, and

setting down her crutches begins praying aloud; then the priest enters silently from the sacristy, and, kneeling on the lowest step, begins reciting in a monotonous voice, the "Rosary," *Ave Maria, Gratia plena*, etc. The old woman and ourselves form the only congregation, and even she hobbles out again before the service is over, although it only lasted half an hour. We, however, remained to the end, by which time it was almost dark outside. As we reeled back to the hotel over the uneven pavement, there were sounds of drinking and revelry in almost every house; men singing Bacchanalian songs, or shouting at each other in argument; whilst passing beneath one window we heard, high above other voices, those of Jews—whose intonation we had ere this learnt to recognise—clamouring as usual about money. Again and again the words, "*gulden*," "*hundert tausend*," "*million gulden*," "*joch*," and "*massen von geld*," reached our ears.

I dare say we did the inhabitants of Tokay great injustice, for they were doubtless harmless enough, but we took care on retiring for the night to double-lock our door and look well to the window fastenings, for the whole place somehow had a brigand look.

András's room was next to ours, a fact in which *I* at any rate took comfort. He had prepared a light supper for us by the time we returned, which we partook of pic-nic fashion, in our own room. Esk, our faithful *bányá* (dog), was left in charge of the carriage in the *álas* close by, and, howling terribly during the night, he must, I fear, have disturbed the slumbers of the whole town or village, whichever Tokay may happen to be; but beyond this, no sound broke the stillness of the hours of darkness, and the worthy inhabitants gave us no annoyance whatever.

The church bells awoke us at an early hour the following morning. Looking down into the yard at the rear of the hotel, we see servants walking to and fro, and wading through the mud right valiantly. It is too deep even for top-boots, and they plunge into it with naked feet; but a large dog with long brown hair stalks about gingerly, like a tame bear, and chooses the driest places. The ducks and geese have a fine time of it, and flourish accordingly. On one side of the yard is a shed where the cows are kept, and having seen them milked, we lose for once our relish for "white coffee."

At seven o'clock, András comes to the door with the information that he has made arrangements for us to breakfast at the station restaurant, and recommends us to quit this *elendes dorf* (wretched village) as soon as we can.

Leaving our room after a hasty toilet, and proceeding along the dingy passage, we see two dark objects ascending the stairs and "stopping the way." Tourists possibly; but no! they turn out to be the pet pigs of the establishment, no doubt on their way to the *salle à manger*, situated on the landing. They are, however, checked in their bold career, for on catching sight of us they turn round, and with much demonstration of annoyance, a look of injured innocence, and many a grunt and squeak, they hastily retrace their steps.

Now, however much I may doat on a pig in its proper sphere, I do not quite like him as a domestic animal; but tastes differ, and the Hungarian pig, as we have already seen, is a much more civilised quadruped than his English brother.

At eight o'clock we make our triumphal departure from Tokay, and by dint of "sitting tight," and holding on to the sides of the carriage, succeed in reaching the station without broken bones. We have had rather a hard time of it, taking it altogether, but, happily for us, our philosophy is of that practical kind that seeks, and invariably finds, consolation wherever a particle of it can be found. We had made the discovery of how much human nature can endure and live, which is a knowledge worth acquiring in this "vale of tears;" we had tasted "Imperial Tokay" in the place where it is manufactured, and had seen the worst of the "*honfoglalás*" (Kingdom of Hungary), which is a thing to be proud of.

The kind Hungarian friends with whom we had been lately staying, had made us promise, before leaving them, to pay them a visit on our return; but wishing to go down the Save—the second largest river in Hungary—before the setting in of the autumnal rains, we decide to send a messenger from this place with the dog, and a note of apology for ourselves.

And so, *bányá* mine, we are going to label thee, "This side up, with care," and send thee away, but thou art going to a better home.

For the first time since we had him, Esk refrained from wagging his shaggy tail when I spoke to him. There must have been something in my tone of voice that boded evil; for he looked up at me with his large, earnest eyes, and trembled from head to foot; then, putting his front paws on my knees, he buried his head in my lap.

Poor beast, he had won our affections, and it was hard to part with him now that the moment had come. Having given him a good breakfast, however, and commended him to the tender mercies of the man who was to take him to his new home, we arranged for our own journey south. The train from Kashau was due at ten o'clock, and we decided to travel in it as far as Schemnitz, and then cross the plains in a southerly direction towards the capital, our carriage following us to Miscólsz in the evening, a place at which we meant to break our journey.

As the train slid out of the station, the great basaltic rocks of the volcanic hill of Tokay frowned down upon us with forbidding aspect, and it remained in sight for nearly an hour, when it gradually faded from our view, and appeared but a faint grey cloud on the verge of the horizon.

The plains in the north of Hungary are much more fertile than in the south, and we pass through thousands of acres of waving corn, and pastures as smiling as those of the Bánat. There has been a great deal of rain here, which we have partially escaped in our more northern travels, and the roads, as we approach the towns and villages, are such quagmires that in one place we saw a "shaker" and party of travellers—who had evidently driven from some distant horizon to start by our train—literally buried in the mud, which was half way up the wheels. Whether the unfortunate occupants were able to extricate themselves from their ridiculous position we could not tell. Under the circumstances, it would have been impossible for them to get out and walk. It is therefore not unreasonable to assume, in the silence of history concerning them and their fate, that they are there still.

Wandering about the plains, in proximity to each village,

are large families of geese, the parents waddling with sedate and solemn mien as they follow their tribe of yellow goslings. Whichever way one looks there are geese snowing the distant pastures or swimming in the marshes.

Approaching a village, we observed a vast concourse of people gathered together on its outskirts. A fair is being held, and the ground is inundated to such an extent that the booths are actually standing in water, a day or two's rain being quite sufficient to cause it to lie on the surface, for the soil in this district is already saturated with moisture, in consequence of its proximity to the Theiss. Accustomed to this state of affairs, the people of both sexes, nothing daunted, hold up their petticoats and paddle through the water like ducks. Here and there, in the little patches of green that, like wet islands, rise above the water, are sellers of pottery displaying their wares, and a *colporteur* his tracts, whilst, standing about in groups, are Jews, dragging their long togas in the mire, and gipsy children taking mud baths. Away beyond the fair, with its booths and wet islands and general slush and slipperiness, are thousands of horses, cattle, and pigs—*pet* pigs, affectionately watched over by buxom Magyar females, ankle deep in water. The train stopped in full view of this scene, for no apparent reason so far as we could ascertain, for three-quarters of an hour, and then lumbered on again, and brought us to Mád Zomber—what *insane* names these Hungarian villages have! Once more reaching the solitary plains, we pass through vast tracts of uncultivated land, roamed by immense herds of cattle, which form dark groups on the horizon. On, past a well, on one side of which are a countless number of horses, and on the other of cows; but they do not intermingle in the least.

These vast herds are a never-ending source of astonishment to the English traveller journeying through these thinly-populated districts. Near them stand sheep-dogs, with long hair, pointed noses, and bushy tails, like wolves. Overhead, flights of birds are hovering in the sky. How gracefully they skim through the translucent air! and now they soar away, and hover, rising and falling, in the distance; whilst one or two, less rapid in their flight, get left behind. What is the reason they cry so piteously? See that large bird yonder, following in their wake with outstretched neck! It is a falcon in hot pursuit. It overtakes the one most distant from the rest, seizes it in its cruel grip, and they fall to earth together, the victim and its prey. A tall crane plumes itself on the border of a marsh. A windmill in the distance throws its big arms about languidly in the sultry breeze, and we reach districts cultivated with maize, tobacco, hemp, poppies, and flax, the flowers of the three latter creating with the golden shade of the ripe grain, an exquisite modulation of colour. Every now and then we see in the distance swelling tumuli, commonly called "*Kún halom*" (Cuman-hill), believed by some to contain the tombs of military chieftains of ancient times; by others to be Turkish mounds (*török domb*). The learned, however, attribute to them a still more ancient origin even than the former, and declare that they are the remains of the artificial boundary made by the Romans not only to define the borders of their empire, but also to protect themselves from the incursions of the warlike barbarians of the surrounding countries.

There is evidence that a similar frontier-line extended from Pest to the south-east, towards the mountains of

Transylvania, and the green mounds which we here meet with at regular intervals are the places on which the watch-towers stood that protected the frontier-line. Beneath some of these mounds the dykes on the outside are still visible, which are called by the peasantry *Ordög árka* (devil's ditch).

CHAPTER XLVI.

THE GOLD MINES OF SCHEMNITZ.

A NARROW mountain gorge with irregularly built houses on either side, and churches with red domes and shining cupolas, backed by wondrous mountains, introduce us to Schemnitz.

The street is both steep and rugged, so that, leaving our coachman to find some place below where he can deposit the carriage, we walk leisurely up the hill, where women are sitting surrounded by huge baskets of lilies of the valley and forget-me-nots; whilst other women are selling snow-white lambs, the little creatures, whose legs are tied together, panting piteously as they lie on their backs in baskets much too small to contain them. At length, reaching the hotel, and passing under the archway, we are shown through a yard, up two flights of stone steps, across a balcony built against the steep side of the mountain, and commanding a near view of the shingled roofs of neighbouring houses with their respective cats, and are ushered into a large apartment, where we are welcomed by mediæval celebrities, who, as we enter, gaze at us furtively out of their dark frames, and follow us suspiciously about the room with staring eyes—a most ghostly chamber truly, and one that looks anything but conducive to sleep.

Although we have ascended at least thirty steps, we still find ourselves on a level with the heads of persons walking

in the street; a window at the end of the room looking out upon a fountain where women stand gossiping and slopping, exchanging salutations with the passers-by, and occasionally screaming at the top of their voices at other females leaning far out of windows in the upper stories of the high houses. Pretty girls in red bodices and large white sleeves frilled at the elbow, come tripping down the hill, laughing merrily, and carrying wooden pails to fill with the yellow water of the fountain, its colour *said* to be due to the attrition of the rocks containing gold ore, through which the stream flows that feeds this fountain.

A great deal of gold dust is found in the rivers of Transylvania, caused either by the decomposition of the metalliferous rocks or from the rupture of ore-veins. The upper part of the river Marös is one of the richest streams in Hungary, pieces of the precious metal being sometimes found in it as large as a marble. The gold found in these rivers is, or was until a comparatively recent period, a monopoly in the hands of the gipsies, who paid an annual tax to Government for the privilege. It is found in the greatest abundance after rain, when the sand left by the flood has collected on the edges of the mountain torrents.

This celebrated town, the capital of the mining districts, founded in 745, contains twenty thousand inhabitants. The town itself, together with the mountain on which it is built, is completely undermined, veins of the precious metal traversing it in all directions. In 1865 the quantity of gold raised from the Schemnitz mines was 650 lbs. in weight, and of silver, 13,000 lbs. The mines throughout the whole of Hungary that year produced no less than 5000 lbs. weight of the former, and about 63,000 lbs. of the latter. The mines richest in gold and silver at present are, however, those in the east of Hungary, in the province of Transylvania, the metal found here in the greatest abundance now being lead, in which, however, gold and silver, to some extent, are always intermingled.

There are two principal adits, the upper and the lower.

Having applied for permission to view the mines at the office immediately opposite the entrance to the latter, we were ushered into an inner apartment where we were vested in two loose long garments like surplices, and, if the truth must be told, very ragged and dirty ones too, in addition to which F. was provided with a species of green felt jelly-bag by way of head gear, the exact pattern of those worn by the ancient Druids. Having resigned ourselves into the hands of a stout foreman of the mines, who gives us both a mining lamp to carry, we issue from the office with the farewell salutation from those within of "*glück auf!*" an expression invariably used by the miners to each other on descending the mines, and which literally means "Happy return to day-light!"

As we crossed the street in this strange guise we wondered what our friends at home would think was happening to us if we could have been photographed at that instant! The passers-by however were evidently accustomed to such apparitions, for they took no notice of us, nor did they even turn their heads as they also exclaimed "*glück auf!*" and we vanished in the darkness.

This adit, which is worked by Government, extends to galleries and other adits. The passage is about eight feet high by four broad; but, the floor being only roughly covered with planks, beneath which water rushes, progress is neither a pleasant nor easy task.

The mountain perforated by these mines is of Trachyte formation and contains Plutonic rock, which geologists affirm must have been sent up from beneath by volcanic agency after the deposition of the Tertiary deposits. It is in this Plutonic rock that the veins exist which contain the precious metals.

No fewer than three thousand families—the greater number of whom are Slovaks—are employed in the various Schemnitz mines, twelve of which are worked by Government, the others belonging to private companies. After following our guide through the damp, dark passage by a gradual but continuous descent of about eighteen hundred feet, we came to the huge iron tube through which the water flows that drains the mines, and the noise was almost deafening. We were here joined by a second guide, and at length reached a staircase leading to the machinery and a still lower level. As we descended and stood by the immense wheel, we looked down into a black and, to our eye, measureless abyss; bridged by a narrow and frail platform on which the man stood who was working the machinery. As he stood there alone with his one feeble lamp—no one within ear-shot—there was something appalling in the thought of his being there day after day without any companionship save that of the great broad, black wheel, which keeps turning slowly round and round in endless revolution to the deafening splash of waters, and we wondered he did not actually go mad. His fate seemed somehow much more terrible than that of the men who were working far beneath in the depths of the earth, for they were not alone but in companies. As a rule, the men work alternately twelve and eight hours a day, but in some portions, the mines are so hot and unhealthy that they are only allowed to work fourteen days at a time, when they are changed, the heat and foul air acting very prejudicially upon their health. How can they work, these poor creatures, all their lives in this living grave? As we saw them with their feeble lamps hacking away at the hard rock, I realised for the first time, with what labour and misery the beautiful metals are procured with which we so unthinkingly adorn ourselves.

The gigantic wheel to which—after having descended deeper into the mine—we have just returned, pumps the water out of the passages, the water being utilised by means of a smaller wheel, to raise the ore from the lower adits. The ore is first placed in large square sacks, and, after being raised, is shunted through a hole in the rock into another adit, where a train-truck waits to receive it, after which it is sent either to Neusohl or Kremnitz to be smelted.

These mines were also begun by the Romans, who, having in those days no such force as dynamite or gunpowder within their command, drilled some of these passages, as in the cobalt mines of Dobsina, by the slow method of chisel and hammer. Such portions even yet are easily distinguishable by the smoothness and evenness of their surface.

In the "Roselia," the oldest of all the mines here, coins, lamps, and even articles of dress of the Roman period have been found. There is also a cavern of considerable extent likewise attributed to Roman excavation, a process believed to have been accomplished by fire and vinegar, a method alluded to by Pliny, the rocks having been evidently split and not hewn, traces of fire in both caverns and passages being still visible.

But, however interesting and instructive our exploits had been, we felt thankful when, after having traversed the mine a distance of no less than three thousand six hundred feet, we once more saw the sweet, fair day-light gleaming through the aperture, and knew that our journey through the dark and toilsome regions of the night was accomplished.

There is a mining school at Schemnitz founded by Maria Theresa, where two hundred students receive a gratuitous and liberal education. The branches taught, besides metallurgy, mineralogy, and mining, being chemistry, mathematics, drawing, and surveying. The students wear a uniform of dark green, turned up with red; the sleeves of their jackets curiously padded at the shoulders to protect the arms from being grazed by the walls of the mines. They also wear funny little leather aprons behind. Both their caps and jackets are ornamented with the mining *insignia*, a crossed hammer and pickaxe. In full dress, these academical students, the more advanced of whom are called "Practicants," wear black velvet aprons, gold epaulets, and a sabre.

Having explored the mines, the next thing to be done, after an hour or two's rest from fatigue, was to inspect some of the treasure they contain. The mineralogical collection, however, is not so good as might be expected, all the finest specimens being sent to the National Museum of Pest, which possesses the third best collection in Europe; there is, however, a very fair one here, and quite sufficiently good to give the visitor an idea of all the minerals and stones which the mountain holds concealed within its hidden recesses.

The gold is found in various forms, sometimes in round smooth globules the size of shot, embedded in a porous and spongy-looking stone; at others it assumes the most beautiful shapes, simulating a succession of leaflets on a stalk, anaglyphs, and every sort of device conceivable, so exquisitely moulded that it was difficult at first to realise that some had not been wrought by a skilled goldsmith, from special designs; whilst silver is often found in a thin, brittle, and yellowish stone called *spath*, which looks as though it had been moulded from the most beautiful vine, or some other large leaf. More frequently, however, it is seen lying in compact beds, either in small angular pieces of a slightly leaden colour, or in bead-like masses.

It would be impossible to describe the variety and splendour of the minerals, one of the most beautiful stones being the amethyst, which is found in large beds, in which the dark purple rectangular crystals, shooting upwards in cones of equal size, are so polished and regularly formed that they appear as if they had just come out of the hands of the lapidary. Malachite is likewise found in a transition state, together with ocherite, both of which stones are intermingled with globules of gold. These Plutonic rocks also contain opal; which is found in the whitish-grey calcined rock, generally in strata of about four inches thick, where it forms a compact and seeming opaque mass, possessing the appearance—if I may so express it—of petrified and etherealised fire. When seen in its original stratum, opal presents quite a different aspect from that which it assumes after it has passed into the hands of the lapidary, and is far less beautiful to my mind in its *rounded* and artificial form. Of all the stones found in the Hungarian mountains, none impressed us so greatly as this one in its natural state.

It is exceedingly interesting to see the minerals which are used by the professors in lecturing to the mining students. There are the round hollow stones in which crystals are just beginning to form, and others showing the progressive stages of their growth. Amethysts are invariably found, like other crystals, in pebbles, some of which measure half a yard in diameter, and which, on being broken in two, are seen to be thickly lined with lustrous purple stones. There were clayey substances also in every phase of transition, from the primary matter, which in the process of drying had cracked into small squares of equal size, to the fully developed marble, which, when cut through diagonally, formed the most beautiful hexagons, each as perfect as those of a honeycomb, and each hexagon separated from the other by a perfectly white and well-defined line created by a deposit of chalk working its way into the original interstices in the course of —who shall conjecture how many ages?

A wet evening sends us home to our dismal room, where in due time they bring us candles and a pair of snuffers—modern improvements in the manufacture of the former not having apparently extended to Schemnitz. In the feeble, glimmering light, the large room appears even more hobgobliny than ever, whilst the eyes of the ancient celebrities in the picture frames seem to grow larger and to revolve in their sockets as we look at them. To make matters worse, we are perpetually reducing ourselves to a state of darkness whenever it becomes necessary to snuff the candles—which it does about every five minutes—and we realise that, like the wearing of pattens, candle-snuffing is an art which, to be accomplished gracefully, must be acquired in early life.

Fortunately all the rain fell during the night. Towards the small hours we could hear it tearing madly down the street like a mountain torrent, which I should imagine the narrow gorge in which the town is situated must originally have been. Looking out of the window at nine A.M. we see above the mountain a small piece of sky about the size of a pocket-handkerchief. It is all that is visible of that aerial region, but it is intensely and encouragingly blue, and, after breakfast, we sally forth to see the town with its fine old

castle built against the steep hill-side, and looking down at us over the picturesque roofs of the houses, every one of which was formerly a fortification. The castle dates from 1491, and the custodian entertained us with blood-curdling tales of Turkomans and Templars, and told us how that the Christians fought and the infidel marauders fled.

It is the weekly market. Forcing our way through sacks of scarlet pepper, stands of Slovak cheeses—which, moulded in cloths, look precisely like gigantic puddings—baskets running over with pink and white radishes, the classic garlic, and other commodities, we reach the opposite side of the road. The little lambs we saw yesterday have been kept alive for to-day—God knows how—and are lying in the same baskets, only panting more sadly, their heads thrown back and eyes half-open, the whites of which alone are visible. So cruel and piteous a sight makes our hearts ache, and we endeavour by much gesture, to induce their owners to change their constrained positions, and give them a little food. They only think we are beginning a bargain, and lug them out of the baskets by the four legs, which we can see are tied together far too tightly, and then, finding we are not bent on purchasing, they throw them in again, just as if they had been bundles of turnips or vegetables. The lilies of the valley have been freshened up, and the forget-me-nots, reflecting with their meek blue eyes the sky above, appear as though they had but just awakened from their bath of dew. Women, hundreds of women, in dark blue skirts bordered with light green, stand about the stalls, and look like figures painted on old china. Priests, in long black robes which sweep the street, come wriggling in and out of the crowd. Now and then we hear close behind us a plaintive, supplicating voice, uttering words, the meaning of which we cannot understand, save that of "*Christus.*" It is a beggar, asking kreuzers for the love of Him who died for us. And everywhere the people throng and jostle each other in the narrow street. Looking upwards, all is colour, motion, and a sea of heads, above which rise the high houses, with their overhanging roofs, and the black domes and cupolas of the *Rath-haus* and the beautiful old churches, with their lancet windows and porches, entered by long flights of steps. There is a rapid stir in the crowd as way is made for a long country cart, drawn by three donkeys and two small black oxen, the latter forming the wheelers of the rustic team!

In the lateral streets, which are almost as steep as the roofs of houses, we see bullock-waggons laden with hay and corn, and pots and pans innumerable. Up these steeps women struggle and toil, with large, square, wooden pails or baskets attached to their backs, and carrying babies swathed in linen, like small white mummies.

Presently we descry above the sea of heads a tall man, in what has been graphically designated a " stove-pipe " hat.

" *Buval Jankó!* " we hear a Hungarian gentleman observe, in a somewhat amused tone, to a friend standing at his elbow.

He is certainly an Englishman of some sort, we could swear to the cut of his sartorial garments anywhere. Is he an archdeacon, with that high collar and swallow-tailed coat? What an incongruous object he looks amongst all these pretty costumes, so full of colour! No wonder that the Arab who first saw an Englishman in this guise hastened to inform his neighbours and acquaintances that he had seen " his Satanic Majesty with a saucepan on his head, and his tail slit in two!"

Strange as it may appear, he is the only Englishman we have seen during either of our travels in Hungary, and it is quite impossible to pass him by without a greeting.

His speech soon reveals the mystery of his *genre*. He belongs to the " Society of Friends," and is, he informs us, a travelling agent for a firm in Birmingham.

CHAPTER XLVII.

THE "CALVARY."

RETURNING to the hotel we hire a carriage to take us to the foot of a mountain forming one of the most conspicuous objects in the neighbourhood of this interesting town, and upon which is a "calvary," well worthy a visit. Climbing the rugged street with some difficulty, we pass under the old tower, where a blind man sits, telling his beads "for the love of God;" but with a mental eye open to the possibility of stray kreuzers.

At the base of the steepest part of the mountain is an avenue of trees leading to the first of the line of small chapels which contain representations of the "stations of the Cross." At this point, one of the horses began kicking so violently, and had evidently made up its mind so firmly not to proceed another inch, that we were obliged to alight. Possibly the thought of the steep ascent caused it to arrive at this decision, or perhaps it was a stern Protestant and objected to "Calvaries" on principle.

A hot and fatiguing pilgrimage up a narrow path, takes us past the fourteen stations, all of which describe most touchingly the scenes in our Saviour's passion. The figures, which are either plaster or carved in wood, standing out completely in relief, being, in no one instance, grotesque in either form or colour, but most skilfully and artistically devised.

The first " station " represents the Garden of Gethsemane, where the Saviour is kneeling in agony, whilst the Disciples sleep. In the chapel where He is being crowned with thorns, the sight, as we look through the grating, is quite startling, the figures and their grouping are so painfully natural. In the centre sits the meek and patient sufferer, surrounded by Roman soldiers. A real halter and chain are round His neck, and a Jewish beggar dressed in brown rags, squatting in the corner and pulling the cord with which the Holy hands are tied, is so life-like in his rags, and in the patches of his coarse gabardine, and so villanous in the expression of his wrinkled, dirty countenance, and the satanic smile of derision with which he regards the pale Saviour, from whom drops of blood are falling, that it is difficult to realise He is not an actual living person.

Not far from the summit of the mountain is the "Nailing to the Cross," in the representation of which incident not a detail is wanting. One man is hammering a nail into the right hand, and another is boring a hole through the left with a gimlet; whilst the low brows and square chins of those who are doing the cruel deed, make us wonder from what class the artists can possibly have taken their models.

Then comes the large chapel on the extreme summit, containing the "Crucifixion." The three crosses stand on a large block of real rock, beneath which and on a level with the ground is a small grating, behind which souls are represented grilling in the flames of purgatory, the only really grotesque thing about the whole.

Walking round to the other side of the chapel, and entering by another door, we find the "Entombment," and then another tableau of the pale and lifeless form lying in the sepulchre with the angels watching beside Him, and the women in the distance bringing spices.

Before several of the "stations" were persons kneeling, tears falling down the cheeks of some, and there is no doubt that the vivid representation by these life-size lay-figures of these touching incidents, bring them before the minds of the ignorant in a manner we cold Protestants can hardly understand, and I must confess that I could myself witness few of these scenes so graphically portrayed without deep emotion.

Two hours have passed away ere we descend the zig-zag path, and traversing the avenue reach our carriage, for we tarried long upon the sacred heights to see the view, which is wonderful, of the fine old town, nestling in its amphitheatre of mountains, and the little houses of the miners dotting the green slopes, and nestling amongst trees. The horse again kicked on our way back, from which I infer that the first little demonstration was an exhibition of temper rather than one of sentiment.

Passing by the kitchen of the hotel which is near the entrance, we observe, lying on the table amongst sundry joints of meat, vegetables, and other comestibles, what appears to be a cod divested of its tail and trussed for boiling, but which now proves on closer inspection to be the cook's chrysalis of a baby that she had placed there for safety. The little creature was as stiff as a board and could not have moved so much as a finger or a toe to save its life. It looked quite happy however in its small mummy-wrappers and smiled sweetly as I spoke to it, seeming as though in its little heart it had a mind to "crow" if it could only have expanded.

"Why don't you hang it up to a door-nail, or to the wall

there?" inquires F. "It is dangerous here, you might pop it into a pot by mistake."

At which the mother only laughed and looked down upon her infant so lovingly that I half expected to see a halo of glory around her head, the look of love was so ineffable.

It was a bright starlight night, and, a dinner partaken of, we wandered out to see how the old place looked by lamp-light. Here and there a feeble light glimmering through some window threw its reflection across the uneven street, and made the quaint old archways stand out weird and grim. High above us the lofty and precipitous mountains frowned down upon the townlike prison walls, and almost shut out the sky. Strolling up and down the narrow streets, we pass miners on their homeward way; whilst at the fountain, women stand gossiping as they fill their pitchers even at this late hour of night. Now and then we come to a tavern where miners are singing their celebrated songs in hoarse rough voices, the theme of which is invariably the dangers to which they are exposed. The airs were sad, and as we listened there seemed something very pathetic in the thought that the perils to which the lives of these poor fellows are exposed, should even form the subject of their thoughts during their hours of recreation.

The lights in the many-storied old houses now begin to die out one by one, and presently a bell, the tone of which is the deepest and most sonorous I ever heard, begins to toll slowly.

"It cannot be the hour it is striking," exclaimed F., as in slow and measured beat it reached the eleventh stroke. He took out his watch and held it up to the light thrown from a window of a little wine-shop, where three men sitting on a bench were drinking.

"It is the '*Todtenglocke*' (death knell)," said some one in German that moment passing by, as it continued to toll out the tidings that another soul was departing, and summoned the inhabitants to pray for its repose. And the slow and solemn "boom" went rolling and echoing up the gorge, as one swelling buttress after another caught the wave of sound and sent it on, and up, and up, until it seemed to die away amidst the stars.

The three men, impelled possibly by its solemn warning, left the shop, and went staggering homewards; and we ourselves felt it was high time to "turn in," if we were to get any rest at all, as we had to be up again at four o'clock on the morrow to meet the train at Altsohl, to which place we purposed driving.

What a ghastly-looking meal is breakfast by candle-light! The large *salle-à-manger*, lighted at one end only; the long stretch of gloom beyond; the dark doorways which appear to lead to mysterious and unknown caverns; the ghostly old wooden presses standing against the wall; the last night's crumbs lying still unswept upon the floor; and the marks of wine upon the tablecloth—how wretched it all is!

The coffee is gritty and cold, the butter is flabby, and the rolls have a peculiar flavour of last night about them. Getting up in the small hours is, however, as nothing compared with the discomfort and unsavouriness of the breakfast with which one feels compelled to fortify oneself before starting on the journey. Above all, how cadaverous in the dim light look the guests who sit beside one, and who are also condemned to make an equally early start! What a gloomy and dishevelled band we appear, as we sit in moody silence, each possessed of a vague and undefined sensation of melancholy and ill-usage, as though something doleful were about to happen to us, the precise nature of which we cannot define!

Emerging from the dark room, we find it is daylight

outside, but the Schemnitz world is still asleep, as we walk down the silent street to join our carriage. Above the summits of the mountains a long vermilion streak proclaims that the sun has risen, though yet invisible to us, and there is a solemn feeling in the cold, still air as though the spirit of the "passing bell" had not yet died away. All nature seems to join in telling its sad meaning. The morning star recounts it as it disappears within the veil The crescent moon foreshadows it, as it sinks beneath the hills. The great silence tells it. Yes! the very echo of our footsteps preaches the sad, unwelcome doctrine, that "all is passing away."

We feel much more cheery, however, by the time we reach the bottom of the hill, and see our carriage—to which *two* horses only are harnessed this time—and András's nimble little figure dodging from one side to the other, as he arranges the cushions for us, and makes all "taut" for starting, and we are quite jolly again when once more jolting along the road to the music of the horses' bells.

Clattering under the old gateway, we soon reach the open country, and see the train ascending the hill on the opposite side of the narrow valley. How the engine puffs and snorts, and what difficulty it seems to have in dragging itself up the steep incline! It scarcely appears to move at all, as, cantering down the hill, we quickly leave it far behind. On the way our progress is momentarily arrested by a little procession, which, leaving the main road, is wending its way upwards by a mountain path. It is the "Kost" being carried to a dying person. Peasant women follow, with little children clinging to their skirts, some holding lighted tapers, and all walking with heads bent low. How picturesque, but how melancholy at the same time, are all Roman Catholic countries!

At Altsohl we find all the women in full costume, the day being evidently a festival of some sort. There is a great display of ravishing little top-boots in scarlet and yellow leather, and brilliant *peltz rökel*—short sheepskin jackets, worked not only in coloured silks, but in gold and silver thread. The men, too, are in their Sunday-best, with feathers and flowers in their hats, and smoking their holiday pipes.

At Altsohl station another painful scene awaits us. More emigrants are starting for "Amurica," that country whose streets are paved with gold. As usual, there are not enough carriages to convey them, and the agony of the men, women, and children who come to see the last of them is prolonged. At length the bell rings. Friends embrace each other passionately, and weep like children. The emigrants take their places, and the train moves slowly from the platform. The last look is given through the carriage windows. A thrilling cry of pain goes up from those left behind—it haunted us for many a long day after—and we whirl away, the very wheels as they rotate, seeming to echo the words of the Hungarian whom we met at Schemnitz: "They die by a fence—they die by a fence!"

CHAPTER XLVIII.

THE MODERN BABEL.

IT is Fair-day in the Hungarian capital, and the hotels are as full as they can cram. There is not an inch of space left anywhere. The restaurants, as we pass them, are so choked with human life, half savage, half civilised, that not even an eel, were it ever so hungry, could manage to insinuate itself, suppose it had the *courage* to face so polyglot an assemblage.

In the streets the traveller is jostled not only by Hungarians of each nationality, Magyars, Slovaks, Ruthenians, Széklers, Wallachs, Croatians, Serbs, and Illyrians—a "mosaic of nations" which, constituting the inhabitants of the entire Austro-Hungarian dominions, numbers upwards of 150,000— but Germans, Poles, Muscovites, Bohemians, Frenchmen, Italians, Turks, Heretics, and Infidels. There are Jews and gipsies by the thousand, German Jews, Hungarian Jews in the costume of the *Magyar-orság*, Polish Jews, in black toga and corkscrew curls, from the province of Gallicia, Transylvanian Jews, in greasy brown cloth dressing-gown and sandalled feet, looking like dissipated Capuchin friars out for a holiday, and who evidently ignore the maxim concerning the proximity of cleanliness to godliness no less than their Christian brethren.

There are men in hats made of rushes, others with conical-shaped hats of fur, the precise pattern of that worn by Robinson Crusoe; others again wearing large broad ones like Spanish *sombreros*. There are men whose pale olive complexions proclaim them to be Greeks. There are Turks and Bosnians wearing the becoming fez, and here and there an Arab in a turban, besides whom there are also men from Upper Hungary whose long hair hanging to the waist is plaited in four tails, and who wear immense leather belts and sandals, and such wonderful garments, that they must be seen even to be believed in; men, too, from the country of Somogy clad in blanket-like cloaks, like those of Bedouins, whilst working their way in and out amongst the crowd, their looks bold and defiant, are numerous Magyars in snow-white petticoats fringed or embroidered at the edges. There are women, too, with coloured scarves coiled gracefully round the head; women—beautiful women, whose raven hair is covered with gold coins, flashing and quivering in the sunlight! Women again—natives of Pest—wearing dark-blue kerchiefs so disposed as to conceal the whole face, with the exception of eyes, nose, and mouth, and who only need the addition of a *yashmak* to give them the appearance of veritable daughters of the Prophet. What a medley! and what a Babel of tongues greets the ear of the stranger as he stands in the thick of the fair. At these fairs, four of which take place annually, no fewer than twenty-eight thousand strangers pour into Pest.

No wonder that *mein Herr* Dulovic shook his head and intimated that he could not take us in as we dashed up to the door of his hotel one morning in a droszky and pair, some Armenians having previously engaged the room we had occupied for two days at the "*Königinn von England*," a circumstance that compelled us to seek shelter in some other hotel.

The little old man was well-nigh beside himself; his tow-coloured wig almost stood on end, and his countenance was suffused by a warm dew as he endeavoured to withstand the importunities of three other "parties," who had arrived at the same moment, on the same errand as ourselves.

We however, as may be remembered, had stayed at this small but well-ordered hotel once before, and, as old acquaintances, had no intention of being turned away. Moreover we were *Ángolok*, and just at that time the English nation happened to be at an unusual premium in the estimation of the Hungarains.

"Stay! Yes! No! Yes!" exclaimed Herr Dulovic, hesitatingly—"If you do not mind——"

"Mind?" broke in F., descending from the carriage. "We don't mind anything at such a time as this," adding, as we follow mein Herr up the stairs and into a chamber of such limited dimensions that to have swung even a cat in it one must have taken that animal by the head and not by the tail, "*Si on ne peut pas avoir ce qu'on veux, il faut prendre ce qu'on peut.*"

After a hurried repast we stroll out to have a peep at the fair, which, save in the matter of costumes and diversity of peoples and tongues, differs little from that of other countries. There are the same long avenues of booths, containing every conceivable article for man or beast. Stands of juicy melons, pomegranates and oranges from Croatia, presided over by girls and stately women, looking like Druidical priestesses in their long white robes; booths of *édességek* (sweet-meats); booths of imitation jewellery much frequented by the Magyar girls; booths of hard-ware, and wooden utensils, belonging to nut-brown specimens of the wandering tribe; Slovak cheese, carpets from Servia, bacon from Slavonia, booths of ready-made under-clothing, sheepskin *bundas*, *pelz-röckel*, and beautifully embroidered cloaks; high boots for men, and others for women and girls, with scarlet and yellow sides, trimmed with coquet-tish little rosettes, not to speak of Turkish-looking slippers worn by the women of Szegedin. There are Jews in the characters of money-lenders and sellers of *bijouterie*; gipsies in that of horse-dealers, cunning-looking men with long whips ornamented with bows of many-coloured ribbons, and gourds hanging from their girdles; there are shepherds, too, splendid looking fellows with forms like those of Roman athletes; besides which are men in coarse gabardines directing games of chance, acrobats by the dozen, and the off-scourings of the four winds of heaven. What a hurly-burly!

Along the banks of the Danube, however, an entirely novel scene presents itself to our gaze. For the space of half a mile boats and barges are moored together in close proximity; some of them are heavy, flat-bottomed craft, whilst others, gaudily painted in red, white, and green, look like miniature Chinese junks. These boats and barges, in conjunction with the *quai*, form a market-place of themselves for articles consisting chiefly of the produce of the country; wines, badacsony, from the Platten-See; the white wines of Transylvania, and the more delicious ones of Tokay; *slivovitz* and *fenüviz*, a spirit made from juniper-berries; tobacco, wool, hides, and other commodities "far too numerous to mention."

Beyond, there are the usual vast herds of sheep, pigs, and cattle, guarded by wild, top-booted graziers and strange, fierce-looking shepherds; whilst outside the fair the road is lined with vehicles of every description.

Opposite is a booth where a sheep is being roasted whole, while on stands arranged in front are savoury "gipsy roasts," consisting of small pieces of hot meat for the refection of the hungry. Hard by is a seller of macaroni soup, ladling out her steaming esculent to numerous comers; and near her a stout Magyar *Frau* vending "*Tisch-wein.*"

It is when the fires of sunset have faded in the west, and the curtain of night has dropped upon the most beautiful scene in the world—the Blocksberg and the Danube and the rock-built citadel of Buda—that the real fun begins. By that time the stern business of the day is over, the bargaining has come to an end till the morrow, and the whole twenty-eight thousand visitors give themselves up to pleasure. In the warm shadow of the booths merry groups stand idly chatting. Managers of theatres shout and scream and yell. Marionettes whirl and twirl and curtsey, and move their heads up and down with sudden jerks, and go through their little antics with the same melancholy precision as elsewhere. Acrobats climb poles and perform juggling tricks to the astonished multitude. In the eating-booths the fires gleam like "mad Sarabands," and the people cooking the gipsy roasts stand out against them like black imps.

Passing the Jägerhorn on our way back to our hotel, we find the *Cziganok* are sawing away there as usual, whilst the people sitting beside the snowy tables pave the way for night-mares as they devour their "*gebratene Ente*" and "*geschmortes Lämmerchen.*" It is worth while entering to see the costumes and various physiognomies of the visitors: the soft, caressing, and almost effeminate features of the Sláv from the South, and the pale, olive-complexioned Greek, contrasting forcibly with the robust and majestic Magyars—off-shoots of a kingly race—with their frank and manly countenances.

On reaching the hotel, we find ourselves unexpectedly plunged in the lap of luxury, a Hungarian gentleman having offered to exchange our little chamber *au quatrième* all amongst the chimneys and the cats, for his own handsome and commodious room on the first floor, one of the thousand acts of kindness we received whilst travelling in this country. There is no city where there is greater amusement and gaiety than Pest, particularly in the winter, when the "nobles" bring their families to the Capital from their country chateaux. At this season there is a perpetual round of balls and entertainments, skating being the favourite occupation during the hours of day. In May the *beau monde* return to their country seats, and the traveller may then look in vain for the beautiful horses and handsome equipages, which in the winter months brighten the streets of the city.

Pest, too, is the seat of the National Government. Accompanied by a member of the Diet, to whom we had a letter of introduction, we visited the Lower House at the time when the Delegates were sitting. Received at the entrance hall by a number of lackeys, dressed in a handsome Hussar uniform of black and scarlet, we were at once shown to the visitors' gallery. Many of the members wore the black cloth *attila*, and embroidered waistcoat, but by far the greater number the severe garments of Western Europe, even the nobles having relinquished the brilliant costumes with which they formerly sat in Assembly.

There are 441 Delegates, all of whom are chosen irrespective of religious sects. Of this number 39 are Croatians, who speak in their native language—Slavonian.

The Magyars, as a rule, evince great calmness in council. Their warm and impulsive natures, however, and susceptibility to excitement, render them victims to the most violent and rapid changes of temperament, and, even in the midst of the calmest deliberation, they not unfrequently manifest the wildest outbursts of feeling.

On the occasion of our visit, the debate was rather a noisy one, and the President's bell was in frequent requisition, but the very instant Baron Sennyei rose to speak, the most perfect silence reigned, and the eyes of every Delegate in the House were steadily fixed upon him. He is a great politician and the present leader of the Conservative party, or what is called *Mérsékett ellenzék* (moderate adverse party), and is spoken of as the one who will, in all probability, be chosen President of the Council at the next election.

The Magyar language, which is spoken by almost $6\frac{1}{4}$ millions of inhabitants, or 40 per cent. of the entire population, is forcible, energetic, and capable of the most impassioned eloquence, and although pathetic in its tones when spoken in conversation, when declaimed it becomes bold and emphatic. It is copious in idiomatic expressions, and rich in its vocabulary of words. Although the Magyar language possesses no auxiliary verb "to have," no primitive possessive pronouns, no gender for the distinction of sexes, and scarcely any true declension for objective terms, yet it is said to surpass every Teutonic, Slavonic, Italic, and Indo-

European language in the richness of its verbal formations. Of all the letters in the alphabet, *k* is the one most conspicuously heard, and all the more so from the fact of its coming at the end of so many words, being generally used to denote the plural.

The Magyar language, if for no other reason, would be deeply interesting to the stranger from the fact of its being the only non-Aryan tongue throughout Europe (if we except that of the Finns) in which Christian rites are performed and Parliamentary debates carried on, and also from its having been established in Europe and subjected to Aryan influences for nearly a thousand years, without having lost its essential Turanian features, its etymology and syntax still preserving their ancient characteristics.

Until forty-five years ago, Latin was the language universally used throughout Hungary in all proceedings connected with law and diplomacy. The country having at one period been under the dominion of two foreign powers, viz., the Austrian and Mahomedan, a common language was necessary for these deliberations. By mutual consent, therefore, the mediæval Latin was adopted, and but for this the three languages spoken in the country, viz., Magyar, German, and Turkish, would necessarily have created great confusion.

In fact, so commonly was it in use until twenty or thirty years ago, that it was called "*Stataria*," whilst Magyar itself was even taught by the means of Latin, the grammar being designated "*Hungarica*."

In some parts of Hungary, even in comparatively recent times, Latin was used by the peasantry to converse with persons belonging to nationalities other than their own, whilst the Huns, whose language was a harsh and barren idiom, likewise strove to make Latin—which was spoken in Pannonia in the time of Augustus—the medium of communication with their fellows.

After we had remained listening some time to the expressive utterances of Baron Sennyei, Herr Franz Pulszky—a man of considerable note, not only in his own country, but in many European circles—conducted us to the Upper House, situated over the National Museum. where sit the nobles. The gallery surrounding the grand staircase by which the room and its antechambers are approached is adorned with fresco-paintings—very creditably executed by Hungarian artists—representing the history of the civilisation of Hungary and, beginning with the entry of the Huns into the country, portraying the various epochs of history, and ending with the revolutionary period of 1848.

Our cicerone was one whose features proclaimed that nature had destined him for no ordinary career. Pointing to a fresco situated in one of the most conspicuous places, viz., close to the entrance of the Chamber of Debate, he exclaims:

"You see there the great leader of our Patriotic party."

"What, *Kossuth* here, and Louis Batthyani?" we cried as we observed a figure bearing the palm branch of martyrdom, and knew at once for whom it was intended.

"Yes, and *I* am here," he added significantly. "The Austrian Government made a great fuss about it at first, but was obliged to give in at last." And as I looked up at the commanding figure of the revolutionary leader haranguing the populace, I must say I could not help wondering it had done so.

The picture in question besides Kossuth represented Deák,

Széchenyi, Louis Batthyani, who was executed at Temesvár, and Petófy, the poet of the Revolution.

It was pleasant to hear the very grateful terms in which Herr Pulszky alluded to the Emperor of Austria for having spared his life. He was condemned to death on two occasions, once to be shot and the other to be hanged. He had, however, the honour of being burnt in effigy.

The Hall of Assembly, though small, is a very handsomely decorated apartment. On the lowest tier stand the chairs of crimson and gold, where sit the Cardinals, whilst on the desks in front of the seats above we recognised the familiar names of Graf Festitics and Prince Windishgraitz, which, on those gentlemen paying a visit to England some years ago, were, as might have been anticipated, converted into the more intelligible, if not euphemistic ones, of "Count Fiddlesticks," and "Prince Windowscratch."

It is singular that Count Andrassy—the correct pronunciation of whose name is *Andrasshy*—though a Magyar and also condemned to death for the part he took in the insurrection under Kossuth, should until recently have filled the post of Prime Minister to the Austrian Government, an anomalous position one can scarcely understand any Hungarian patriot occupying with their very natural repugnance to the Austrian supremacy.

CHAPTER XLIX.

O'BUDA.

FAIR-TIME is by no means the most pleasant at which to visit the capital, and we were right glad to learn one morning soon after our arrival that it was over. Oh, the dust and muddle and hurry-skurry of the whole business of packing up! But even that too is almost over now. The booths have disappeared; the pedlars have shouldered their wares, and the acrobats their bundles; the young ladies in pink tights have resumed their top-boots; the Mesdames Jarley have packed up their wax-works, and the decapitated bodies of Bem, Kossuth, Matthias Corvinus, and Joan of Arc, stripped of their finery and with their heads carefully stowed away elsewhere, are lying in boxes filled with straw, and jogging along the road in dreary fellowship. All are gone off to the next fair. Nor will they have long to rest on their laurels, for there are two thousand fairs in Hungary every year. Little is left to remind us of the existence of this one but sundry heaps of dust and straw mingled with scraps of paper of various colours which the wind has benevolently blown under doorways and into safe snug corners, and all things have shaken down and resumed their wonted complexion in bright, beautiful Pest. Persons come and go as usual. In the markets, vendors of *Tisch-wein* and hot macaroni soup assert their former sway, and Magyar women, once more left alone, shine forth in solitary glory, in all the convolutions of their short but voluminous petticoats.

It is amusing to linger about the square and regard the "common objects," sturdy Magyar matrons bargaining over their purchases, as they stand at the stalls on which repose whole yards of bread and miles of sausage, or see them turn-

ing over the contents of the vegetable baskets guarded by female rustics, sitting under huge umbrellas. Equipped in their top-boots which extend above the knee, and which are well greased to resist the manifold vicissitudes of Hungarian roads, these Magyar females resemble groups of Amazons, rather than peaceful house-wives.

A propos of these Magyar sisters of ours I never could determine at all satisfactorily to my own mind whether the enormous rotundity of hip is due to a peculiar type of human form, or to extraneous matter in the shape of pads or pillows. I incline to the latter theory, but I seldom saw a full-blown specimen of the *genus* without wishing to solve the mystery. As they go marching home with their purchases, one cannot help thinking what admirable weapons the long, narrow, crusty loaves would make which they carry under their arms; these and three quarters of a yard of sausage— an edible made of raw meat, well flavoured with garlic, and so compressed as to assume almost the hardness and heaviness of iron—might furnish implements of warfare for an army; and appear to be exactly the kind of weapons with which the ancient inhabitants of Eastern Hungary defended themselves against the Romans in A.D. 103 as seen in the sculptures on Trajan's Column at Rome.

Steamers ply constantly throughout the day between Pest and Ofen, as well as Promontorium and other towns and villages in the neighbourhood of Pest, and few things are more interesting than to stand on the long steps of the quays and watch their arrival and departure. Here stand or sit groups of men and women waiting for the steamers to take them to their respective destinations, and I never grew tired of sketching them, for they occasionally formed themselves into groups that were perfectly statuesque. I never knew people— to make use of artistic phraseology—who "composed" so well.

Embarking on these boats may sometimes be seen not only Bosnians, Servians, and natives of the Sublime Porte; but occasionally an Albanian in gay and martial attire with a sabre at his side and pistol in his girdle, and now and then a Dervish. Indeed at no hour of the day are these splendid quays devoid of interest; whilst lying close into the shore are gaily painted fishing-boats looking like exaggerated Dutch toys.

Sitting on one of the benches at the place of embarkation for Promontorium, enveloped from head to foot in his long black cloak, we often observed an exiled Pole—a refugee from that part of his hapless country upon which Russia has set her iron grasp. He never spoke, but sat moodily watching the river flowing by, his thoughts evidently far away, and was verily the saddest spectacle we saw the whole time we were at Pest. There are a number of Polish refugees in this charming little capital, and it is easy to recognise them, their downcast but resigned look, more eloquent far than any spoken demonstration of sorrow, plainly indicating who and what they were. Taciturn always, it was seldom we could engage them in conversation, but if fortunate enough to do so, their incessant themes were loss of nationality and love of country. " Unpaternal" as are most continental Governments in their treatment of political refugees, Austro-Hungary is a very favourite place of exile with the Poles; nor is this altogether strange, for the Hungarians naturally sympathise with the Poles as a people situated in some measure similarly to themselves, besides which it is said that the Austrian Government is far more indulgent to political refugees than the Prussian. Probably Austria is influenced in some degree —as well she may—by the remembrance of the assistance Poland once afforded her in the hour of her greatest need, when in 1683 she was almost overwhelmed by 300,000 Turks and Tartars who had already made a breach in her walls.

Every night as we retired to our room in Hôtel Dolovics we observed, resting on a door-mat on the same floor as that on which our own room was situated, a solitary boot. What silent pathos was there in it! It was a small boot too, a woman's, and its loneliness haunted me somehow, and kept me awake thinking of it. I did not feel half so much for the wearer as for the lonely thing itself, which in the solitude of its *sole* seemed even more than human. We never saw the wearer, though we watched long and patiently; at last, one night, we found it gone. It had moved off our stage, and was once more on its lonely walk through life. Upon inquiring of the manager of the hotel, who occupied a gloomy little office glazed in at the top of the stairs, he satisfied our curiosity by informing us that it belonged to a lady residing in the north of Hungary, whose leg had been amputated in childhood in consequence of injuries sustained from grape-shot, at the commencement of the bombardment of the city in 1849, during the war between the Imperial troops and the Revolutionists—a struggle which resulted in the gallant Magyars making themselves masters of the Citadel of Buda, on whose ramparts, after a three-weeks' heavily-sustained combat on both sides, the Hungarian flag floated over the city.

During the troublous annals of their history the Magyars have invariably displayed dashing heroism, noble self-sacrifice, and loving devotion to their country, but in no instance, perhaps, so notably as in the struggles of 1848–9, when, although numbering as a nation only six millions and a quarter, they fought for their independence against the combined forces of Russia and Austria, and notwithstanding the immense resources at their foes' command, succeeded for a while in not only asserting their national independence, but in quelling at the same time the insurrection of their own subjects the Wallachians, Slavonians, and "Saxons" of Transylvania.

In the square at Buda there stands a cross erected in memory of General Henzi and his Croatian compatriots who, fighting on the side of the Imperialists, fell during that sanguinary conflict. Pest suffered severely on this occasion, and its wretched inhabitants, who had so often been driven away by the inundations—a foe scarcely less terrible—now fled in terror by thousands and tens of thousands from the shells which—the Austrians once more in possession of the fortress—were directed towards the city by one hundred pieces of ordnance stationed on the heights of Buda.

The Hungarians are scarcely likely, I should say, to unite in another struggle for their national independence, unless they are indifferent to the fate of their magnificent city, for, since the last revolution when they succeeded in becoming masters for a while of their citadel, the Austrian Government has taken warning and erected fortifications on the summit of the Blocksberg which command not only the city but the fortress itself. The Hungarians speak of these fortifications with contempt, but this, I fancy, is a piece of very natural bravado, for the position of these ramparts not only renders them invulnerable in themselves, but the capital thus menaced could not possibly hold its own against a bombardment from the heights which command it on all sides.

I was sitting on the banks of the Danube one morning, opposite the Blocksberg, peacefully sketching the boats on the river, when I was startled by a voice behind me saying in German:

"I will thank you for your card."

I had been conscious for some time past that I was not alone, but, thinking I was merely surrounded by the usual curious spectators, I went on quietly with my occupation; but now turning round I see standing beside me a soldier in the Austrian uniform.

"For what purpose do you wish my card?" I demanded.

"You are taking the plan of our new fortress yonder," was the reply.

"Well, and what if I am?"

"You must have some object in doing so. What may it be?"

"I do not like to see it there," I replied, just to hear what he would say. "It is an ugly object, and I would like to have it knocked down."

He coloured deeply, and again demanded my card, or name and address.

"*Jó Isten!*" here broke in an old woman piously, setting

down her basket, and elevating her hands and eyes the better to give full expression to her feelings,—" as though we hadn't trouble enough in '48! the *Nagyságos Asszony* (foreign lady) must needs take the measure of the fortress;" whilst a child squatting down beside me set up a piteous howl. One of the spruce young waiters from the *café* at the corner of the Petöfi tér also came out to see what could be the matter, together with a cook, and sundry other menials from other establishments hard by, all of whom, taking their stations on the steps in front of me, appeared to think I was gifted with the power of seeing through opaque substances, till I was finally hemmed in by a hot and eager crowd, all anxious to hear the upshot of the parley.

Beginning to fear I might have gone too far in thus venturing to jest with an Austrian soldier, on such an awful subject as the fortifications of the Imperial Government, I endeavoured to pour oil on the troubled waters by at once declaring my nationality, and informing him that I was an English lady.

"You speak German too well to be English," he retorted curtly. "Show me your passport, *Madame*."

"I do not usually carry it about with me," I replied meekly; "but if you do not mind waiting a few moments till I have finished sketching these boats, you can, if you will, accompany me to my hotel, where I can show it you, or, if you prefer it, you can come with me to the British Consulate, which is nearer. My nationality is known there, for the Vice-Consul signed a document for us this very morning."

He waited patiently and civilly whilst I coolly put the

finishing touches to my sketch, when, having packed up, we walked off together.

Before we had proceeded very far, however, I saw F. coming down the Pfarr Kirche Platz, on his way to meet me. As may be imagined he was greatly astonished to see me in the company of an Austrian gendarme; but fortunately having our passport with him, he was able at once to convince my interrogator as to my nationality, who, after inscribing our names in his pocket-book, made a polite bow, and went on his way.

During our stay at this pleasant city, we often made excursions up and down the river, scarcely a day passing without our going by steamer to O'Buda or Alt Ofen, the latter being the German appellation for this straggling town or village, which being literally interpreted means "Old Stove," a name given to it probably on account of the hot springs which since time immemorial have existed here, or else from there having formerly been numerous lime-kilns in the neighbourhood. Of much more ancient origin than even Buda itself, it somehow had a strange and weird sort of fascination for us, such an odd old place as it is, so still, so silent, everything in it so arid and parched, that it looked as though it had been baking for centuries past in its own oven! Surely time must have passed it by with folded wing, for, as we wander through its almost deserted thoroughfares, the very atmosphere seems to tell of a long-forgotten past. Yet, silent as it now is, these hills must at one time have resounded to the murmur of many voices, as well as to bright music and revelry, for Alt Ofen was once, as we have seen, a city of kings.

Recent excavations bear witness to the fact that a city

formerly stood here capable of containing two hundred thousand inhabitants, a number equalling the population of Buda and Pest together at the present time. It was known to the Romans as Aquincum, and there exist in the vicinity many interesting Roman remains, amongst which is an aqueduct, one mile and a half long, whose pillars are still partially standing, together with a Roman amphitheatre larger than that of Pompeii, containing numerous Roman inscriptions, proving that a temple of Nemesis once existed in its immediate vicinity. A bust of the goddess has also been discovered, together with one of Jupiter, whilst in the amphitheatre itself, some of the stone benches are not only inscribed with numbers, but with the names of the persons to whom the seats belonged. But our days began to be numbered, and the time sped only too swiftly, as we loitered now on the banks of the river, now in the beautiful Magarethen Island or Stadtwäldchen, eating ices in the *kiosks*, till at length the time not only drew near but the last day of our visit had actually arrived, and an excursion to the Kaiserbad was all that was left for us.

It is not easy to tear oneself away from this interesting place, with all its historical associations and elements of novelty to the stranger; for there is an individuality about it which renders it unlike every other city in the world. The Hungarians, too, with their singular pedigree, how different they are in themselves from the dwellers of all other cities in Europe! and what warm and kindly natures they possess! Verily, all things conspire to render Pest a charming place of sojourn.

CHAPTER L.

THE WITCHES' CARNIVAL.

OF all the pleasure resorts in the neighbourhood of Pest, none is so great a favourite as the Kaiserbad, on account of its mineral springs, which are recommended as a cure for almost every ill to which frail humanity is prone. To the passing stranger, however, who only sees the outward aspect of the frequenters of these baths, and knows not the inward miseries they suffer, the only malady the majority of them would seem to possess, as he watches them regaling themselves at the restaurant, and notes with what marvellous rapidity one viand after another is made to disappear, is that of insatiable hunger.

As we sit in the pleasant gardens the flowering trees and shrubs waft their perfume over us, and in the tepid pool the lotus, which opened wide its fan-like leaves to catch the noon-day sun, now spreads them wider still as they drink in gratefully the falling dews.

The neighbourhood of the Kaiserbad is not only interesting as containing one of the old Turkish baths, but also on account of the belief held by Hungarian archæologists that it was originally founded by the Romans. Above the gardens is a small octangular building surmounted by a cupola, the tomb of Sheikh Gül Baba, a Mussulman Saint, who died nearly two hundred years ago, and whose resting place is protected from Christian desecration by a special clause in the Treaty of Karlowitz of 1699. Hither come once a year a number of pilgrim dervishes to pay homage to the "holy shrine."

To the Turks also is due the true Egyptian Lotus which grows here, for they brought it from the Nile and placed it in a pool formed by the hot springs, where, protected from the effects of the cold atmosphere by the high temperature of the water, it blooms freely as at Grosswardein.

Not an inch of soil here but has been the scene of some sanguinary struggle between the Christian and the Turk. Never was resistance more desperate than that made by the latter, nor triumph of the Christian arms more complete.

During this siege, one of the most memorable in history, and which continued for three months without any cessation, under the leadership of the Duke of Lorraine, many English officers joined the Imperial forces, together with volunteers from almost every nation in Europe, all firmly bent on expelling the Ottoman foe. Every Hungarian who could wield a sword went forth to the conflict, till the Turks, compelled at length to surrender, fled across the Danube and were engulphed by thousands in that mighty stream.

The moon had risen by the time we left the gardens of the Kaiserbad and found ourselves in the quiet streets of Buda. In the quaint old square, fantastic shadows, thrown by the gabled houses, lay sharply defined upon the dusty ground. In the small square windows, burning red, gleamed here and there a solitary light, contrasting strangely with the silvery moonlight; whilst above, the palpitating stars shone pale from out their purple deeps, and looked down upon the ruined amphitheatre with its rugged lines.

On the Danube, boats and barges moored along its margin lay black upon its surface, and now and then heaved and tossed as a passing steamer, displacing the water, made them rock, and knock against each other. All else was as still as in the dead of night. At long intervals a foot-passenger came walking by, but with the usual greeting he, too, passed on his way, and soon became lost to view in the gloomy shadow of the hill.

Leaving Buda and the regal palace with its terraced gardens and majestic flights of steps behind, we soon reach the suspension bridge, and find the stream of busy life still flowing there. Carriages are thundering through the tunnel beneath the Schlossberg to and from the station, and people passing and repassing the bridge on their homeward way. We, however, drawn thither by a mysterious fascination, are about to climb the Blocksberg, for this, according to German fable, is the night when witches dance upon its heights.

Scrambling up the steep, rough road through the Raitzenstadt, with its funny little houses and white gables, like the tents of an army (a quarter inhabited exclusively by Servians), we pass a ghastly "calvary," and soon arrive at the summit of the mountain.

The view of Pest and the surrounding country never appears so beautiful as from the heights of the Blocksberg on a moonlight night. The noble city lying peacefully beneath, the rigid lines of its solid blocks of masonry and tall black cupolas cutting sharp into the sapphire sky, the deep brown shadows where the streets run parallel, the brilliant lights of the restaurants and cafés illumining the opposite houses with almost prismatic hues, the broad Danube rolling onwards its majestic waves till it loses itself in the pale and misty distance, the wooded islands sleeping calmly on its surface, and the lamps upon the bridge, linking together as with a chain of diamonds the ancient and

modern cities into one; all form a scene to go home and dream about.

It was from this well-chosen spot, which commands both sides of the Danube, that Görgei, the military leader of the insurrectionary party, with his forty thousand troops and battery of artillery from Kömorn shelled the fortress of Buda, then in the hands of the Imperialists, and succeeded after a prolonged siege of twenty-one days in hoisting on its ramparts the standard of Hungarian liberty.

The outer walls of the bastion have a very imposing aspect, being pierced at every few steps with holes for cannon, which seem perpetually to menace the inhabitants of the twin-cities lying so peacefully beneath. Wherever one gazes from below, these fortifications, crowning the mountain, form the most conspicuous object, reminding the Hungarians, not only of their signal defeat, but also of what they have to expect should they ever again attempt to regain their national independence. I must confess, that with my sympathies ever on the side of the Hungarians, these fortifications were, to me, a most objectionable spectacle. For although the powers of governing the Hungarian kingdom are now equally divided between the two nations, so long as the sovereign power is vested in the House of Hapsburg, the term "dual-monarchy" will in many respects continue to be a miserable misnomer.

As a portion of the Austrian empire, Hungary, however, is not badly off, and there are those who think her people have reason to be grateful to Austria for its clemency after the insurrection of '48-9. It is, however, only natural that the Hungarians should wish their vast and beautiful country to be again governed by a king of its own, instead of one of an alien race. They complain, and very naturally too, of the liquidation of the Austrian national debt, for which the Hungarian Ministry, to a certain extent, became responsible in 1867, but which debt includes many millions which were raised abroad for the purpose of enabling the Austrian Government to subjugate them.

The Magyars are wont to attribute to Austria every ill from which they suffer. Amongst the higher classes, however, as may naturally be supposed, there is greater toleration in matters political; but, on speaking of the "dual-monarchy" to a Magyar merchant, with whom we were once travelling, he said—summing up all in that melancholy inflexion of voice which is so characteristic of the Hungarians—"Ah, well! we are married to a wife we do not like, but we must bear with her, for divorce is impossible."

It is, however, only fair to say that the Hungarians invariably speak of the Emperor of Austria in terms of great respect, and it is to be regretted that Prince Rudolf, the heir to the throne, is not as popular as his royal father.

It was a fortunate stroke of policy, that of Deák's advising Francis Joseph to allow himself to be crowned King of Hungary at Pest in 1876. He knew well the feelings of his countrymen, and that that alone would enable the Emperor to find his way into the hearts of the Hungarian people, who would never recognise him as their true king until he had, like their early monarchs, been crowned with the sacred diadem of St. Stephen.

How singular and dazzling a pageant must have been the royal procession to "Coronation Hill," formed as it was of the representatives of the various nationalities all dressed in their ancient costumes. How splendid those of the Delegates in their *mentes* and *dolmans* of rich blue or ruby velvet, trimmed with sable and ermine! The nobles, clad in silver coats of mail and mantles of leopard's skin, fastened across the chest with magnificent diamond clasps, their caps adorned with waving plumes, and the trappings of their chargers, like those of Attila of old, adorned with precious stones. Following the King came the archbishops and Prince Primate on horseback, arrayed in their gorgeous vestments and gold mitres, bearing in their hands their gem-bespangled croziers. Reaching the mound, formed of earth brought from the various provinces of the kingdom, the King, giving spurs to his horse, dashed up the eminence, the sacred crown upon his head, and robed in the coronation mantle of light blue silk, embroidered by Gisela, the wife of St. Stephen, a garment which, kept under safe guardianship with the crown in the Castle of Buda, is never repaired except by royal hands. Facing the four quarters of the globe he waved his sword in each direction in accordance with the custom of Hungary's ancient kings and in token that he would defend the country from foes from whatever side they might come.

The Empress is greatly beloved. She speaks their language thoroughly, is beautiful, and flatters their vanity—one of the weak points in the Magyar character—not only by professing a fondness for them, but by spending a portion of every year in the palace of Gondölö, near Pest. On the other hand, I have occasionally heard the Empress's delight in field-sports deprecated in no measured terms. It is said that they are the only subjects upon which she ever converses at Court, which some of the Hungarians regard as not only unfeminine, but *mauvais ton*.

As we saunter round the bastions of the Blocksberg, all is so silent that the rumble of carriages still crossing the bridge reaches us even on these dizzy heights. Beyond the city the full, round moon, shining upon some stretch of fresh green herbage or ripening corn, transforms it into pale tints of chrysoprase, the mighty Alföld stretching away in one unbroken level to Belgrade. Dark clouds, however, are rising from the south, and a cool refreshing breeze is springing up from the same direction.

At length, stationing ourselves under the lee of the northern ramparts for shelter, we were both immersed in deep thought, when we were startled by an Austrian soldier on patrol, who, appearing suddenly and mysteriously from out the shadow of the great walls near which we were loitering, demanded in a loud and peremptory tone, in German—

"*Wer geht da?*" (Who goes there?)

"We are only English travellers, admiring the prospect," we replied in the same language.

"You have been a long time about it," continued he, sarcastically; "and I should think you must have made yourselves acquainted with it by this time;" adding after a few moments' pause, "You have been hovering about here for the last hour and a half at the very least."

"Probably," I replied, "for we have come to see the witches dance to-night. You need not be afraid of our laying a train to blow up these precious fortifications of yours; we have no dynamite with us."

"I will thank you for your cards," was the only rejoinder.

Instead of complying with his request, however, F. withdrew from his pocket our passport, which since my little encounter on the quai he invariably carries with him, and which evidently made on this officious and sensitive offshoot of the Austrian Government such an impression, with its veritable British lion and unicorn easily distinguishable in the clear moonlight, that with a polite bow he exclaimed—

"*Passieren Sie!*"

Soon after this little episode, whilst continuing our stroll, a sudden change came over the spirit of the scene.

The clouds we had observed rising from the south awhile ago, but which as we stood behind the northern ramparts we had failed to see approaching us with rapid strides, had now silently stolen upon us and obscured the moon's disk. The wind, too, increased rapidly, and began to blow against the bastions with reports like that of musketry. It was a weird spot, this black and silent mountain summit, as the dense clouds scudded past.

"We are in for a storm!" cried F., throwing the end of his cigar away. "Perhaps this is the witches' herald. If they don't turn out on such a night as this, all I can say is they ought."

"Yes; here they come," he added, with a laugh; "or, at any rate, their broomsticks,"—as the wind, suddenly blowing almost to a hurricane, caught up a cluster of stalks of Indian corn that had been lying on the ground, and hurled them high in air.

As we turned our faces homewards with all speed, the thunder began to peal, and, approaching the *Raitzenstadt*, a signboard, which had become loosened from its fastening, suddenly flapping against the wall of a cavernous doorway with a great noise, made us start. Reaching a small warehouse, we entered it for shelter.

The storm was destined to be of short duration, for, deviating slightly from its course, it travelled towards the mountains of Buda, the thunder reverberating grandly, till the hills, answering each other with sounds like the roar of artillery, seemed to be the scene of a bombardment. The clouds, too, swept past, following the storm, and as we issued from the *Raitzenstadt*, the heavens were again clear, and the wind had laid itself down exhausted.

CHAPTER LI.

PARTINGS.

AS we crossed the suspension bridge for the last time on our way from Pest on the morning of our departure, the sun had risen, but the shadows still lingered beneath the white colonnades and archways that flank the Palace Gardens. On the Danube sleepy little fishing boats were floating with sails still furled, but on the quays, men were busy unloading merchandise from the larger boats that lay alongside.

We had bidden a sorrowing adieu to our carriage the previous evening, and as we looked at it for the last time, and the remembrance of our pleasant picnics and roadside bivouacs came floating back upon the mind, we almost wept over it, for it was akin to parting with an old and valued friend.

Our last journey had tried its enfeebled constitution sorely, and looking at it we felt its work was done. It would no longer rumble along the road to the merry jingle of horses' bells. The patches which András had sewn over the rents in its poor old hood, no longer excluded the rain; it was leaky in every pore, and the canvas in some places hanging to it in ragged filaments gave to the whole, a woebegone appearance indeed.

We were once more on our way to Füred, there to await the departure of the Austrian Lloyd's Steamer on the Save, and had scarcely taken our seats when we heard a plaintive voice saying in rather questionable German and still more questionable grammar,

"Would any lady or gentleman be so good as to exchange their seats and allow me to sit in this carriage? I am *so* afraid to travel near the engine."

Looking out of the window, I recognise the typical Englishwoman at last. There she is, arrayed in the typical brown ulster, large straw hat of the mushroom species, and green gauze veil. Nothing wanting to render the type complete.

"All right!" replied the manly voice of a Magyar seated in the farthest corner, evidently glad of an opportunity of befriending an unprotected female; "take my seat, I'll go into the next carriage."

She too was on her way to Füred, having just arrived from Vienna, and we soon ascertained that she was an "unappropriated blessing," roaming about the "wide wide world" as "unappropriated blessings" sometimes will; whilst a maid, who accompanied her in her wanderings, was seated in the next carriage with András.

The landing-place at Füred on this occasion of our visit presented a most animated scene, and was thronged with people in gay attire. We had secured rooms some weeks previously in the same hotel, or rather boarding-house, for strictly speaking there are no hotels here; but for which it is not likely we should have found accommodation, for the little place is evidently as full as it can cram.

On the landing, amongst the loiterers who were either there to meet their friends or watch the new arrivals, we recognised the imposing form of András's "better half," who had come to greet her lord and master. He did not, however, appear to be so glad to meet his Katicza as husband should; on the contrary the previous evening he had presented himself with a doleful countenance, and entreated us to take him with us to Ángolország.

"How could he leave his *edves kedves* (sweet, beloved) master and mistress?" the warm-hearted little man in his sorrow at parting with us adding another adjective to his usual form of address—"He would be our butler, our cook, our groom," in short our everything. He would be scarcely any expense to his *edves kedves uram* and *asszonyom*," he only wanted black bread, bacon and kurkurnty soup; and as to clothes!—he had plenty of strong, home-spun *gatyák*, etc., etc., a pair of *czimák* (top-boots) once a year was all he would need; and as he completed the category, we could not help smiling inwardly at the thought of the sensation his appearance would create amongst the English natives with his embroidered petticoats and feather-adorned cap, and with a sore heart we told the little man he must return to his Hungarian master and to the bosom of his family.

Greatly to our surprise and delight we found here the friends with whom we had stayed in the north of Hungary, and with whom in the evening we strolled down to the lake. To the right was the bold promontory of Tihany sloping its rugged cliffs into the bosom of the lake and bearing on its summit the Benedictine Monastery founded by King Andreas I. in 1055, one of the very earliest Christian institutions established in this country.

These Benedictines are said to have been the chief agents in the conversion to Christianity of the heathen hordes who fixed their abode on the Alföld in the 9th century. The breeze blowing from the south-west wafts over the still, blue waters the distant and plaintive sound of the monastery bell, as it tolls the *Ave Maria*, calling up within us a feeling of deep reverence for the descendants of the first preachers of the cross in this once heathen land. There are some, however, who ascribe the first germ of Christianity in this land to the Eastern Church and the Byzantine Greeks, many of whom it is well known were in Hungary previous to the adoption by the Magyars of the new religion. But whether the glory of Hungary's original conversion to Christianity is due to the Benedictines or not, they were at any rate the principal means of keeping alive and spreading that faith which in various modifications is now held by all the nationalities of this vast country. It was, moreover, to the teaching of this order that the Hungarians are indebted for the first lessons in both architecture and agriculture, for, whilst instilling into their minds the doctrines of Christianity, they taught them the dignity and importance of labour, and just as we ourselves are indebted to the Benedictines for many of our beautiful churches, and the majority of our abbeys, the Hungarians owe to these early Christian monks the greatest architectural achievements their country possesses.

As we saunter along the margin of the lake the weird and banshee strains of a gipsy band reach us, which the echoes give back in muffled harmony. On calm and peaceful nights like the present, the air in this vicinity is said to resound with the enchanting songs of fairies who live in the rocky fastnesses of Tihany. How delightful to find ourselves in a land where fairies still exist! The lake also is believed to be the abode of Naiads; whilst that of Neusiedler, near Presburg, is said to contain within its watery depths whole palaces of gold and precious stones. This being a happy country where these fascinating little people abound, it might reasonably have been expected, since the gipsies had favoured us with a serenade, that they also would have turned out to bid us welcome. Possibly they did so, but our eyes, blinded by the hard, stern civilisation of the West, were not at any rate permitted to see nor our ears hear them; or we may, perhaps, have sought at too early an hour for those dissipated spirits. There is more than one superstition believed in concerning this lake, nor is it to be wondered at. There are phenomena, too, peculiar to it which give it a very eery character, one of them being that it is occasionally violently agitated without any apparent cause, and the other that in the winter the ice which covers it sometimes bursts with a loud report.

These phenomena are the more remarkable from the fact of its being so shallow, spreading itself out as it does over no less an area than four hundred square miles.

The water-drinkers were up betimes, and from earliest dawn there was such a tramping of feet in the corridor outside the door, that sleep any longer was out of the question. I wonder what particular qualities the waters are supposed to possess at that unearthly hour? Opening the window, I let in the sweet morning air. The lake is sleeping calmly below, the long line of distant shore scarcely perceptible, whilst horizon and sky are blended into one. In the marshes beyond the lake, the white vapours which hovered over them in the darkness, now rising, begin to take shape, and, separating into fleecy cones, wear the appearance of a procession of phantoms, or attendant spirits of Night, as, scarcely touching the surface of the earth, they glide away to that mysterious region where they hide themselves till evening comes again.

In spite of the earliness of the hour, a small, flat-bottomed boat comes skimming along close to the shore, filled with fishing-nets, baskets, and men, muffled up in sheepskins, their heads covered with woollen caps with long flaps to them.

A little later, and the priest is seen taking his matutinal walk. He exchanges salutations with the doctor of the bathing establishment, who stands in the portico beneath. And now the abbey bell with muffled beat again comes floating over the still air, as it summons the worthy monks to matins! How full of romance and sentiment is their cloistered dwelling, and of beauty its surroundings!

But the sun is up, and, looking like part of the morning, comes the chambermaid. Following the pretty custom of the country, she stoops and kisses my hand, and then presents a small tray on which is placed "white coffee," the milk in some way or other being whipped to a froth.

As I sit by the open window it is amusing to watch the

people pass. All little Füred is astir by this time, and an important-looking personage comes stalking along, followed by a dog. His figure, pompous and comfortable, is enveloped in a long cloak lined with some beautiful fur resembling sable, which sways backwards and forwards, with the regularity of a pendulum. He is evidently a person of distinction, the *polgár mester* (mayor) probably or *biró* of Dorf-Füred, a village not far distant. Coming from an opposite direction is another, but somewhat less pompous individual, also accompanied by his own particular quadruped. They meet and exchange salutations in the most elaborate and approved method of the Hungarian period; they begin talking confidently, on municipal matters probably, or more likely still the condition of the dykes, a much vexed question at the present time, and a source of never-ending dispute and clamour amongst the various municipalities of the kingdom.

Presently, after a quarter of an hour has elapsed, the colloquy apparently draws to a close; they bestow upon each other a parting benediction, at which the dogs—without so much as raising their heads—open their eyes drowsily and then close them again. They know by experience there are many last words to be said before the real farewell is taken, and they are perfectly right. The disputants separate, and walk in contrary directions, but only to turn back and resume the argument for awhile, and then repeat the ceremony of leave-taking. The whole process has been gone through many times, when there comes at length a peculiar flourish of the walking stick, and a wave of the hand indicative of the conclusion of the whole matter, upon which the dogs jump up in an instant, and follow the heels of their respective masters.

Another lovely day, of which we make the most—for the

summer heats are passing and the rains of autumn will soon be here—tempts us to make an excursion to the monastery of *Sacer Mons Pannonæ*, the chief monastic institution of the country, dedicated to St. Martin, and erected, so it is said, on the precise spot on which the dwelling of the parents of St. Martin stood.

There would, however, appear to have been some slight confusion in the minds of historians concerning the birth-place of this charitable and amiable saint, a manuscript in the library of the monastery itself declaring him to have been born in a town at the *foot* of the hill; whereas his biographer and disciple Sulpicius Severus contends that he was born in a district more remote, namely, at a place called in the present day Steinamanger.

Whatever place may have had the honour of giving him birth, here at any rate he dwelt in manhood, and although born of heathen parents and having entered the Roman army, he became a soldier of the cross, and fighting against Arianism, which was rife in Pannonia in the 4th century, became in the reign of Constantine the Great the light of the Western Church.

The monastery is situated on the spur of a mountain which forms one of the chain enclosing the Hungarian plains to the west, and beneath which lie the forests of Bakony, of unenviable notoriety as the hiding place of Hungarian brigands.

Hither come swarms of pilgrims weak in the knees and otherwise shaky in the lower extremities, hobbling up the steep hill-side, to sit and shiver in a marble chair contained in a crypt beneath the abbey, and in which the Saint is said to have sat during mass. To recline in this chair with a minimum of clothing is said to be a cure for rheumatism—probably acting on the homœopathic principle "Like cures like;" a remedy that even rivals the baths of Füred, and moreover possesses the additional advantage of being gratuitous.

The present monastery is the third which has been erected on this site, the first having been destroyed by the Pagans, the secret warfare that had been going on between Christianity and Paganism during the reign of King András I., having come to an open rebellion in that of King Béla. The second was demolished by the Turks; whilst the one now standing is interesting as having been built by the Abbot Urias who made himself so conspicuous in the " Holy War."

In addition to the statue of the patron saint, who as usual is represented in the act of giving his mantle to the beggar, the church contains two others of Hungary's mediæval kings, both of whom were canonised by the Pope, viz., St. Stephen, and St. Ladislaus.

Our last day at Füred has also come, and, like all things pleasant, far too speedily. We have bid a sorrowful adieu to our honest little guide, who with his belongings has gone back to his master, taking with him a substantial token of our appreciation of his services, and we are only waiting the steamer's signal to cross the lake on our way to Croatia ere we turn our backs upon the classic land of Attila and Arpád and bend our steps towards the region of the setting sun.

The service at the hotel was charged for on the bill, and I need scarcely say paid for also; but who could resist giving a *douceur* to the bright-eyed chamber-maid who kissed our hands when she brought our white coffee every morning, and who happens to be brushing away an imaginary cobweb just outside our bedroom door as we make our exit, and looking up so sweetly, wishes us a pleasant journey;—or the civil waiter who happens to be in the middle of the stairs and who wishes us a speedy return;—or the porters who pant so exceedingly, as they carry our luggage down to the steamer and stand mopping their faces with their large full white sleeves;—or the boots, who helps to stow it away;—or the shoes, or in short anybody, and everybody—who, I ask, could resist the bestowal of a few kreuzers upon these civil people as they shower *lebewohls* and *auf wiedersehens* upon us as we depart? We at any rate are not of those strong-minded children of men.

CHAPTER LII.

AGRAM.

EVENING has come, and the still, smooth waters of the Save, reflecting the sky, are like an upturned shield of gold. Not a ripple laves the shore. The black ibis and crested grebe have gone to roost in the low brushwood that fringes it on either side. Not a zephyr stirs the slender stems of the pampas-grass. All nature is still, but over the corn-fields comes the sound of voices, singing a Slavonian melody, slow and sweet, like an evening hymn, which, rising and falling in pathetic cadence, is in wondrous harmony with the scene.

Casting our eyes in the direction of the sound we see a number of reapers, whose sickles flash in the setting sun as they lop the golden grain, the women, wearing scarlet kerchiefs round their heads, looking like poppies in the corn. They are singing in unison a *piesma*, one of those national ballads which have descended from the ancient troubadours, or *guslars* as they are here designated.

To the right rise undulating hills resting their summits on the saffron sky; and from a belt of forest at their base now comes the distant jingling of bells, upon which the reapers, leaving their sickles on the ground, traverse a narrow pathway through the *heide-korn* and wend their way homewards. We watch them crossing the darkling landscape in picturesque procession till they are nearly out of sight, and then turn our faces towards Agram, for since the sun has sunk to rest, miasmatic vapours have been slowly rising from the marshes. In the vicinity of this placid stream, fevers lurk, and the "pestilence that walketh in darkness" waits not for the night.

As we hastily pursue our way towards the little Croatian capital, the distant throb of a *kobsa* comes wafted over the calm waters, and the voice of a peasant singing in a clear rich tenor, as he accompanies himself on his simple instrument. Floating on the glassy bosom of the stream a small black speck now comes in sight. It is a *bredvos*, containing happy peasants on their way from Agram or some village on the opposite bank; and the musical "burr" of the *kobsa* comes nearer, for the boat, a heavy flat-bottomed craft almost as broad as it is long, with its large square prow rising high above the water, makes for the shore.

These ballads, which the traveller hears continually in Croatia, and said to be older than old Homer himself, are the very mainspring of national life, and are the chief means of keeping alive in the hearts of the Slávs, that yearning after national unity of which in these days we hear so much.

To the left of the river are the plains on which a lonely shepherd's hut and two water-lifts are seen standing out black against the sky, but to the right are clusters of wooden huts roofed with shingles, and lying beneath blue mountains. On the balconies, overshadowed by sheltering eaves, the dwellers sit or stand, the bright colour of their costumes gleaming warmly in contrast with the prevailing gloom, for night is falling fast. As we approach the capital, lights are burning in many a window, whilst away in the west and above the irregularly built houses, though the sun set fully an hour ago, a long streak of intense carmine melting into orange reminds us of the far East.

The summer nights are delightful in Agram itself, and resemble those at Venice. The air is balmy, the sky soft and tender, and the great stars, flashing out of the purple sky, scintillate with the changeful splendour of the ruby, the topaz, and the emerald.

Reaching the outskirts of the little city, the most important place on the Save, our way takes us through the long street that leads to the Jellachich Platz, so called from a Ban of that name, who once ruled the province as Viceroy. Let us stroll into the restaurant of the hotel "K'Carnu Austrianskomn!" The instant we do so we realise our distance from the civilised

West, for on asking for a newspaper, several are instantly handed to us, every one of which is either in Windic or Croat, the latter called *hrvatsky*, being the colloquial dialect of the district. Although Agram is the centre of Slavonic literature, the language spoken here is less pure than that spoken by the Slávs of the south-east.

No fewer than nine periodicals are published in this thriving little capital, whilst a Literary Society has recently been formed for the purpose of circulating books, journals, and pamphlets throughout the Sláv provinces, to further which clubs and reading rooms have been established in almost every village. Like the Magyars, the Croatians are very jealous of German influence, and the publication of books and papers in that language is in every way discouraged.

Croatia enjoys a political autonomy, and has a Diet of its own, of which every Croatian noble is a member, the affairs of the State being vested in the Ban. The Croatians are bent on self-improvement, and one of their greatest ambitions is to become independent of Austria in the way that Hungary is, and to form with these nations a triple-monarchy. In religious tenets they belong exclusively to the Greek and Roman Catholic Churches; using, as Slávs of the Western Church, what is termed the Glagolic alphabet in contra-distinction to that used by the Bulgarians, invented by Cyrillus. The most ancient and pure Slavonic is found in what is called the "Ecclesiastical Slavonic" or "Old Bulgarian," into which the Bible was translated in the middle of the 9th century.

This clean, bright little city contains between eighteen and twenty thousand inhabitants, and consists of an upper and lower town. The former is built on the side of a rocky hill, so steep that the houses in the narrow streets, which rise abruptly tier above tier and are approached by long flights of zig-zag steps, look down the chimneys of those on the opposite side of the way. This part of the city, which was once fortified, constituted the citadel. It is now, however, occupied by the *canaille* of Agram, and this quarter may be said to rival ancient Cologne in its variety of perfumes that are not found in either Messrs. Rimmel or Piesse and Lubin's distilleries. Climbing the steep and rugged steps, we pass groups of people sitting at their doorways in the evening air; whilst the moon, prodigal of her gifts, bears her blessing up the unwholesome, narrow streets, and silvers each crazy tenement with a touch as soft and loving as though it were the abode of kings. Making our way upwards, and passing the quarter of the "great unwashed," we at length reach broad, clean streets and lofty houses, and come to the Palace of the Ban, the various public offices, the Academy of Law, and the Museum. On another hill, separated by a narrow sandy gorge, and surrounded by fortifications and high battlemented walls, stand the Cathedral and Palace of the Archbishop. Exposed for centuries to the incursions of the Turks, many of the churches of Croatia, like those of Transylvania, were strongly fortified.

Beyond the foreground of picturesque house-tops, the Save, creating a shimmering pathway across the plains, is seen winding its way towards the Bosnian Mountains, whose outlines are softly pencilled on the sky. This river, taking its rise on the confines of Istria, after flowing through Croatia, divides Slavonia from Bosnia, and still forms the boundary between Christianity and Islam.

The Save also forms with the Theiss one of the principal tributaries of the Danube, and, swelling its waters by emptying itself into the mightier river at Semlin, is one cause of the disastrous inundations which so frequently occur in the region of the Alföld.

It is Sunday, and, like the Protestant Debrecziners, the Agramese, combining the service of God and Mammon, on this day hold their weekly market. The streets are one blaze of colour, and it is to be doubted whether even Rome itself, before the sharp traits of her people began to be obliterated by modern innovations, presented a more splendid spectacle. It is well we planned that our last wanderings in the Austro-Hungarian dominions should be in Croatia, for the costumes are far more beautiful here than any we have hitherto met with on any of our travels, this scene alone being worth coming all the way from Ángolország to see.

Looking down the long straight street that leads to the Jellachich Platz, we find it thronged with people hurrying to the market, and the predominating tints of their costumes, white, scarlet, and green, are rendered all the more striking by the black, curled lamb's wool, with which portions of their dress are trimmed.

The women are attired in short white skirts, stiffly starched, and fluted to the waist, over which a long straight calico frontal is worn, trimmed with broad horizontal stripes of scarlet braid, laid on in a gradation of widths, the white full bodice, embroidered at the throat, being covered with innumerable rows of coral beads. Over this is generally worn a small white jacket of white kid, bordered with the black lamb's wool before mentioned, a beautiful fleece resembling that known in England under the rather vague term of "Astracan." The jacket in question is made so as to leave the front of the bodice exposed to view with its wealth of coral beads, and is not only one mass of the richest embroidery in various coloured silks, but small pieces of silver foil in the shape of stars are also added, which glisten in the sunshine. In addition to all, the fronts of this costly article of attire called a "*cabanitza*" are adorned all over with scarlet tassels. The girls wear a scarlet kerchief round the head, but the married women a very imposing and effective head-dress, which in some respects resembles the square white *taglia* worn by the Neapolitan women, but much larger, consisting of a large square of muslin or calico, trimmed either with lace and scarlet braid supported on two curiously shaped pieces of wood called "horns," round which the back hair is coiled. Nothing can be more becoming or dignified than this covering for the head, and a group of women thus attired form pictures that an artist would love to portray. How their dazzling, spotlessly white, and fan-like petticoats glisten as they trudge merrily along, some carrying long white bundles in their arms, which on closer inspection turn out to be *bambinos*, swathed in yards and yards of home-spun linen, whilst others, like graceful Caryatids, are supporting on their Juno-like heads large flat round baskets filled with fruit or vegetables. Even the old women wear embroidered bodices and scarlet and white skirts. Yonder sit a group of ancient Amazons in close conclave, who may have been amongst those who in 1848 clad themselves in the panoply of war, and went forth to aid their husbands in the battle against Kossuth, singing patriotic songs, and improvising others as they marched towards the Imperial city.

The Croatian men also figure largely in embroidery. Their brown or black cloth tunics are handsomely worked in scarlet; whilst, slung over the shoulder by a cord of the same colour, is a large square bag, designated a "*torba*," which, hanging at the side, is completely covered with little scarlet tassels an inch and a half long. These Croatians, male and female, except in the matter of jewellery, are more given up to the pomps and vanities of this wicked world than even the Hamelsdorf girls themselves.

In the square, peasants from the country round have been arranging their goods since break of day, and the whole place, from its gaiety and bustle, wears the appearance of an annual fair, rather than that of a weekly market. All is so bright, so gay, with such a delicious and harmonious mingling of colour, that we look down at our own hideous garments of the civilised West with their Quaker-like sobriety and sartorial gloom, with feelings almost akin to shame. Verily there is no prettier sight in the universe than Agram on a Sunday morning; but the traveller must be no sluggard, and must be up and out at seven o'clock, the hour when the villagers come trooping in. At ten the market is over, and, obedient to the summons of the bells, the people flock to church, and kneeling down before the service commences may be seen devoutly praying, the men on one side of the church, the women on the other, whilst kneeling on the steps of the altar may be seen a small but promiscuous gathering of men, women, and children.

"Who are they?" I inquired in German of a lady who was sitting on the same bench with me in a church close to the market, and pointing to the group round the altar, all of whom seemed to be oppressed with sorrow of some sort.

"They are poor country-people," she replied softy, "and have some especial blessing to ask, some member of their family is sick or dying. Look at that young woman to the right of the altar! She has brought her sick baby and laid it beneath the picture of the 'Good Shepherd.' Ah! surely He will have pity," and crossing herself devoutly she too knelt down to pray.

Gazing in the direction indicated I saw the wee thing lying helplessly in its bandages, its tiny face so pale and wan, that the former might in truth have been its winding-sheet. In the centre of the group two little boys were kneeling side by side, their small hands clasped and their heads bent low. They came

into the church alone, and, making their way at once to the altar, threw themselves on their knees. What grief was theirs, we wondered, and what blessing had they come to seek? There was a silent pathos about these lonely children that moved me even to tears.

Mass is sung in the Slavonic tongue, a concession granted by the popes to these Yougo-Slávs, in recognition of their heroic struggles against the Osmanlis, and nothing can be more beautiful and touching than their deep, slow chanting.

The country round Agram is very picturesque. A little beyond the city lies the peaceful valley of St. Xavier, together with that of Tuskanac, with their fragments of feudal castles, backed by a lofty hill crowned with pines.

Hiring a passing carriage, we drive towards the cool waters of the Save. Shadows are lengthening across the plains, and the

villagers, crowding into the boats, are being ferried to the nearest church, possibly two or three miles away. Far away on the hills the narrow zig-zag paths are indicated by strings of people coming in the same direction, and we soon reach a church, in the enclosure of which numbers of persons have already assembled waiting the arrival of the priest; stately girls and women in their beautiful scarlet and white garments and square headgear, looking like Druidical priestesses in their white fluted skirts, one and all affording a living mass of rich and varied colour. *

Our steamer, which starts at six A.M. to-morrow, awaits us on the Kulpa at the junction of that river with the Save, a few miles further down the stream. Returning to the hotel, we pick up our luggage, and meet the steamer by the train which leaves for Sissek at nine o'clock.

After passing Agram, the Save spreads itself out till it seems to encircle the whole district in its embrace, reminding us of the Lagoons at Venice. The moon is full, and, as the train rolls us along, everything is so calm, so peaceful, and presents such an even surface to the eye, that we appear to be surrounded by a broad sheet of silver.

Sissek—a miserable place with wide unpaved streets—contains many objects of interest to the archæologist. The village of Old Sissek, which adjoins it, contains numerous remains of pillars and ancient buildings of Roman origin, together with a Roman causeway of massive masonry by which it is approached.

On arrival, making our way at once to our steamer the "*Zrini*," we soon discern her amongst the dark objects with which she is surrounded.

Sissek, though possessing a population of little more than 1200, contains, at this time of year, when the harvest is being gathered in, almost as many thousand. Being the centre of the corn trade, it is here that the huge flat-bottomed boats freighted with grain are unloaded, the men employed, called Latianer,

* These pages were written just before the terrible earthquakse, which not only rendered many of the inhabitants homeless by reducing their houses to a heap of ruins, but which, by the violence of the shocks and their frequent occurrence, kept the inhabitants in such a state of alarm that, on four occasions, panic-stricken they fled from the city and encamped in the plains beyond.

coming each year to Sissek for this purpose and leaving as soon as the season has passed. After being unloaded the corn is conveyed by train to its destination, a great deal finding its way to the English market.

A curious scene surrounds us. There are boats with houses on their decks, others lying empty on their sides and half heeled over, and others again close alongside taking in cargo. Here and there coloured lights are twinkling faintly from the masts of smaller boats, and far down the river's reach more lights are burning where caravans of merchants are bivouacking on the shore. In an hour's time all is still, the vessels have finished taking in their cargo, and no sound is heard save the voices of boatmen weighing anchor, and the soft lapping of ripples driven by the zephyrs of night against the steamer's side.

At six o'clock A.M. the "*Zrini*" bursts from her moorings, and, soon leaving the Kulpa, bounds like a captive let loose into the waters of the Save.

More singular far than on the Danube boats is the motley assemblage that greets the eye of the traveller as he cruises in one of the steamers on the Save. Close to us, with their long chibouks standing by their sides, are two Turks, or Osmanlis as they prefer being called, for the term Turk is one of ridicule, signifying "rustic." Beside them sit a trio of young Servian ladies, dressed in black velvet jackets with large hanging sleeves richly embroidered in silver. Standing near the galley are a group of Albanians, warlike, magnificent-looking men armed to the teeth, with square shoulders and limbs like athletes. There are also men whose erect carriage, resembling that of the Serbs, and frank open brows, proclaim them to belong to Montenegro, that brave and independent little nation, which, although consituting a portion of the border-land that fringed the dominions of European Turkey, has never, like the other Sláv nations of the South, submitted to its rule. As they walk the deck it is easy to see they have never been a subject people. Their dress is a white tunic encircled by a shawl at the waist, blue trousers tied in at the knee, and a small round cap with a crimson crown adorned with gilt ornaments, the latter worn as a symbol of their national freedom. Until lately they also wore an emblem of mourning for the subject condition of their Sláv brethren, the Serbs, to the vassalage of Turkey.

On the forecastle is a mass of human life quite Eastern in its aspect: bright intelligent little Turks full of life and animation; heavy Bulgarians with downcast eyes and beetling brows, who, sitting apart, hold communication with no one; Armenians, Illyrians, Bosnians, Croatians, Hungarians, and uncivilised-looking men from the villages lower down the Save.

Occupying one side of the stern is a huge heap of sheep-skins and striped blankets, which we imagine must be covering passengers' luggage or bales of merchandise. Presently however the heap of what we supposed to be inert matter moves slightly, and a little hand appears and then a small Oriental-looking head, for beneath these blankets and sheep-skin rugs a Greek family were lying huddled together.

There is a little boy on board who interests us greatly. From early morning we had noticed him sitting silently on his bundle, and apparently alone. There was something in the expression of his face that attracted our attention, as he sat with his head slightly elevated and his eyes directed upwards. What could he be gazing at so intently in the dazzling sunlit sky? Making my way towards him through the groups of passengers, some of whom were gambling with curious cards, others singing softly to themselves or lying at full length fast asleep, I reached the spot where he was seated, and at once perceived that he was blind. No one appeared to take any notice of him, as, with pale face and that vacant, and infinitely pathetic expression which one sees in the countenances of the blind, he sat alone.

Standing against the bulwarks smoking was a man who from his uniform I recognised as a corporal in the Austrian army. Addressing me in German, and pointing to the child, as though he had been a bale of merchandise, he said,

"He was put on board at Jassenovatz."

"Where is he going?" I inquired.

"How should I know," was the rejoinder, as, shrugging his shoulders, he walked across to some other part of the ship, adding, as he did so, that he supposed "*somebody* would meet him *somewhere*."

He was in fact a piece of goods "to be left till called for." Taking his small hand in mine, I led him to the other side of the deck under the shadow of the awning. What an odd quaint little specimen of humanity he was, with his loose brown garments, cut precisely like those of his elders, and his funny shapeless little shoes such as all the Sláv peasantry wear, consisting of a flat piece of hide laced into shape at toe and heel, with leather thongs!

At this moment the captain, passing by, enlightened me further as to the history of this waif of humanity.

"That little urchin," said he, looking down kindly upon him, "is a *Minnesinger* or *guslar* as they call them in Croatia; the Yougo-Slávs dedicate from their infancy to the Muses all male children who are born blind. As soon as they are old enough to handle anything, a small mandoline is given them, which they are taught to play, after which they are taken every day into the woods, where they are left till evening to commune in their little hearts with nature. In due time they become poets, or at any rate rhapsodists, singing of the things they never saw, and, when grown up, are sent forth to earn their livelihood, like the troubadours of old, by singing from place to place and asking alms by the wayside.

"It is not difficult for a Sláv to become a poet; he takes in poetic sentiment like a rivulet does water from its source. The first sounds he is conscious of are those of his mother singing to him as she rocks his cradle, or trudges along to market with him tucked under her arm a stiff little bundle. Then as she watches the dawning of intelligence in his infant face, her mother-language is that of poetry, which she improvises at the moment, and so, though he never saw the flowers, nor the snow-capped mountains, nor the flowing streams and rivers, he describes them out of his inner consciousness and the influence which the varied sounds of nature have upon his mind."

The interest this little *guslar* awakened in us soon became general, and, seated high upon a heap of rugs, he was made to sing in his childish voice some of the sweet and simple Slavonian melodies.

CHAPTER LIII.

THE IMPALED RAÏA.

HARK to the measured tramp of feet as the Slavonian peasants whirl and twirl in the intricate mazes of the *kolo*, the national dance of the Slävs! Bright eyes flash beneath heavy lashes, bosoms heave, hearts go pit-a-pat, the charms and beads that hang round the women's necks rise and fall in unison with the rapid movement, fire-flies dart about the steamer's deck, now hovering on the bulwarks, and now playing at hide-and-seek above the head of the dancers. On the margin of the river, glow-worms begin to light their lamps and scintillate in the bushes; whilst over on the Bosnian hills long rows of fires are flickering where the gipsies have pitched their encampments.

Faster and faster go the feet; louder and louder sounds the "burr" of the *kobsa*. The bag-pipes, played by a Wallachian shepherd, drone out their harsh music, above which the shrill little *svira** tries hard to hold its own, and pours forth its plaintive pipings in a feeble and somewhat intermittent treble.

The theme of the *kolo* is the same as that of the Csárdás, love expressed in rollicking pantomime. The dance was got up by a number of peasants who came on board at

* A small flageolet.

Xupanje, but who left us again at a village further down the stream.

While the dancing was going on, our attention was attracted to a gispy woman, who, taking no apparent interest in the proceedings around her, was sitting apart, close to the bows of the steamer. Almost masculine in stature, and with the prominent features which so many of the Bosnian gipsies possess, she looked, with her large lustrous eyes fixed immovably upon the horizon, like some Sibyl prophesying dark things to the night.

Excited by the strains of music that followed the *kolo*, the little guslar took up his tiny instrument—a mere toy—and began singing some more ballads, which won for him no end of kreuzers and applause. At ten o'clock, however, all was silent, every one being asleep, with the exception of a tall and sturdy young Montenegrin, who was standing against the galley smoking, as motionless as a statue, his eyes fixed intently upon the fading hills. Was he thinking of his beloved *Vaterland*— the land of Slavo-Serv liberty, and of its *Tserna Gora*, that dark pine-covered mountain from which his brave little country takes his name? Judging from the small amount of luggage carried by the other passengers, which consisted, as a rule, solely of a gourd or leather bottle, a rug, and an iron pot containing food for their journey, our Montenegrin must have been an emigrant, so numerous are the bundles with which he is surrounded. His gun was slung across his shoulder, and from his shawl-girdle hung some other weapon. But he, too, soon spread his *straka* on the deck, as the large cloak that forms the Montenegrins' outer garment is called, and turning to the east, he makes the sign of the Greek cross, and, lying down, is soon fast asleep.

The night was delicious, the air fresh, but without chill. We had come to anchor opposite a dense belt of forest on the Slavonian side, through which the moon, penetrating here and there between the boughs, shone like silver spray. Everything was calm and dreamy. Occasionally a night-bird, roosting within its leafy labyrinths, uttered a plaintive cry, or a fish rose with a sudden plash; but these sounds seemed in complete harmony with the silence, and, retiring to our cabins, we soon subsided into the general slumber, and did not awake until the sun, shooting golden arrows through our window, summoned us on deck.

To the right, gently undulating hills, which constitute a portion of the Diarnic Alps, and on whose summits snow lies for nine months in the year, now begin to unfold themselves in a solemn rhythm.

We left Croatia behind long ago, and on our right the shore wears an Oriental appearance, for we have reached Bosnia —" Golden Bosnia," as it is familiarly called—whose efforts, together with those of Herzegovina, to obtain emancipation from Mahomedan oppression and misrule, called forth the sympathies of Europe, and elicited the diplomatic action of the great Powers on her behalf.

The shores of this river are especially interesting in a historical point of view. It was on the conquest of Bosnia by the Osmanlis, who at that time spread themselves over the whole district of the Save, that the Military Frontier was established, or rather systematically organised, by Ferdinand of Austria. Extending from the shores of the Adriatic to Moldavia, it embraced Slavonia and Transylvania, as well as a portion of Croatia and the southern belt of Dalmatia, thus covering an area of nearly a thousand miles. At distances of about half a mile apart, we see the Military Frontier posts, which previous to the Treaty of Berlin were vigilantly guarded. They consist of small wooden houses raised on stakes, and surrounded by a verandah in which the guard patrolled. By the side of each house is still seen a high pole to which straw and wood are tied, and which, when ignited, formed a primitive mode of signalling at night to neighbouring frontier-posts on the occurrence of local disturbances of a political character. On the advance of an invading foe the guard of one station signalled to the next, and so on, till the whole line, apprised of the danger, arose to arms and hastened to the threatened district; from three to four hours being the time which is said to have been occupied in communicating from one end of the frontier to the other; whilst during the day when disturbances arose, the wild tocsin—with which every guard-post was provided—resounding along the banks of the river, called the border regiments to arms.

In consequence of the geographical positions of the Danube and the Save, the immediate districts of the rivers were from an early period infested by bands of fugitives from neighbouring countries who lived principally by war and plunder, but whom the Hungarian Government under Matthias Corvinus—that great champion of Christendom against Mahomedan invasion—permitted to remain on condition of their defending the boundaries from the inroads of barbarian hordes from the East. The system adopted was precisely that of the ancient Romans in the defence of their frontiers on the shores of the Rhine and the Danube. These border men-at-arms received no pay, but had fiefs allotted to them on the payment of a heavy tax to the State, and also on the condition of furnishing a certain number of guards. The owners of the fiefs were united under a chieftain who governed the little commonwealth, which generally consisted of fifty families. In times of peace, forty thousand men were on duty at the various posts, but in case of war the whole military force was capable of furnishing two hundred thousand men, all of whom were compelled, if necessary, to serve in the regular army. Under Austria, this border-line became one of the most perfect military institutions of modern times, whereby not only two hundred thousand men were added to her standing army without any cost whatever to the Empire, but a complete system was formed for the maintenance of quarantine. Since the organisation of this frontier line by Austria, the plague, which formerly was seldom absent from Hungary more than twenty years together, has not once visited that country.

On the Bosnian shore we also see at regular intervals the guard posts, which, previous to the Treaty of Berlin, were similarly used by the Turks to protect their frontier lands from Austrian invasion.

What a splendid country Bosnia is, with its luxuriant vegetation and fertile soil. Hundreds of miles of it have never as yet been turned by either spade or plough. Nothing is wanting to render it a happy and prosperous country but colonists to bring its rich virgin soil under cultivation. The population of Bosnia is small, scarcely amounting to one million, of whom thirty-five thousand are Jews, and twelve thousand gipsies, the former being descendants of refugees from Italy and Spain. The remaining inhabitants are divided between Mahomedans and Christians, a Sláv people, the original inhabitants of the country, who speak a Sláv dialect, containing a large admixture of Turkish words. There are no sons of the Prophet so truly bigoted, strange as it may seem, as these Slávs of

Bosnia, although they only embraced Islam to protect themselves from persecution, and their property from spoliation when invaded by the Turks. More fanatical far than even the true-born Turk himself, the Bosnian Mahomedan persecutes in his turn his Christian compatriot, the *raïa*, and calls him "dog."

The *raïas*, who form the Christian portion of the Sláv population of Bosnia, the greater number of whom belong to the Greek Church, constitute almost exclusively the peasant class. Although the former feudal system, of which these *raïas* were the serfs, was abolished by the reforms of 1852, yet forced labour still exists to some extent in Bosnia, the imperious Infidel obliging the Christian *raïa* to work for him almost at the point of the bayonet.

The condition of these poor Bosnian peasantry is consequently still one of the most humiliating servitude, and is very little mended. Not only are they oppressed by the Mussulman population but they are impoverished by their ecclesiastical superiors, the *popas*, who impose burdens on them grievous to be borne, and who on non-payment of their imposition are said not unfrequently to refuse them the rites and consolations of religion. Between the intimidation of their ghostly advisers and the vengeance and cruelty of the Mahomedans, the poor *raïas* still have a hard time of it, and are kept in a state of perpetual poverty and fear.

The banks on the left or Slávonian side, the extreme south-east of which territory we skirted when traversing the Danube, are extremely picturesque. We pass numerous villages, the houses of which, built on stakes, are all gables, balconies, and palisades. In the open windows of these dwellings a woman is occasionally seen, her bright costume creating a charming bit of colour set in its dark wooden frame-work, whilst on the Bosnian shore a long caravan is seen preparing for the day's march, consisting of thirty or forty people and as many mules. How picturesque they are, with their Eastern-looking packs, and deep, rich brown colouring, as they stand grouped in one mass against the background of glowing horizon!

The dense primeval forests which have been skirting us for some hours now give place to morasses, and leaving these behind

we enter a sandy region roamed by pigs. A number of these animals, the precise colour of the sand, come down to drink, driven by a man enveloped in a mantle made of long finely split grass, which, forming a fringe many inches thick, is plaited at the neck, and reaches almost to the heels. This garment, believed by the learned to be the very first that was invented, is also occasionally worn by the shepherds on the Croatian plains. Wherever we cast our eyes there are pigs, pigs, pigs: canary-coloured pigs; pigs with long golden hair (probably the embodied spirits of the water-nymphs, transmigrated into these domestic pachyderms, which the Slávs, like the ancient Greeks, still believe sit upon the banks of the Save, and, combing their golden tresses, sing sweetly to lure the unwary boatman into the shifting sands); sienna coloured pigs; pigs of every gradation of yellow and light brown, surrounded by little families of pink piglets, whose bodies, not yet impregnated with the prevailing sand, seem not to belong to the same genus as their progenitors, as one and all stand out in bold relief and artistic contrast against the intense blue sky.

On arriving at Bertsch, I lose my little guslar, a woman carrying a distaff—which, like the women of Transylvania, a Sláv is seldom seen without—having come on board to fetch him. Before he left I threw into his bundle a quantity of Turkish sweetmeats, given me by a Bosnian gentleman, which must I fear have sown the seed for a rich harvest of indigestion and night-mares sufficient to drown his little pipe and extinguish his muse for many a day to come.

Reaching the province of Syrmien, whose banks skirt us on the Hungarian side, a group of Amazons with red and blue scarfs, folded round their heads like turbans, are standing knee-deep in the water washing their *chuddas,* just as they are seen to do in the Ganges. They scuttle away at our approach, and hide in the low bushes which are growing in the sandy soil, whence they gaze at us furtively like Miriams and the maidens of Pharaoh's daughter. The shore here is covered with hundreds of pigs, no longer golden, but grimly black, with long bushy hair and hanging tails, looking from a little distance like bears. We have now left the region of sand behind, and again enter a morass, the abode of myriads of wild fowl, numbers of which are taking their bath on the confines of the river, or diving for fish; the shore being literally edged with them as by a fringe. More tame by far than the human bipeds of Syrmien, they take no notice whatever of our approach. A raft passes close to them, but they do not move; whilst an eagle standing alone, its great yellow feet planted on a small green promontory, was so lost in contemplation that it did not stir for full a quarter of an hour, but remained as immovable as if it had been the Sphinx beneath the pyramids of Gezah.

At every turn in the river we are reminded of our gradual approach to the East. Women, walking in the roadway or coming down to the river's brink for water, now wear yack-mashes, and the Austro-Hungarian traits have almost died out. Presently we see, apparently standing alone with no habitation within sight, a long pole, to which is lashed what appears from a distance to be a human form, and our minds involuntarily revert to the famous newspaper controversy of "Impaled Bosnian" *versus* "faggot of haricot beans."

There he was sure enough, his black hair standing on end, as well it might, and his loose, Oriental-like garments fluttering in the breeze, with his poor wizened legs dangling black and helpless. It was a blood-curdling sight, and fain would we have turned our eyes in the contrary direction, but no! we would be brave and view through a field-glass this unfortunate *raïa*— another victim to Mahomedan cruelty and barbarism. We would view him in all his ghastly details, in order that we might expose the horrors of the deed throughout the length and breadth of Christendom. Our courage almost fails us, but we raise the glass, through which we see the sickening picture. Across the breast, his epitaph was written in black letters painted rudely on a narrow strip of board. What are the tragic words? They are Slávish for " good cheer for man and beast," and point to a small, one-storied "*gastina*" or way-side inn now seen amongst a cluster of low bushes!

The resemblance was complete and the object of our commiseration a veritable fact, until with calm eyes we were able to  dissect him limb by limb. His head was formed of a bundle of sticks, that doubtless when originally placed there were freshly gathered boughs, but from which the leaves since dropped had left simply a little bundle of dry twigs which formed a capital shock head of hair. The upper part of his body consisted of a piece of old sacking, and his flowing nether garments of a sheaf of Indian corn without the ears, the long, pointed leaves of which, bleached by the sun, fluttered in the air; the narrow board, by dividing the body, formed the waistbelt, and the legs, which hung black and helplessly, were two somewhat crooked stakes, to which the whole fabric was tied previous to its being hoisted to the pole.

Plenty more victims to "impalement" saw we on our farther progress down the Save, but we henceforth witnessed them with stoical indifference, and they no longer awoke our pity or moved us to tears.

The time occupied in steaming down the Save is twenty-six hours, and we are fast reaching our destination. Already ambitious Servia lies to our right. We have passed Schabatz with its hospital and gymnasium, for since this brave little race of Slávs have achieved their independence, they are imitating the civilised West in many of its national institutions. After steaming into a flock of wild swans, we turn another bend of the river, and Belgrade, with its fortress-crowned hill, comes in sight, over which, thank God, the banner of Slavo-Serb liberty at last floats in the breeze. The Save now ends its career, and empties itself into the beautiful Danube, which here looks like the ocean.

As we steam under the citadel of Belgrade with its minarets and towers, which for centuries has been alternately the bulwark of Christendom and the advanced post of the Infidel, a gun booming from its battlemented heights reverberated against the promontory of Semlin, the last Hungarian town on the banks of the Danube, and, stepping on shore, the red, white, and green colours of the kingdom of St. Stephen no longer float over us, for we have planted our feet on Servian soil.

FINIS.

www.ingramcontent.com/pod-product-compliance
Lightning Source LLC
Chambersburg PA
CBHW030741230426
4366TCB00007B/799